Introduction to
Criminal Justice
Information Systems

Introduction to Criminal Justice Information Systems

Ralph Ioimo, DPA

Auburn University
Montgomery, Alabama, USA

CRC Press
Taylor & Francis Group
Boca Raton   London   New York

CRC Press is an imprint of the
Taylor & Francis Group, an **informa** business

CRC Press
Taylor & Francis Group
6000 Broken Sound Parkway NW, Suite 300
Boca Raton, FL 33487-2742

First issued in paperback 2020

© 2016 by Taylor & Francis Group, LLC
CRC Press is an imprint of Taylor & Francis Group, an Informa business

No claim to original U.S. Government works

ISBN-13: 978-1-4987-4881-0 (hbk)
ISBN-13: 978-0-367-59708-5 (pbk)

Visit the Taylor & Francis Web site at
http://www.taylorandfrancis.com

and the CRC Press Web site at
http://www.crcpress.com

This book is dedicated to my father, who was a great source of encouragement throughout my life. He always knew that I could achieve things even when I didn't think I could. I am sure he is looking down at me today with a big smile and saying, "See, I told you that you could do it." Thank you, Dad.

Contents

Preface... xvii
Acknowledgments xix
Author... xxi

Chapter 1 Overview of criminal justice information systems.............. 1
Introduction 1
The evolution of CJISs 2
    Development of criminal history systems...................................... 4
    Evolution of CAD systems 6
    Record management systems 7
    Mobile computing 9
Exploring criminal justice enterprise computing 11
    Court management systems 11
    Correction management systems... 13
Data warehousing and data mining 14
Workgroup applications in criminal justice agencies....................... 15
    Property and evidence systems 15
    Crime analysis and geographic mapping systems..................... 16
    Automated fingerprint identification systems and live scan devices... 16
    Mug shot systems.. 16
    Facial recognition systems 17
    Citation collection systems 18
    Case and investigation management systems 19
Current trends in CJISs 20
References 22

Chapter 2 Justice information system standards and national
            systems.. 25
Introduction 25
Hypertext markup language... 26
Extensible markup language... 27
    Global Justice XML Data Model.. 28
    National Information Exchange Model 31

Regional Data Exchange... 36
Law Enforcement Information Sharing Program 36
National Crime Information Center 2000..................................... 37
Uniform Crime Reports 41
Part 1 crimes... 41
Part 2 crimes... 42
Law Enforcement Online... 46
National Law Enforcement Telecommunication System 47
Law Enforcement Information Technology Standards Council 47
World Wide Web 49
References 50

Chapter 3   9-1-1: Its history, current status, and the next generation 53
Introduction 53
Basic 9-1-1: How it works... 55
Enhanced 9-1-1.. 56
Challenges faced by the 9-1-1 system 58
Private branch exchange systems 59
TTY/TDD communications 60
Cellular phone technology... 61
Voice over Internet protocol.. 64
Next generation 9-1-1 66
References 71

Chapter 4   Police computer-aided dispatch systems.......................... 73
Introduction 73
System performance requirements 74
Administrative functions.. 75
Window configurations.. 75
Squad or shift activation 76
Code table management... 76
Unit recommendation and validation tables............................. 77
Training support... 78
Calls for service data transfer 78
CAD system baseline functions.. 78
Activity logging... 78
Audit trail 80
User-definable expert advisor 80
Library function 80
Card file 81
Command line.. 83
Online messaging/conferencing... 84

Call entry process 84
  Basic required data elements... 84
  Call receipt methodologies 85
    Receipt of 9-1-1 calls 85
    Receipt of calls on 7/10-digit phone lines 86
    Call receipt through mobile computers (on-view events) 87
    Call receipt through voice radio................................... 87
  Minimum required data elements...................................... 87
  Call priority.. 87
  Ability to add or modify information to a call in progress 88
  Duplicate call detection.. 88
  CAD geofile processing... 89
  Hazard information file 90
  Premise information file.. 90
  Premise history file 91
  Call scheduling... 91
Dispatch process 91
  Basic data elements 92
  Command area dispatch.. 92
  Call pending queue... 93
  Unit status monitoring 93
  Status timers 94
  Available units window 95
  Event history 95
  Nonpatrol units 96
  Unit history 96
  Unit recommendation.. 96
  Officer history.. 96
  System status management... 97
Supervisory function... 98
  Supervisory workstation... 98
  Supervisor monitoring capability....................................... 98
  Emergency alert... 98
Administrative function 99
  Code table management.. 99
  Unit validation and recommendation tables................... 100
CAD mapping.. 100
  GPS/AVL requirements 102
  Access to internal databases... 102
  Access to external databases... 103
References 103

Chapter 5   Police record management systems **105**
Introduction 105
Enterprise information system 106
   Calls for service 107
      Linkages to other modules 107
   Master name index 108
      Known associates 112
   Interfaces 114
   Master vehicle index 114
      Interfaces 116
   Master location index 116
   Incidents 119
   Arrest 121
      Linkages to other modules 122
      Interfaces 124
   Juvenile contact 124
   Known offender 125
      Linkages to other modules 125
      Interfaces 126
   Field interview reports 126
   Citations 126
      Linkages to other modules 127
      Interfaces 127
   Wants, warrants, and protective orders 127
      Interfaces 128
Reference 129

Chapter 6   Police workgroup applications **131**
Workgroup applications 131
   Crime analysis and geographic information systems 132
      Interfaces 136
   Automated fingerprint identification systems 136
   Mug shot systems 139
   Property and evidence 140
      Linkages to other modules 144
      Interfaces 145
   Case management 145
      Linkages 146
   Investigation, vice, intelligence, and narcotic systems 149
      Interfaces 151
   Pawnshop 151
      Linkages to other modules 152

False alarms 153
   Linkages to other modules... 154
Subpoena tracking module.. 154
   Linkages to other modules... 155
Summary.. 155
References 156

Chapter 7   Mobile computing..157
Introduction 157
History of mobile computing 157
Data radio and wireless technology as transport mediums 162
   Mobile computing security... 165
Mobile computing and dispatch operations 165
Field report writing 167
The mobile office 168
   Crime analysis information.. 170
   Digital photography.. 170
   Wireless mobile video 171
   Biometric tools 172
   Reference information 172
   Briefing information 172
   Cellular telephones 173
The future of mobile computing...174
   Convertible laptops 174
   Tablet personal computers (PC) 174
   Personal digital assistance 176
   Voice to text and text to voice 176
   Technology integration..178
References 178

Chapter 8   Crime analysis and crime mapping 181
Introduction 181
The history of crime analysis 182
Intelligence analysis... 185
Intelligence-led policing.. 186
GISs and crime mapping 187
Crime mapping types... 189
Crime analysis and information technology 193
Information technology and crime analysis............................... 195
   Tactical crime analysis.. 196
   Strategic crime analysis.. 197
   Operations analysis... 198

    Administrative crime analysis 200
    Predictive policing 202
    Intelligence analysis... 204
References 205

Chapter 9   Corrections information technology.................................. 207
Introduction 207
History of correction information technology 208
Jail booking/intake systems 208
    Jail booking/intake components... 209
    Subject name 209
    Subject's alias 211
    Personal information 211
    Inmate classification 211
        Suicide attempts.. 212
        Gang affiliation 212
    Medical history... 213
    Personal property... 213
Corrections management information systems 214
    Inmate tracking 215
        Cell tracking.. 215
        Movement tracking 215
        Inmate identification 216
        Disciplinary tracking 217
        Visitor tracking 217
        Prisoner phone logs... 218
        Medical tracking... 218
Doctors, dentists, and nurses 220
Inmate medical billing 220
Inmate accounting 221
Commissary and food service management 221
    Commissary.. 222
        Commissary inventory tracking subsystem 222
        Commissary privileges.. 222
        Commissary transactions 222
Sentence management.. 223
    Sentence compliance 223
    Inmate rehabilitation training... 224
    Inmate release and reintegration 225
    Victim information and victim notification 225
Schedule management 226
    Court scheduling... 226
    Medical and dental scheduling.. 227
    Work release.. 228

Community CMS 228
Presentencing investigation.. 229
Case management 229
Master name index.. 229
Case file... 229
Jail and prison management external systems interface requirements 230
Integration with AFISs and mug shot systems.. 230
References 231

Chapter 10 Prosecutor information management systems.................233
Prosecutorial system.. 233
History of prosecutorial systems.. 233
Prosecutor record management information system overview.............. 234
Case manager.. 234
Master name index.. 235
Victim and witness tracking... 235
Analysis and disposition.. 239
Master calendaring 239
Attorney assignment 243
Property and evidence tracking... 243
Document management... 243
Juror tracking... 246
Discovery tracking 246
Worthless checks.. 246
Restitution tracking 249
Child support module 249
Reports.. 252
Preformatted reports.. 252
Ad hoc report generator 252
Transfer data to external report generators... 254
Internet capabilities.. 254
Data warehousing and data mining capability 255
References 255

Chapter 11 Court management information systems...........................257
Introduction 257
Court docket module.. 259
Master name index 263
Sentencing and rulings 265
Work credit payments... 276
Cash bond.. 276
Unallocated 276
Multipayment 276
Garnishment 277

Warrants 277
Electronic ticketing 281
Court minutes 281
Court scheduling 281
Ad hoc search capability 284
Standardized reports 285
Integrated justice information systems and court management
software 285
References 285

**Chapter 12 The challenges of implementing a criminal justice
information system 287**
Critical success factors in implementing criminal justice
information systems 287
Functional requirement specification 288
Development of an FRS 288
    Business issues 288
    Functional issues 290
    Technical issues 291
Development of the request for proposal 292
Implementing the system 293
The role of the "executive" champion 293
The role of the project manager 294
The end user and managing their expectations 295
Project planning 297
Scope creep and how to manage it 298
Test plans and procedures 300
Bringing a new system operational 302
System documentation 303
Daily support for installed systems 304
Change management ensuring systems are used to their fullest
potential 305
User groups and criminal justice information systems 306
Managing system growth and budgeting for change 307
References 308

Chapter 13 The future of technology in law enforcement 309
Introduction 309
Driving forces influencing technology adoption 310
    Changes in policing models 310
    Environmental factors driving innovation 311
        Cloud computing and administrative functions 312
        Cloud computing and mission critical functions 312

The pervasive use of video 314
   Video surveillance and monitoring 314
   Automated license plate readers 315
   Mobile video systems 315
Further development of social media 316
Smartphone and tablet technology 317
Collaboration technologies 319
Continuing innovation 320
References 321

Index 323

Preface

During my lifetime, there were two events that influenced my future in information technology. In 1966, while I was in high school, I took a personal typing course, not realizing how important knowing how to type would become in our information technology age. Then in 1972, as I was preparing to graduate from college and had put off taking a math course until my final quarter at California Polytechnic University, San Luis Obispo, California, I was granted permission to substitute that math course with a computer science programming course. These two events became critical to my future and my contribution to criminal justice information systems.

In 1976, I transferred from the patrol unit to the planning, training, and research unit in the police department I was working for at the time. The first task the chief of police assigned me was to prove with empirical data that our department was in need of additional police officers. That is when I designed a patrol workload study that measured not only the number of calls for services we handled on a given shift but also the time consumed in handling these calls for service and other officer-generated activity. Here is where I put to use that computer science course that I took in my last quarter in college. I went to the city engineer and told him what we needed to do, and together he and I wrote a program on a Hewlett Packard 9830 Programmable Calculator in a new language called BASIC. The program captured the data pertaining to each call, and from this information, we were able to confirm that the officers spent 94% of their time on calls for service and officer-generated activities and 5% on administrative activities, leaving no time for unobligated patrol.

The Law Enforcement Assistance Administration declared the Patrol Workload Study a National Exemplary Project. The importance of this study is that I was asked to chair the National Steering Committee for the nation's first generic police record management system known as Police Operations Support System Elementary (POSSE). POSSE became the standard that is at the base of all record management systems to this day. Since these early days, I have had the pleasure of helping to implement information technologies in criminal justice agencies throughout the United States.

Criminal justice information systems have come a long way since the early days. Information technology permeates every aspect of the criminal justice environment as it does our everyday lives. The intent of this book is to provide an overview of the various software systems and technologies used in today's criminal justice environment and to suggest where this technology will evolve to in the future.

Acknowledgments

Professionally, I want to thank Paul Wormeli for his assistance in providing information used in this book. Paul is a pioneer in criminal justice information systems, and together we have implemented hundreds of criminal justice information systems across this nation. Together we have also conceived new technologies that public safety agencies use today but have no idea where the concepts that gave birth to these technologies came from. Paul has led the nation in promoting criminal justice information systems and continues to be a visionary in this field.

I also would like to thank the following firms for contributing the product examples used in this edition:

- CrimeStar Corporation: a software firm that provides computer-aided dispatch, police records management systems, field mobile computing systems, and jail management systems.
- Microfirm Software Corporation: a software firm that provided the various screen samples from their prosecutor information system.
- PTS Solutions: a software firm that provided the various screen samples from their court management system.

Personally, I also want to thank my family for their support and understanding throughout the many years while I traveled across the country implementing information technology systems for justice agencies and for their patience with me on vacations when I was working in support of these agencies.

Author

 **Dr. Ralph E. Ioimo** was a deputy chief of police in Simi Valley, California. He assisted the nation in establishing the first standardized police records management system and has participated in state and national steering committees on public safety automation. He has lectured at numerous state and national conferences and symposiums on public safety technology issues and published in both trade and academic journals on a variety of information technology issues. Dr. Ioimo was also the first executive director of the Integrated Justice Information Systems (IJIS) Institute in Ashburn, Virginia, and has been involved in helping the U.S. Department of Justice in defining and guiding the future IJIS direction. Dr. Ioimo also brings his extensive law enforcement experience, technology consulting experience, and academic background together to provide unique approaches to system implementation consulting.

Author contact information
Ralph E. Ioimo, DPA
Auburn University at Montgomery
161 Riverwood Lane
Alexander City, AL 35010, USA
(334) 354-4134
(334) 394-5457 Fax
rioimo@aum.edu

Author

chapter one

Overview of criminal justice information systems

The importance of information systems in a modern criminal justice environment spans every aspect of the criminal justice service delivery system.

List of definitions

CAD—computer-aided dispatch
CMS—court management system
COBOL—a programming language
FBI—Federal Bureau of Investigation
GJXDM—Global Justice Extensible Markup Language Data Model
GUI—graphical user interface
IJIS—integrated justice information system
JMS—jail management system
Mainframe—large central servers that supported terminals directly attached to the computer
NCIC 2000—National Crime Information Center
N-DEx—Law Enforcement National Database Exchange
NIEM—National Information Exchange Model
POSSE—Police Operations Support System Elementary
PROMIS—Prosecution Management Information Systems
RMS—record management system
Time slice—computer processor time required to complete a task

Introduction

Information systems are an essential part of today's criminal justice system. An information system is a process that uses information technology to capture, transmit, store, retrieve, manipulate, or display information used in one or more business processes (Alter, 1996). In today's environment, without information systems, the components of the criminal justice system would grind to a halt. For purposes of this text, we define the criminal justice systems to be comprised of the police, prosecutors, courts, and corrections.

Criminal justice agencies depend on information technology to perform their daily functions, similar to their business counterparts. As the world moves deeper into the information age, the need to manage information becomes ever more critical. There is no greater reliance on information technology than that found in the criminal justice system. Information technology is what makes the management of information in these environments possible. Without information technology, the criminal justice system and all subcomponents would grind to a halt.

The focus of this book is on the information systems used by criminal justice agencies. We discuss business applications used within each component of the criminal justice system wherein all members of each agency rely upon for common information. We also examine the workgroup applications that criminal justice agencies use to perform tasks related to a specific workgroup function.

This book focuses on the current information technology trends within the criminal justice information systems (CJISs). We examine information sharing between the various criminal justice agencies across disparate systems and how the use of new technologies inspired new approaches to sharing data between each of the criminal justice agencies. These exciting new technologies have given way to improved information-sharing efforts that enhance the effectiveness of the justice system.

We will begin exploring CJISs in this section by reviewing the following:

- The evolution of CJISs
- Exploring the criminal justice enterprise databases
- Exploring workgroup applications used in criminal justice agencies
- The current trends in CJISs

The evolution of CJISs

Like most information systems, CJISs evolved over time. Perhaps the earliest use of information technology occurred in New Orleans with the development of an electronic data processing device. The system was not a computer but a vacuum tube–operated calculator with a punch-card sorter and collator. New Orleans Police Department used this tool to summarize arrests and warrants (Brown, 2000). Throughout the 1950s, isolated uses of automated information systems existed, mostly among the larger justice agencies throughout the country. These customized software packages provided statistical information to the agencies they served. These systems were mainframe based and shared with other government departments. Only large cities could afford their own information systems, so there were few criminal justice agencies computerized before the late 1970s when computer technology started to become affordable to medium and small cities.

In the large agency environments, criminal justice software resided on the city or county's mainframe and was under the control of the data processing department, which reported to the finance or general services department within local government. Access to these systems occurred through terminals connected to a central server. Figure 1.1 depicts a typical mainframe environment of these early days.

These early information systems were under the total control of a data processing department. If end users sought reports, they would print the information on the master printer located in the data processing facilities; there was no local printer capability. These shared resources often competed for "time slices" on the mainframe. A "time slice" refers to computer processor time needed to complete a processing task (Whisenand & Tamaru, 1970). Computer time was under the management and control of the data processing department. Programs running on the mainframe received a priority assigned by a data processing operator. As an example, when the data processing shop ran the payroll checks, it had priority. The other applications had to wait until the payroll checks completed before they could complete their processing. Other city or county applications took precedence over the justice applications, and because the justice

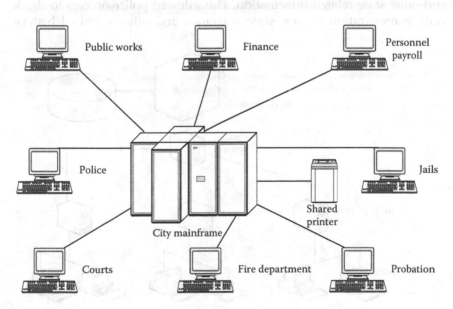

Figure 1.1 Central server environment.

agency did not have control of the mainframe, there was rarely anything an organization could do about these delays.

Development of criminal history systems

The Federal Bureau of Investigation (FBI) developed the first nationally recognized CJIS known as, the National Crime Information Center (NCIC). The NCIC is a national information network operated by the FBI since 1967, which provides criminal justice agencies throughout the country with access to information on stolen vehicles and stolen property, wanted persons, and missing persons (Chu, 2001). The FBI provides each state with access to NCIC. Each state provides access to the counties, and local agencies can access the state system through their own computers. Figure 1.2 depicts the NCIC information flow.

Initially, local agencies accessed NCIC via a teletype machine. Data returns printed in a single line format with data separated by forward slashes (/). The abbreviation of data meant operators had to know the abbreviations or look them up in a manual (Whisenand & Tamaru, 1970).

Many states, and some larger police jurisdictions, created their own criminal information systems, which allowed local agencies to obtain criminal information at the state and local levels but were not a part of the NCIC system. Many of the state systems provided access to the Department of Motor Vehicles (DMV) information, state arrest data and other state related information. This allowed police officers to check vehicle registration details, state warrants, and other criminal history

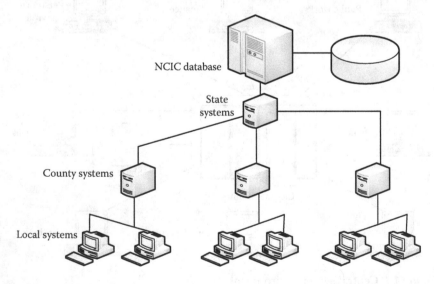

Figure 1.2 NCIC information flow.

information. Officers in the field provided dispatchers with the person's name and driver's license number, and the dispatcher entered the individual through the teletype into the state and NCIC systems and would get potential wants and warrants from the state and national systems. With links to the DMV, they would also get a driver's license and vehicle registration details. Today, every state has a CJIS specific to that state's requirements but usually contains similar information as to what NCIC provides at the federal level.

Several prominent local wants and warrant systems were developed in the 1960s and 1970s, such as the City of Los Angeles, the Automated Wants and Warrant System, and the Police Information Network system developed by the San Francisco and Oakland area police agencies (Whisenand & Tamaru, 1970). Today, there are many similar systems throughout the United States. With the emphasis on information sharing that has expanded since 9/11, these local systems provide their information to the state and federal systems.

In 1971, the FBI added a computerized criminal history (CCH) file, containing records of individual offenders' criminal histories. The CCH program gradually developed; only 12 states and the federal government contributed records to the system until recently. With the Community Oriented Policing Services Making Officer Redeployment (COPS/MORE) program implemented by the Clinton administration, many states rewrote their CCH systems and now regularly access the FBI system.

In the 1990s, the FBI completely reengineered NCIC and released NCIC 2000. NCIC 2000 is the latest version of this system. In reengineering NCIC, the FBI added significantly more capability to match technology advances. NCIC 2000 now has the capability of providing mug shots of wanted suspects, which can be sent directly to field officers that have laptops in their vehicles. They also provided single fingerprint identification capability. If the officer has a fingerprint cradle in his or her vehicle, the officer can place the subject's finger in the cradle, transmit the fingerprint to NCIC, and quickly obtain want or warrant information on that individual (FBI, n.d.a).

Another crucial database supported by the FBI is the "Combined DNA Index System" known as CODIS. One part of CODIS is the National DNA Index System or NDIS. NDIS contains the DNA profiles contributed by federal, state, and local participating forensic laboratories (FBI, n.d.b). Upon collecting DNA samples, the agency submits them to the state for analysis, and CODIS searches for a match. CODIS matches a target DNA evidence against the DNA records contained in the database. Once CODIS identifies a match, the laboratories involved in the match exchange information to verify the match and to establish coordination between their two agencies (FBI, n.d.b).

Since 9/11, law enforcement has recognized the need to share information on criminal activity between justice agencies. The importance of sharing information about crimes and criminals is a key factor in the fight against terrorism. This brought about the creation of new databases to assist in this task. A vital national database developed to promote this information sharing supported by the FBI is the Law Enforcement National Database Exchange (N-DEx). N-DEx is a repository of criminal justice records, available in a secure online environment, managed by the FBI's Criminal Justice Information Services (CJIS) Division (FBI, n.d.c). N-DEx brings together information such as incident and case reports, arrest reports, computer-aided dispatch (CAD) calls, traffic citations, narratives, photos, supplements, booking and incarceration data, and parole/probation information. In addition, N-DEx automatically correlates and resolves data from open and closed reports to determine relationships between people, vehicles/property, locations, and/or crime characteristics. It also supports multijurisdictional task forces—enhancing national information sharing, links between regional and state systems, and effective regional information sharing (FBI, n.d.c).

Information-sharing technologies are the wave of the future in CJIS databases. A vital part of CJIS databases are criminal justice history systems, which is addressed throughout this book.

Evolution of CAD systems

CAD was one of the first significant applications built for police. A CAD system aids communication center personnel in the performance of their duties. Before CAD systems, call takers manually wrote down information provided by the caller. This information included the location and call type as well the caller information. The call taker would time-stamp a card that they placed in a time clock with the date and time they received the call. In most dispatch centers, the dispatchers had several card slots for each unit they controlled. The dispatcher would place the awaiting call into one of these slots, and when a unit became available, they would read the information aloud over the radio for the intended unit and time-stamp the card to confirm the date and time they dispatched the unit. When the unit arrived on the scene and notified the dispatcher that they arrived, the dispatcher would time-stamp the call card to show the time the unit arrived. Finally, when the unit cleared the call, they would advise dispatch that they were clear of the call and would provide a disposition. The dispatcher again would time-stamp the card with the time the officer(s) cleared the call and then manually enter the final disposition on the dispatch card.

The dispatcher also made notes about calls in progress and officer-generated activities such as traffic stops, on what communication centers referred to as a "radio log." At the end of the shift, the dispatcher would turn in their handwritten radio log to a clerical person. That person typed the logged information and produced a daily activity log. The log depicts all activities occurring on a shift. Management relied upon this log for a variety of purposes. They often referred back to these logs to provide the press information associated with an event.

Although there were many variations of the previously mentioned process, the same basic steps took place in most police agencies. It was a laborious process and rarely accurately reflected all the activities associated with an event. In addition to the activities described earlier, call takers and dispatchers manually accessed other supporting data and information contained in volumes of reference manuals. The generation of management reports from the data captured was an exhausting, manual processing of the captured data. Computer-aided dispatching significantly streamlined this process and provided massive amounts of data to the call takers, dispatchers, supervisors, and management personnel.

The installation of the first CAD system occurred in 1968, in the South Bay Regional Communication Center. The company that built this system was Planning Research Corporation (PRC) and for years was the only supplier of CAD systems. This was a mainframe-based system written in assembler language (Whisenand & Tamaru, 1970). This early system provided the ability to capture the call information and forward it to a pending queue, prioritizing the call based on a predetermine criteria. The CAD system captured officer-generated activities and allowed the dispatchers to monitor officer activities and show where units were at any given time. Units, not assigned to a call, appeared in an "available units" list. The system was able to recommend units based on the location of the call and the unit assigned to that beat. These systems brought efficiency to the busy dispatch center environment. Management obtained vital information in the form of preformatted reports.

The bottom line was these new CAD systems began the automation of the communication center. The evolution of CAD systems advanced rapidly throughout the 1980s. With today's advanced technologies, CAD systems provide capabilities never thought possible in 1968. Chapter 5 fully describes the current and future capabilities of CAD systems.

Record management systems

Record management systems (RMSs) are a significant part of each criminal justice agency. Until the mid-1970s, there was no standard definition of an RMS for any criminal justice agency, not even within a single discipline. The majority of the justice agencies kept manual records. Most justice agencies could not afford expensive information technology. If they had any information technology at all, agencies shared it with other governmental entities (Whisenand & Tamaru, 1970). Most of these systems provided management information such as, crime statistics, number of cases prosecuted, number of inmates incarcerated, and other similar statistics.

The National Advisory Commission on Criminal Justice Standards and Goals called for the need for criminal justice agencies to automate their information processes. They emphasized the need to be able to share information across agencies and justice disciplines. The commission defined a set of standards they recommended justice agencies follow in the development of information technology and RMSs (National Advisory Commission on Criminal Justice Standards and Goals, 1973). The Law Enforcement Assistance Administration (LEAA) began to fund the development of RMSs for police, prosecutors, courts, and corrections. By the mid-1970s, LEAA realized that funding the development of software applications without a solid definition of what these systems should accomplish was wasting precious federal funds. A more concentrated and coordinated effort was necessary to achieve the goal of automating the criminal justice system and sharing of information between the various agencies. As a result, in the late 1970s, LEAA funded the development of several computer software initiatives for the development of generic police and prosecutor RMSs.

The timing of these initiatives was pivotal in that the cost of computer systems was rapidly declining while their capabilities were rising. During this time, minicomputers were rapidly replacing mainframes, and microcomputers just entered the computer market. This would make information technology affordable to most criminal justice agencies. In the mid-1970s, software development was expensive. LEAA determined that if the federal government funded the development of RMS systems, justice agencies would have the ability to adapt this software to their environment. This would limit costs to the purchase of hardware and any customizations to the public domain software that was necessary for their agency. The public domain software would also be available to software companies, and these companies could make enhancements to this software and market those enhancements as they saw fit. As a result, LEAA funded the development of two key information systems:

- POSSE—Police Operations Support System Elementary, a police RMS
- PROMIS—Prosecution Management Information Systems, software for district attorney records management

The development of court and jail/corrections management software systems did not happen the same way.

The 1980s saw a significant expansion of information systems for criminal justice agencies. They were primarily COBOL systems built on minicomputers. They were character based and used a central server for all processing and data storage. Several companies began to enter the criminal justice software market. As they did, each company built their systems on selected hardware platforms. This made these systems highly proprietary. Systems developed on a Hewlett-Packard platform could not be easily transferred to an IBM platform without a significant software rewrite.

These early systems used flat file data structures, which made searching for data across files extremely difficult. As an example, data pertaining to an individual arrested for a crime resided in the arrest file. Similar data for a subject might also exist in the traffic accident file. To obtain information on a single individual required a different search of each file. The mid-1980s brought about advances in database technology, and soon developers overcame these difficulties using relational databases.

In the 1990s, significant changes in hardware and networking technologies occurred and RMSs changed significantly. No longer was it necessary to maintain central servers to handle data processing needs. New system architectures created distributed data processing systems with multiple files servers. The proliferation of the personal computer (PC) provided the ability to use intelligent workstations at the desktop level, linked through high-speed data networks. Software technology also advanced, providing graphical user interfaces. Open System Architectures provided the ability to migrate application software from one hardware platform to another with little difficulty. Criminal justice RMSs advanced significantly during this time. Today these systems represent the latest in information technology and continue to evolve and keep pace with the private sector.

Mobile computing

Like other justice information technologies, mobile computing evolved over time. The original intent of mobile computing was to reduce airtime or time officers spent on the radio. This served two purposes: (1) to reduce radio traffic between field units and emergency services communication centers and (2) to reduce the workload on dispatchers. To accomplish both goals, radio vendors developed message status terminals (MSTs). Early MST devices consisted of five keys that when pressed would provide dispatch with a predefined status. These devices later grew to ten keys but served the same purpose, and that was to inform dispatch of a field unit's status change. These devices provided one-way communications. When a unit came on duty, they would press a key to signify that they were on duty and ready to take calls. This would inform the dispatcher with a light or a status change on the computer signifying they were now available for calls. When the dispatcher dispatched a call to these units, the officers in the unit would press a key that would inform the dispatcher that they received the call. When the unit went in route to the call, the officer would press another key on the MST unit. When the unit arrived on the scene, they would press yet another key, which notified the dispatcher that the unit was on scene. When the field unit cleared the call, they would press another key to signify that they were clear and available for calls. Modifications to this approach existed, but this was the basic function of the MST units. These units were not intelligent devices and could only provide one-way, nonverbal communications with the dispatcher. Later devices had emergency buttons that if pressed would alert the dispatcher that the officer had an emergency.

As information technology progressed, the field mobile computer became intelligent. Many of the radio system providers developed mobile computers for police cars. These devices provided a small monochrome display and could communicate with the CAD system and external information systems such as state criminal history systems, DMV, and of course NCIC. These devices were computers, absent of data storage capabilities, known as mobile data terminals (MDTs). Field officers had the ability to communicate with dispatch and other mobile units. Dispatchers sent all the data associated with a call for service directly to the MDT. Officers silently communicated with dispatchers and other operations personnel. They could also communicate between units and supervisors on the system. A strong enhancement brought about by MDTs was the ability for officers in the field to inquire into local, state, and national databases without interference from communications.

In the mid-1980s, agencies began to replace MDTs with laptop computers. Laptops are intelligent devices with disk storage capabilities as well as communications capabilities. The usefulness of laptops is that officers can remove these devices from the vehicle and use them to write reports in a victim's home or other place. When laptops include disk storage, officers have the ability to store additional reference information.

More recently is the introduction of tablet PCs to the fray of mobile computing technologies. This device is similar to a laptop computer and has the same computing capabilities but uses a stylus as an input device as well as touch screen capability. Tablets allow officers to write reports in a fashion similar to paper reports. Several public safety software vendors developed electronic report forms similar to the paper forms these devices are in the process of replacing. Other handheld devices such as personal digital assistants (PDA) are entering service in public safety, which are found as a part of all modern cell phone technology currently on the market. These devices are smaller versions of the tablet PC used for automated citation generation, field reporting, and other similar tasks.

Since the 1980s, mobile computing advanced significantly. These devices became more powerful and have the ability to store large amounts of data. Adding to these advances in mobile computing is the ability to use transport mediums. One of these mediums is a broad-spectrum radio operating in the 700- and 800-MHz band range with high-speed data throughput capabilities. Alternatives to private radio also emerged for data transport, such as cellular digitized packet data, code division multiple access, and 802.11a-g wireless networking, also known as Wi-Fi. The Federal Communication Commission also added the 700-MHz radio spectrum to public safety, which provides additional data transmission capability that will allow officers to use their laptop computers in the field at desktop speed. Other proprietary technology emerged such as 4.9 GHz, which provides high-speed data transmission, similar to 802.11a-g. These new technologies significantly enhanced the field officer's computing capacity.

Exploring criminal justice enterprise computing

The term "record management system" developed in the early days of criminal justice information technology. This term developed because the initial attempts at computerizing criminal justice agencies began with the computerization of record keeping functions within these agencies. It is a term that most still apply when referring to the central computing system within a justice agency. Although record management continues to be a significant part of CJISs, it no longer represents the sole focus of these systems. An appropriate term for these computer systems that encompass an entire organization is an enterprise computing system (Turban, 1995). An enterprise computing system encompasses information system components that everyone in a criminal justice agency needs to obtain to perform their jobs. As an example, a master name index is a file or subsystem that contains all the names of subjects with whom a justice agency has had previous dealings. Another example is the incident report that follows a case through all justice agencies. Each agency maintains an incident report, documenting the events associated with an incident. The incident report is part of the enterprise database and accessible to all persons and workgroups throughout the justice agency. Figure 1.3 depicts a police enterprise computing system.

Court management systems

The managing of the courts is a significant undertaking that requires significant information technology support. Court management systems (CMSs) typically track all activities pertaining to court operations. This includes maintaining both civil and criminal records. They track everything involved in a court case, including defendant, plaintiff, other parties, offenses, fines, court costs, minutes, and court orders. These systems are as complex as police RMSs and include interfaces to various external systems.

CMSs incorporate many of the following components:

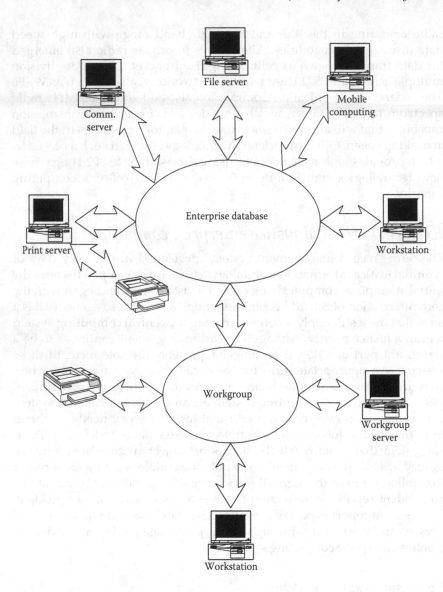

Figure 1.3 Enterprise computing system.

- Case files
- Court docketing
- Defendant files
- Plaintiff files
- Warrants and protective orders
- Affidavits

- Accounting system (fines, payments, etc.)
- Courtroom scheduling
- Personnel management
- Numerous reports

Each of these components serves both as stand-alone modules of a CMS and integrates with both internal and external systems.

CMSs integrate with other information technology components. As an example, CMSs integrate with fingerprint identification systems, mug shot systems, probation management systems, document imaging, and other similar technologies. CMSs also interface to external systems such as the following:

- Police RMSs
- Jail management systems
- Probation management systems
- National and state criminal history databases
- DMV

In Chapter 12, we discuss all aspects of CMSs and the way this technology is moving. CMSs are leading the way in establishing criminal justice standards for data exchange. The new technologies associated with court systems have a significant impact on the criminal justice system.

Correction management systems

Correction management systems provide jails and prisons with the ability to manage the intake and the long-term housing of prisoners. Jails differ from prisons in that they house two different types of inmates. Jails house people who stand accused of a crime but not yet convicted. They also hold those convicted of a crime and who are serving their sentence at the county or city jail. Prisons, on the other hand, are either state or federal institutions that house prisoners already convicted of a crime. Each facility has both similar and different needs that information technology must address.

Correction management systems automate the collection, control, and production of essential jail and prison operational and management information. These solutions help corrections administrators track inmates and guests and manage cell and population information, and they record and generate audit trails for legal protection. Correction management systems typically consist of the following:

- Inmate management
- Track inmates

- Find inmates
- Inmate release
- Cell checks
- Inmate movement
- Facility management
- Booking processing
- Commissary management
- Account management
- Visitor management
- Medical records

Like other criminal justice systems, corrections management systems link to other subsystems. As an example, corrections management systems typically require access to the following:

- Electronic imaging systems
- Automated fingerprint identification systems
- Bar code systems
- Mug shot systems
- Intranet
- Office automation tools

In addition to these other systems that corrections requires the ability to access, most correction management systems require access to external databases such as the following:

- NCIC
- State criminal history systems
- Court systems
- Other databases as required locally

Correction management systems focus on the operations of a jail or prison. Like other criminal justice systems, they evolved over time. Today they are the mainstream of jails and prisons. Chapter 9 provides detailed discussions on jail and prison management systems.

Data warehousing and data mining

Data mining is a term used to describe knowledge discovery in databases, knowledge extraction, data archaeology, data exploration, data pattern processing, data dredging, information harvesting, and software (Turban & Aronson, 1998). Central to today's CJISs is the ability to store large volumes of data and to be able to access that information in a multitude of ways. Justice agencies have always had difficulty in accessing information. In the manual systems of yesterday, it was almost an impossible task to get information from handwritten reports, particularly from the narrative portion of the report. Similarly, the volumes of these reports often necessitated that criminal justice agencies purge these data from the manual archives. Agencies often lease, purchase, or build physical warehouses to accommodate archived data. To access this information requires knowing the case numbers, arrest numbers, or names of the individuals associated with an incident. The information was not terribly useful for investigations or other purposes. Obtaining information required manually searching each of the stored reports, which made accessing these data difficult.

Data mining and data warehousing provide justice agencies with the ability to access data in a variety of ways. Chapter 2 discusses the ways in which the various justice agencies use data mining and warehousing.

Workgroup applications in criminal justice agencies

Workgroup applications are typically standalone applications that perform or support a function. Workgroup applications go beyond the scope of enterprise computing systems. These may consist of information that is specific to a group, functions not performed by other units or maintain information that prohibited from being a part of the enterprise computing system.

Criminal justice agencies implement workgroup applications in that they typically operate as standalone systems although they are dependent on their enterprise database for information. As CJISs progress, workgroup applications develop.

The following is a summary of typical workgroup applications in use within justice agencies.

Property and evidence systems

Police and sheriff departments throughout the country use property and evidence systems. These systems require access to the enterprise computing system and to external systems for access to other justice systems. Property and evidence systems track the location of property contained within the property and evidence room. These systems typically support bar code readers and digital photography for the storage of pictures of pieces of property. Property and evidence systems also interface with court systems and case management systems for case disposition information. They also maintain property custody information. The primary purpose of the property and evidence systems is to control and manage the property and evidence within a property room.

In Chapter 6, the author describes the state-of-the-art technology for property and evidence systems and its integration with the enterprise computing system.

Crime analysis and geographic mapping systems

Crime analysis mapping systems provide crime analysts with the ability to plot the locations of crimes, the suspects that commit those crimes, as well as provide predictions of crime by the time of the day and day of the week. Mapping systems link to the enterprise database and draw information from external systems. These mapping systems provide the crime analyst with the ability to geographically assess the crime patterns. Recent trends are to provide these crime maps on the mobile computers that allow officers to view the crime patterns spatially. Crime analysis systems also provide the crime analysts with the ability to perform crime suspect correlations and pattern analysis. They can generate crime analysis bulletins and other relevant information needed in the field.

Within this book, the reader will learn how justice agencies use crime analysis systems and the future direction of this technology.

Automated fingerprint identification systems and live scan devices

Automated fingerprint identification systems (AFIS) capture and store fingerprint data. Fingerprints are the most accurate way to identify an individual (Ashbaugh, 1991). Each criminal justice agency requires the ability to make positive identifications. AFIS and access to them make these identifications possible. The primary system categorizes fingerprints and stores them in a retrievable format. AFIS are most effective when they contain a large number of fingerprints. That is why regional AFIS are the most cost effective.

Live scan devices provide the ability to capture fingerprint data and to search AFIS databases. Local agencies typically maintain a live scan device to capture fingerprints and transmit the fingerprint data to and search the AFIS database. Live scan is a significant improvement in fingerprint technology. It provides the ability to capture the fingerprint information by placing the subject's fingers on a glass scanner and then scanning the prints. Smaller scanning devices also have the ability to scan single prints. Linking live scan devices to external databases, such as the FBI's NCIC 2000, provides the ability to search locally and at the national level.

Both live scan and AFIS are workgroup applications that are expanding throughout the justice community. We will explore this technology in detail in Chapter 6.

Mug shot systems

Mug shot systems typically provide justice agencies the ability to photograph individuals and categorize these photographs. Criminal justice agencies obtain photographs of subjects through a variety of resources. The arrest photograph is the most common, which agencies usually take at the time of booking a person into jail. In the past, booking agencies would take a picture of the subject booked into a jail or of someone under investigation for a crime. A number identifies the subject in the photo by either the booking or case number. Agencies kept the photo in the person's arrest file or as part of a case file. Some criminal justice agencies stored these files in bound book volumes.

Although the manual process for capturing, categorizing, and storing mug shots is still in use in many departments, information technology coupled with digital photography significantly enhanced mug shots and their value in the criminal justice system. Today, there are several automated mug shot systems. These systems have the ability to connect the mug shot to a case.

More importantly, the automation of mug shot systems significantly improved criminal justice agencies ability to access photographs. Mug shot systems provide the ability to produce photo lineups. In the past, investigators put photo lineups together manually, usually selecting photographs from a set of real photographs maintained by the police department. Investigators had to be cautious as to how they put these mug shots together at the risk of misleading the individual viewing the photographs. As an example, the photographs had to be of the same size, with similar background so not to direct a person to a photograph and to the best of the investigator's ability ensure that each of the people depicted in the photos had similar physical characteristics. These photo lineups typically consisted of six photographs, often referred to as a "six-pack."

The automated mug shot systems provide the ability to generate photo lineups. The benefit to computer-generated photo lineups is that the computer compares the description of the primary subject to other mug shot photos. The system then selects the other photos based on the primary suspect's description. The operator enters the identifying information such as race, gender, weight, height, date of birth, distinguishing facial features such as scars, marks, facial hair, etc., and the system selects the like photos to display in a six-pack format. These mug shot systems also serve a variety of other tasks. The Orange County, Florida, sheriff's office is using a mug shot system with a laser printer to produce "wanted" flyers for those sought on warrants. The pictures on these flyers are remarkably clear, with excellent resolution (Dempsy & Frost, 2005; Pavlis, 1992).

Facial recognition systems

Closely aligned with the mug shot systems is the latest biometric technology of facial recognition systems. Facial recognition systems are an advanced technology that allows criminal justice agencies to compare facial features of an individual to a mug shot database. The potential for this new technology is enormous. Facial recognition systems can pick someone's face out of a crowd, remove that face from the rest of the scene, and compare it with a database full of stored images. For this software to work, it has to know what a basic face looks like. Facial recognition software can recognize a face and then measure the various features of each face (Bonsor, 2006).

If a person looks in the mirror, they can see that their face has certain recognizable landmarks. These are the peaks and valleys that make up the different facial features. Visionics defines these landmarks as nodal points. There are approximately 80 nodal points on a human face. Here are a few of the nodal points measured by the software:

- Distance between eyes
- Width of nose
- Depth of eye sockets
- Cheekbones
- Jaw line
- Chin

The measurement of these nodal points creates a numerical code or a string of numbers that represents the face in a database known as a face print (Bonsor, 2006).

Facial recognition software has many uses. It can see through superficial facial disguises such as facial hair. Homeland Security will surely propel this new technology. In Chapter 6, we discuss facial recognition software and mug shot systems in detail.

Citation collection systems

Municipal courts throughout the United States are responsible for tracking and collecting all forms of traffic citations. To facilitate this effort, these courts rely upon citation collection systems. The most modern of these systems allow for the issuing agencies such as police departments to transmit the citation data directly to a citation collection system. The most modern of these systems provide the field officer with a handheld device that ranges from a PDA to a customized ticket writer. These devices electronically manage the citation process from issuance through collection.

Citation collection systems interface to several justice databases for both inquiry and data entry. Typically, when an officer writes a ticket using the specialized devise, the system queries other databases to verify the information and checks for outstanding wants and warrants.

As an example, when an officer enters the personal information of a driver, the system sends off a query to check local, state, and national databases for outstanding wants and warrants attached to the individual. In the case of a parking citation, the system will check the Department of Motor Vehicle records for the registered owner facts and check for stolen vehicle status outstanding wants, warrants, or other holds. When the officer completes the citation, the system automatically sends the data to the local agencies computer and to the court of jurisdiction.

These systems also have the ability to age citations, track payments, and generate warrants or other collection mechanisms. Citation collection systems are extremely popular because they virtually eliminate the need for data entry clerks. They are far more effective at managing the collection process and provide meaningful management information.

Case and investigation management systems

Managing the criminal investigation process is a critical function performed by investigations management. In most departments, the investigation manager assigns cases to investigators based on their area of responsibility such as burglary, robbery, crimes against persons, and other crimes. In the 1970s, the Rand Corporation conducted a study of the investigations process and found that investigator case loads were large, many of the cases assigned to investigators lacked any real possibility of resolution, and most cases investigators were able to solve had a significant number of leads generated from the preliminary investigation (Greenwood & Petersilia, 1975). This study disclosed the need for scrutiny of the investigative process. It found that patrol solves most crimes and those solved by detectives were those with strong leads, usually provided through the preliminary investigation process. Crimes with the strongest leads are most likely candidates for investigators to focus their attention. Those crimes with few leads are not likely to receive any investigator attention. Resulting from this study was the development of managing criminal investigation (MCI) processes. MCI consisted of using solvability factors to aid investigative commanders in deciding which crimes they should assign and which they should inactivate. It also required assigning a review period to check progress on those cases under investigation. MCI required that the agency inform crime victims of the status of their case. If the case lacked solvability, the agency sent a letter to the victim informing him or her that they exhausted all leads, and they placed the case on inactive status unless additional leads developed. If the case met a certain solvability level, the agency sent a letter informing the victim of the case status.

Those agencies that adopted MCI as a process realized significant improvements in the investigative process. Crime clearances increased significantly. In the early implementation of MCI, the agencies manually administered the program. This slowed the investigation process, which required a better means of conducting the MCI process.

With the advancement of information technology occurring at about the same time as the birth of MCI, companies began to create software applications to assist in this process. At first, the system provided basic MCI data, such as solvability factors, and reports that provided case aging information. These systems grew into a significant workgroup application that is now part of every major system on the market. Chapter 6 discusses these case management systems and their application in today's criminal justice information technology environments.

Current trends in CJISs

Current trends within the criminal justice system are clearly moving toward enhancing the ability to share data across the criminal justice agency boundaries. Although CAD, RMS, and mobile computing systems are still growing and advancing in their capabilities, the focus is on the ability to share data across justice agencies. Several new initiatives have been developed, which are bringing about the sharing of information among justice agencies. Advances in technology make sharing of information across disparate systems possible.

Sharing of information among and within each of these justice agencies is critical to efficiency. As an example, it is essential for one police department to know that a man they just arrested for burglary has a history of burglary in the neighboring town and has a court case pending on similar charges in another neighboring community. The courts and the prosecutors need this same sharing of information. Modern information technologies allow this sharing to occur without the need for expensive interface software to exchange information across different hardware and software platforms. Within this book, we explore the various methods used to accomplish this critical information-sharing effort.

In the recent past, criminal justice agencies shared information manually through paper copies of reports. Agencies gleamed data off these reports by manually reviewing them for the information they needed. Often they entered the data into their information systems to fulfill a need in their component of the justice process. As an example, police sends case information to the district attorney's office for prosecution. The district attorney's office entered the data off the police reports into their information systems. Similarly, when the district attorney filed its cases in court, they would provide hard copies of the case and pass them to the court clerk. The court clerk then entered the data contained from these documents into their information systems. This same process repeated itself through each agency within the criminal justice system.

The primary reason these agencies processed data independently was because of the many different information systems available in the market, each promoted by different software providers on different hardware platforms, using different relational databases and written in different software languages. Within a discipline of the criminal justice systems, vendors optimized multiple products for proprietary hardware and operating system platforms. It was common for each police department within a county or region to use a different vendor's software for their enterprise computing systems. Data sharing between police agencies required sophisticated interface software. Electronically sharing these data with other components of the criminal justice system was rare.

The need for criminal justice agencies to access one another's information is essential to the effective processing of information in today's justice environment. In the mid-1990s, the U.S. Department of Justice (DOJ), Office of Justice Programs (OJP), launched a significant integrated justice information system (IJIS) initiative. Developments with new technologies such as Microsoft's Extensible Markup Language, known as XML, opened new doors to the ability to share data across differing systems. This new technology became the impetus behind the IJIS movement. Sharing data between and among criminal justice agencies brings about many benefits. Appropriately implemented, IJIS enhances the ability to share information. Sharing information provides numerous benefits. Integration also significantly improves the consistency and reliability of information and enables instant access by key decision makers (Roberts, 2004).

Although XML provides the necessary tools to exchange data, the ability to exchange data requires the definition of standard data elements and data schema. This required the justice community to come together and agree on a set of data elements that all could use regardless of hardware or software platform. The U.S. DOJ, through the OJP, recognized the importance of defining these data elements. Together with the Global Justice Information Sharing Initiative, DOJ contracted Georgia Tech Research Institute to develop the Global Justice Extensible Markup Language Data Model (GJXDM). OJP created the Structure Task Force (GXSTF), which worked closely with researchers at the Georgia Tech Research Institute. The GXSTF issues new releases and evaluates each version of the GJXDM. The GXSTF solicits feedback from technical experts and practitioners in both industry and government and authorizes GJXDM changes based on this feedback. Future releases contain all approved additions, deletions, and modifications, with a cumulative change log published along with each release. When GXSTF approves a reasonable number of updates, they release a new version (U.S. Department of Justice, Office of Justice Programs, Bureau of Justice Assistance, n.d.).

The GJXDM is an XML standard designed specifically for criminal justice information exchanges, providing law enforcement, public safety agencies, prosecutors, public defenders, and the judicial branch with a tool that effectively shares data and information in a timely manner (U.S. Department of Justice, Office of Justice Programs, Bureau of Justice Assistance, n.d.). The GJXDM removes the individual agency burden of creating information exchange standards, and because of its extensibility, there is more flexibility to deal with unique agency requirements and changes. By use of a common vocabulary understood system to system, GJXDM enables access from various sources and reuse in multiple applications (U.S. Department of Justice, Office of Justice Programs, Bureau of Justice Assistance, n.d.). This new technology opened new data exchange capabilities among all justice agencies and will significantly improve information exchange capabilities among all criminal justice agencies.

In 2001, the Department of Homeland Security and the DOJ came together and significantly expanded the GJXDM concept and developed the National Information Exchange Model (NIEM; http://www.niem.gov). NIEM is an outgrowth of the U.S. DOJ's GJXDM project. NIEM is expanding to include other federal and state agencies such as the Office of the Director of National Intelligence, FBI, Texas, Florida, New York, Pennsylvania, California, and others (National Information Exchange Model, n.d.). NIEM provides the operational tools and proven methodologies to establish and implement standards to allow real-time information sharing (National Information Exchange Model, n.d.). All new systems developed and implemented in Justice, Homeland Security, and related agencies require NIEM compliance. Companies that provide software systems to these agencies have or are in the process of making their software NIEM compliant.

The chapters that follow fully discuss these applications, and their use is explained.

References

Alter, S. (1996). *Information Systems: A Management Perspective*. (2nd ed.). Menlo Park, CA: The Benjamin/Cummings Publishing Company Inc.

Ashbaugh, D. R. (1991). Ridgeology. *Journal of Forensic Identification, 41* (1), 16–64.

Bonsor, K. (2006). *How Facial Recognition Works*. Retrieved from http://computer.howstuffworks.com/facial-recognition1.htm.

Brown, M. (2000). Criminal Justice Discovers Information Technology. *The Nature of Crime: Continuity and Change*, Volume 1. Retrieved from http://inventors.about.com/od/fstartinventions/a/forensic_4.htm.

Chu, J. (2001). *Law Enforcement Information Technology, A Managerial, Operational, and Practitioner Guide*. Washington, DC: CRC Press.

Dempsy, J. S., & Frost, L. S. (2005). *An Introduction to Policing*. Belmont, CA: Thomson Wadsorth.

FBI. (n.d.a). *Press Release*. Retrieved from https://www.fbi.gov/pressrel/press rel99/ncic2000.htm.

FBI. (n.d.b). *Frequently Asked Questions on the CODIS Program and the National DNA Index System*. Retrieved from The FBI Newsletter: https://www.fbi.gov /about-us/lab/biometric-analysis/codis/codis-and-ndis-fact-sheet.

FBI. (n.d.c). *N-DEx: The Leader in National Information Sharing*. Retrieved from The FBI Newsletter: https://www.fbi.gov/about-us/cjis/n-dex.

Greenwood, P. W., & Petersilia, J. (1975). *The Criminal Investigation Process. Volume I: Summary and Policy Implications*. Santa Monica, CA: Rand Corporation Publications.

Microsoft. (n.d.). *Government*. Retrieved from http://www.microsoft.com /industry/government/public.

National Advisory Commission on Criminal Justice Standards and Goals. (1973). *Criminal Justice Systems*. Washington, DC: U.S. Government Printing Office.

National Information Exchange Model. (n.d.). Technical NIEM. Retrieved from http://www.niem.gov.

Pavlis, J. J. (1992). Mug-shot imaging systems. *FBI Law Enforcement Bulletin* (August), 20–22.

Roberts, G. (2004). *Integration in the Context of Justice Information Systems: A Common Understanding*. Sacramento, CA: Search Group, Inc.

Turban, E. (1995). *Decision Support and Expert Systems, Management Support Systems*. (4th ed.). Englewood Cliffs, NJ: Prentice Hall.

Turban, E., & Aronson, J. E. (1998). *Decision Support Systems and Intelligent Systems*. (5th ed.). Upper Saddle River, NJ: Prentice Hall.

U.S. Department of Justice, Office of Justice Programs, Bureau of Justice Assistance. (n.d.). *Building Exchange Content using the Global JXDM: A User Guide for Practitioners and Developers*. Retrieved from http://it.ojp.gov/Search?q=GXSTF.

Whisenand, P. M., & Tamaru, T. T. (1970). *Automated Police Information Systems*. New York, John Wiley & Sons, Inc.

chapter two

Justice information system standards and national systems

Justice information standards have evolved over the years. Standards have been developed that criminal justice information systems must adhere to in serving criminal justice agencies and for the sharing of data.

List of definitions

GJXDM—global justice extensible markup language data model
HTML—hypertext markup language
LEITSC—Law Enforcement Information Standards Council
NCIC 2000—National Crime Information Center 2000
N-DEx—National Data Exchange
NIBRS—National Incident-Based Reporting System
NIEM—National Information Exchange Model
WWW—World Wide Web
XML—extensible markup language

Introduction

In the earlier days of criminal justice automation, the development of systems occurred without standards. The exchange of information between systems was difficult and a significant software development effort was required to share data. Because of this, the integration of systems was limited. As technology progressed, there were a number of advancements that improved the ability to share data. To share information effectively, it became necessary to establish data exchange standards. These exchange standards significantly improved the ability to share information.

As we describe the various systems in use today within the criminal justice agencies, it is necessary to understand the technologies used by these systems. The following subsections describe new standards and tools that are in place and their use in the criminal justice information system is demonstrated. Also discussed are the standards that the criminal justice community adapted for their use with information technology.

Hypertext markup language

To follow the presentation of data across different hardware platforms, it is necessary to understand how hypertext markup language (HTML) has contributed to this capability. HTML is a standard used to develop Web browsers. HTML has allowed the Internet to operate across different hardware platforms. HTML is not a programming language but rather a "markup" language (TuTarz.com, n.d.). A markup language uses markup tags to describe the contents on a page in such a way that a computer can display the information (w3schools, n.d.b; Foster, 2005). The purpose of a data tag is to give meaning to the displayed data (McCrea & Brasseur, 2003). A tag is a label placed around information on a screen. There is no processing of this information other than to display it on the screen. The following is an example of an HTML screen using tags:

```
<html>
<body>
<p><b>PSCI periodically has press releases that allow you to
see our latest activities. These releases inform you of our
clients' progress as well as providing other industry-
related happenings. We encourage you to click on the link to
view these releases.
</b></p></body><html>
```

The <html> appears at the beginning of the markup tag and again at the end of the tag. At the beginning of the tag, it opens the tag, and at the end it closes the tag.

Next, the presentation of the body <body> of what is to be displayed. At the end of the passage, we close the body of text with </body>. If the reader looks at the paragraph itself, the reader will see a <p> (paragraph) and a <b> (bold) at both the beginning and the end. This displays the body as a paragraph that is in bold lettering. To develop pages on a web site to include colors, writing formats, and other presentation functions that can be transferred through the Internet requires the use of HTML tags.

HTML provides the ability to make a perfect web site (Foster, 2005). The web provides an easy, user-friendly manner in which to search, download/upload documents, communicate with other people, shop, and do research all by way of the computer (Pattavina, 2005). HTML allows images and objects to be embedded and can be used to create interactive forms. It provides a way to create structured documents by denoting structural semantics for text such as headings, paragraphs, lists, links, quotes, and other items. It can embed scripts in languages such as JavaScript, which affects the behavior of HTML web pages (W3C, n.d.). HTML is the cornerstone of web browsers.

Criminal Justice Agencies throughout the United States have developed web sites to provide information to citizens. Some agencies have even used this technology to develop citizen reporting capabilities where citizens can report minor crimes over the Internet. HTML, along with other technologies, makes this possible. HTML allows data to be displayed the same way on different types of computers. This has significantly enhanced the Criminal Justice System's ability to share information with citizens, as well as with other criminal justice agencies.

Criminal Justice Agencies also use Intranets, which is an Internet that limits access internally to the organization to share working information that is relevant to daily operations. HTML makes all of this possible. There are investigative web sites restricted to criminal justice agencies. These web sites provide the ability for agencies to share information despite different technologies, through the use of HTML displays.

Extensible markup language

Extensible markup language (XML) is to data what HTML is to the presentation of data. Although HTML deals with the presentation of data, XML transports and stores data and focuses on what the data is (oncorsi.aslromab.it/). XML works in conjunction with HTML. It uses a similar coding structure as HTML. The difference is that the programmer defines the XML tags. In reality, XML does not do anything; it structures, stores, and transports information (w3schools, n.d.c). The following is a sample of XML:

```
<note>
<to>Love</to>
<from>Jani</from>
<heading>Reminder</heading>
<body>Don't forget me this weekend!</body>
</note>
```

The note above is self-descriptive. It has sender and receiver information; it also has a heading and a message body (w3schools, n.d.d). This XML document does not DO anything. It is just information wrapped in tags. Someone must write a piece of software to send, receive or display the information (w3schools, n.d.d).

XML is another vital tool that has significantly enhanced data-sharing capabilities among justice agencies. It is the basis of the National Information Exchange Model (NIEM) and the global justice extensible markup language data model (GJXDM), which we will discuss later in this chapter. This technology has become so pivotal to information sharing in the criminal justice environment that the federal government has required that any software purchased using federal funds must support the NIEM standard, and thus use XML for data exchange.

The strength of XML is that it promotes data-sharing by storing data in everyday language, which allows diverse systems to exchange data (w3schools, n.d.a). This is critical to criminal justice agencies. In the past, it was extremely difficult to exchange information between various criminal justice agencies. Police departments could not electronically exchange information with other police departments that were on different systems. They could not exchange information with prosecutors or courts. There have been many barriers to the exchange of data—field names, data element size, and numeric versus character-based fields—all presented problems to data exchange. Often an agency would pay significant sums of money to software firms to make this exchange possible, only to have their investment destroyed when the agency they were exchanging data with changed their software or when they made a software change. XML, as the standard for all, eliminates or significantly reduces this problem.

Although XML provides an exceptional means of exchanging data within the criminal justice system, it is not a panacea; there are issues that must be addressed. One of the main concerns associated with XML is performance. XML performance can be sluggish and provide slower data delivery. Large databases intensify this sluggish performance. In the criminal justice environments, large databases are common; therefore, this is a significant issue. The concerns over XML performance have promoted a number of concepts to help improve performance. One of those is the development of binary XML, which can improve performance but also has issues that can cause difficulties. The core issue is that XML requires more processing power than most systems can support (Newton and Kanareykin, 2007). Newton and Kanareykin (2007) contend that XML offloading much of the processing onto systems specialized for tasks specific to XML increases performance. Nonetheless, although XML is a valuable tool, these issues must be addressed to become effective in a criminal justice environment that typically deals with extremely large databases (De Anza College, n.d.).

Global Justice XML Data Model

The development of XML opened new doors within disciplines for information sharing. Within the criminal justice system, the data exchange model developed was the Global Justice XML Data Model (GJXDM). The development of GJXDM was a collaborative effort that included multiple levels of justice agencies, but the technical development occurred through an Office of Justice Programs (OJP) grant to the Georgia Technical Research Institute (U.S. Department of Justice, Office of Justice Programs, Bureau of Justice Assistance, n.d.a).

The exchange of information has always been something desired by criminal justice agencies. Until the development of XML, this was difficult/impossible to achieve. This was so between police agencies that had different vendors, as well as different justice agencies such as the prosecutor's office, courts, probation, jails, and prisons. In the past, if an agency desired the ability to exchange data between justice agencies, it required the development of a software program that would enable this exchange. In addition to being a significant technical challenge, it was also expensive, with no assurance that future changes in the primary software would not negatively affect the interface program. GJXDM significantly improved this dilemma.

So what is GJXDM and how has it been employed? The GJXDM endeavor began in March 2001 as a reconciliation of data definitions and evolved into a broad two-year effort to develop an XML-based framework. GJXDM enables the entire justice and public safety communities to share information at all levels—laying the foundation for local, state, tribal, and national justice interoperability (U.S. Department of Justice, Office of Justice Programs, Bureau of Justice Assistance, n.d.b).

Through the analysis of various data elements collected from justice agencies, the number of elements was reduced to approximately 2,000 unique data elements and these were incorporated into about 300 data objects, or reusable components, resulting in the Global Justice XML Data Dictionary (GJXDD) (U.S. Department of Justice, Office of Justice Programs, Bureau of Justice Assistance, n.d.b). This data dictionary allows vendors to develop software for the simple exchange of data without the requirement for significant interface software.

GJXDM was not immediately embraced by the companies that provided criminal justice software. These software packages are exceptionally large and extremely complex. It would not be an easy task to become GJXDM compliant. Enhancing legacy systems to be GJXDM compliant meant a significant effort had to be put forth to achieve compliance. This would be costly for most companies to accomplish. In many instances, it meant entirely rewriting their existing systems using the GJXDM Schema. Besides, many companies felt that they would lose their competitive advantage if a competitor's software could easily read their data. What was the advantage for their firm to be GJXDM compliant?

The Department of Justice and the Department of Homeland Security answered this dilemma when they forced compliance by requiring that any software, funded through grants obtained through those organizations, must be GJXDM compliant. In FY 2005, the U.S. Department of Justice (DOJ), Office of Justice Programs (OJP), adopted a new grant condition. This rule required that any OJP grant application with the potential of using XML should use GJXDM to publish the schema to the central OJP repository (U.S. Department of Justice, n.d.). Since the initial announcement, the same special condition language has also been adopted by

DOJ and the Department of Homeland Security (DHS). The underlying requirement of the condition is that data exchange among grant recipients must be constructed to *conform* to the GJXDM (U.S. Department of Justice, n.d.).

Although GJXDM has significantly enhanced the capacity of information exchange and significantly enhanced interoperability within the criminal justice agencies, there are a number of issues. The development of many of the software programs currently available occurred pre-XML and pre-GJXDM. To be GJXDM compliant, a number of vendors have improvised. Typically, the way firms have met GJXDM compliance is by writing an application that translates the data from the legacy software to the GJXDM format. When GJXDM formatted data comes in, it goes through the same exchange server. The server converts the data into the format the legacy system can interpret. Figure 2.1 provides a visual depiction of the conversion server process.

This conversion processing was a temporary way of responding to the GJXDM requirement. Newly developed software avoided this processing. Contractors developing new software or rewriting their old software simply did so by following the GJXDM format. Today, most vendors have rewritten their software following the GJXDM format.

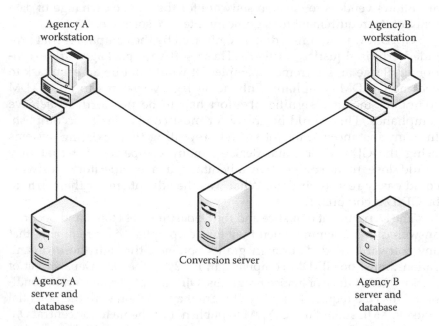

Figure 2.1 GJXDM conversion server.

National Information Exchange Model

The National Information Exchange Model (NIEM) grew from the success of the GJXDM (NIEM, n.d.). GJXDM is part of the NIEM model and focuses on criminal justice data. The overall NIEM schema encompasses GJXDM for criminal justice. It also includes a number of other data elements used by other Homeland Security agencies. In 2007, state, local, and federal officials as well as private sector partners came together to explore how to implement a standard semantic lexicon and the lessons learned to standardize suspicious activity reporting across the nation (Semanticommunity.info, n.d.). The result was to come together and develop an XML-based model that encompassed not only criminal justice agencies but also other Homeland Security agencies as well as some private sector firms that worked closely within these environments. The purpose of this partnership was to share critical information at key decision points throughout the whole of the justice, public safety, emergency and disaster management, intelligence, and homeland security enterprise (U.S. Department of Justice, Office of Justice Programs, Bureau of Justice Assistance, n.d.b).

NIEM is now the standard for information exchange in the criminal justice environment as well as other governmental and homeland security entities. NIEM has been and continues to be enhanced. This technology has significantly enhanced the sharing of information without the costly interfaces experienced with legacy systems. For those interested in using, implementing, and applying NIEM standards, there is a web site that they can access, NIEM.gov. The web site provides technical support for those wishing to develop software utilizing the NIEM standards N-DEx (National Data Exchange).

Since 9/11, the importance of information sharing among criminal justice agencies intensified and its importance has become more widely recognized. In 2008, the idea of an information sharing system that would allow justice agencies to share information as might be required, came to fruition. This resulted in the development of an information sharing tool known as National Information Exchange, better known as N-DEx. The N-DEx is a repository for critical law enforcement information. "N-DEx brings together data such as incident and case reports, arrest reports, computer-aided dispatch calls, traffic citations, narratives, photos, supplements, booking and incarceration data, and parole/probation information. Additionally, N-DEx automatically correlates and resolves data from open and closed reports to detect relationships between people, vehicles/property, locations, and/or crime characteristics. It also supports multi-jurisdictional task forces—enhancing national information sharing, links between local and state systems, and virtual regional information sharing" (FBI, n.d.a).

Law enforcement benefits of N-DEx can be classified in three main categories: investigative uses, strategic uses, and tactical uses.

1. Investigative uses of N-DEx include the ability to
   a. Conduct nationwide searches across jurisdictions, gathering information from various aspects of the criminal justice life cycle via a single access point
   b. Search names, IDs, people, phone numbers, tattoos, associates, cars, boats, other property, etc.
   c. Search by modus operandi, and
   d. Receive notifications and collaborate with others on similar investigations
2. Strategic uses of N-DEx include the ability to
   a. Coordinate task forces
   b. Identify crime trends
   c. Use geo-visualization and mapping features, and
   d. Facilitate a de-confliction
3. Tactical uses of N-DEx include the ability to
   a. Identify "hotspots" of criminal activity
   b. Assess threat levels of persons or addresses
   c. Form additional investigative partnerships, and
   d. Enhance officer safety both in law enforcement and corrections (FBI, n.d.a)

To better emphasize the value of N-DEx, the following factual scenario demonstrates how multiple agencies across multiple jurisdictions in different states were able to collaborate in solving both a crime and a missing persons report.

July 15, 2010: Waco, Texas

Joanne Keane calls the Waco Police Department to report an individual, John Cooley, missing. Keane describes Cooley—noting his appearance and even the eagle tattoo on his left forearm. Keane even provides officers with a description of the car he drives and its license plate number. The police department collects the service call and transfers it into the N-DEx system.

Dispatched to the Cooley residence, a Waco officer arrives later that day. That Waco officer is not just showing up looking for Cooley, the missing person. Because of the integration of the original Waco service call record into N-DEx, and records processed and correlated automatically, the officer can query N-DEx, and have the original service call, and additional relevant data at the scene, for this service call follow-up.

After determining that Cooley is not at his residence, the agency completed a welfare concern–missing person report, the agency filed and submitted the report to N-DEx. The N-DEx missing person report contains an NCIC reference number, indicating that the Waco Police Department also has an NCIC Missing Person record entered for Cooley. Inclusion of this NCIC reference number in the Waco N-DEx report creates a direct link between the data in both systems.

Integrating disparate systems gives investigators using N-DEx enhanced ability to fight crime and terrorism—and ensure public and officer safety.

July 17, 2010
In pursuit of their missing person, Waco investigators perform a known person search for Cooley in N-DEx, using his name and date of birth.

Waco investigators are looking for leads. Investigators search N-DEx for additional information on Cooley. N-DEx results show the original Waco service call as well as the welfare concern–missing person report created a couple of days ago. It also returns a previous incident, a shoplifting offense committed two years ago in Arkansas, where Cooley had the same vehicle and license plate. Through the leveraged systems interfaces with NCIC and III, the investigator sees the missing person entry from NCIC and the shoplifting offense disposition information from III.

To receive notifications of other activity involving Cooley, Waco investigators create a person subscription for John Cooley. This will notify the investigator of searches performed on or records submitted to N-DEx involving John Cooley.

July 24, 2010: Denton, Texas
The Denton Texas Police Department receives a call. A robbery and homicide have just been reported at a local convenience store, and Denton investigators have few leads. Just a store video retrieved by investigators from the scene.

On the video, investigators identify a 40- to 50-year-old man with a distinct eagle tattoo on his left forearm. Investigators complete the incident report, check-in evidence, and continue the investigation.

Using N-DEx, Denton investigators perform a person search for the suspect using descriptive data, including the eagle tattoo.

This brings up pages of results, including the Denton incident report from the robbery homicide.

Believing the suspect to be local, the investigator then uses a polygon filter for the North Texas region to target the results to a specific geographical area. This yields two results that meet the suspect's physical descriptions, including the eagle tattoo.

The investigator then selects the geo-visualization tool. Viewed on a map, the investigator can see the locations are somewhat apart. The crime scene is on the path that Cooley travels to visit Joanne Keane, who reported him missing in Waco. Although Cooley was unidentified by Denton, Denton obtained Waco's missing person data and demographic information, and followed the lead.

The Denton investigators contact the Waco Police Department. Denton investigators have uploaded their convenience store video to the N-DEx Collaboration area thinking that John Cooley, the missing Waco person, might be their convenience store suspect.

Denton investigators invite the Waco officers to the collaboration area. Maybe together, two cases can be closed today. Waco officers open the collaboration area and download the video.

N-DEx data brought these criminal justice agencies together to collaborate. Working alone, they might have otherwise missed key data to help solve their cases.

Before N-DEx, Denton investigators had to send a copy of the video evidence to the Waco Police Department. Waco Police Department would meet with Denton investigators, to view and discuss the video. In the N-DEx collaborative environment, each agency saves time and money, ensures a secure environment for information sharing, and enhances investigative efficiency. Both agencies avoid the risk of exposing or losing data, and the cost of mail, travel, copying, and time often associated with agency collaboration. With the permission of Denton investigators, Waco investigators show parts of the video revealing the perpetrator's face and tattoo to Joanne Keane, who identifies John Cooley right away.

Waco investigators communicate Keane's confirmation back to Denton investigators. Denton's robbery–homicide suspect is indeed John Cooley. Waco Police now know that John Cooley is not your average health and welfare missing person. They configure an additional N-DEx subscription to notify the department of any changes to the Denton incident report. Waco does not want to miss any opportunity to close a case.

Likewise, Denton investigators update their incident record to indicate John Cooley as a suspect in the robbery–homicide and obtain a warrant for his arrest.

The Denton Police Department include the warrant, also entered in NCIC, in their updated N-DEx incident record along with the NCIC reference number creating a direct link between the data in both systems.

July 30, 2010: Denton, Texas

The Denton Police Department gets their man. Denton officers arrested John Cooley after discovering that he was wanted during a stop at a sobriety checkpoint. This reinforces the known fact that sobriety checkpoints regularly catch much more than just drunk drivers. The arrest of Cooley enables Denton investigators to close their incident report and supplement it with arrest data. The supplemental data helps in the event another police agency might be looking for John Cooley in the future.

N-DEx receipt of this updated Denton incident report data immediately results in subscription notification to the Waco Police Department.

A subsequent person search for John Cooley by Waco Police investigators displays the updated information along with other information on Cooley. This included information in NCIC and III through the N-DEx Leveraged Systems interface. Waco investigators note that the Denton warrant in NCIC is not part of the return, and additional confirmation that Cooley is now in jail.

The N-DEx link visualization—driven by the entity resolution on John Cooley and his vehicle license plate—also shows the links between Cooley and known entities, including those in his recent Denton booking report. The resulting follow-up by the Waco Police Department with the Denton Police Department to confirm the arrest and booking of Cooley and to obtain permission to use these data, allows the Waco Police Department to close their missing person report and clear their NCIC missing person record.

N-DEx allows investigators from various agencies to collaborate and view data to solve crimes and promote public safety. Using N-DEx, criminal justice agencies enhance investigative abilities and maximize resources by leveraging national criminal justice data and analytic resources. The criminal justice community puts information into the right hands for a safer America through the N-DEx system (FBI, n.d.a).

This technology demonstrates how XML, through NIEM/GJXDM, has enhanced criminal justice capabilities through the ability to share information.

Regional Data Exchange

In 2008, we saw the development of a similar Regional Data Exchange (R-DEx) that securely shares sensitive but unclassified crime information between federal agencies while allowing for connection with several existing regional bases, local, and state information-sharing systems to impede criminal and terrorist activities. R-DEx is now operational in several metropolitan areas (U.S. Department of Justice, Office of Justice Programs, Bureau of Justice Assistance, n.d.c).

The R-DEx model functions similarly to the N-DEx model. It typically incorporates federal agencies, such as the FBI, NCIS, DEA, and other federal law enforcement agencies and fosters the sharing of data between local law enforcement agencies and federal law enforcement agencies. It is not as widely known or promoted as N-DEx but attempts to foster regional cooperation.

Law Enforcement Information Sharing Program

The Department of Justice (DOJ) established the Law Enforcement Information Sharing Program, more commonly known as LEISP. The LEISP embraces those technologies that foster information sharing. "LEISP addresses barriers to information sharing and creates a forum for collaboration on coordinating existing and planned systems and unified for information sharing purposes. LEISP delineates guiding principles, a policy framework, and functional requirements that are necessary to facilitate multi-jurisdictional law enforcement information sharing" (United States Department of Justice, 2007) According to the DOJ, "the goal of the Law Enforcement Information Sharing Program (LEISP) is to enable the DOJ to share law enforcement information with its federal, state, local, and tribal law enforcement partners and to facilitate multi-jurisdictional information sharing across the law enforcement and homeland security communities" (United States Department of Justice, 2007).

The LEISP concept consists of three tracks:

1. Track I is the department's internal reform initiative, DOJ, which will closely coordinate information sharing efforts within the department, facilitate sharing of DOJ-held information with law enforcement agencies outside the department, provide connectivity for sharing of information with the Department of Homeland Security

(DHS), and allow the DOJ to present a single face to its information sharing partners.

2. Track II will first incorporate "quick hits" to leverage existing sharing-technology capabilities and then center on building out the services and technology platforms that will enable the department to seamlessly share its information.

3. In Track III, the department will work cooperatively with its federal, state, local, and tribal law enforcement partners to enhance interconnectivity that allows standard, routine information sharing across all jurisdictions on a national basis (United States Department of Justice, 2007).

Information sharing has been a challenging process, to say the least; the events of 9/11 highlighted these critical faults. In the past, criminal justice agencies, local, state, and federal have shared information but often on a limited basis and not without issues. Hoarding of information was common. The function of LEISP is to foster this communication and information sharing between all criminal justice agencies to include local, state, and federal.

National Crime Information Center 2000

The National Crime Information Center (NCIC) became operational in January of 1967. The Federal Bureau of Investigations (FBI) manages and supports the NCIC. Since that time, the NCIC has provided critical information to criminal justice agencies throughout the United States and its territories. It is available to criminal justice agencies 24 hours a day. The NCIC processes approximately 28 billion transactions per year (FBI, n.d.c).

The NCIC database includes 19 files: 7 property files and 12 person files.

- *Article file*—Records on stolen articles and lost public safety, homeland security, and critical infrastructure identification.
- *Gun file*—Records on stolen, lost, and recovered weapons and weapons used in the commission of crimes designated to expel a projectile by air, carbon dioxide, or explosive action.
- *Boat file*—Records on stolen boats.
- *Securities file*—Records on serially numbered stolen, embezzled, used for ransom, or counterfeit securities.
- *Vehicle file*—Records on stolen vehicles, vehicles involved in the commission of crimes, or vehicles that may be seized based on federally issued court orders.
- *Vehicle and boat parts file*—Records on serially numbered stolen vehicle or boat parts.
- *License plate file*—Records on stolen license plates.

- *Missing persons file*—Records on individuals, including children, reported missing to law enforcement, and there is a reasonable concern for their safety.
- *Foreign fugitive file*—Records on persons wanted by another country for a crime that would be a felony if committed in the United States.
- *Identity theft file*—Records containing descriptive and other information that law enforcement personnel can use to determine if an individual is a victim of identity theft or if the individual might be using a false identity.
- *Immigration violator file*—Records on criminal aliens whom immigration authorities have deported and aliens with outstanding administrative warrants of removal.
- *Protection order file*—Records on individuals against whom protection orders have been issued.
- *Supervised release file*—Records on individuals on probation, parole, or supervised release or released on their own recognizance or during pretrial sentencing.
- *Unidentified persons file*—Records on unidentified deceased persons, living persons who are unable to verify their identities, unidentified victims of catastrophes, and recovered body parts. The file cross-references unidentified bodies against records in the Missing Persons File.
- *U.S. Secret Service protective file*—Records containing names and other information on individuals believed to pose a threat to the U.S. president and/or others afforded protection by the U.S. Secret Service.
- *Gang file*—Records on violent gangs and their members.
- *Known or appropriately suspected terrorist file*—Records on known or appropriately suspected terrorists in accordance with HSPD-6.
- *Wanted persons file*—Records on individuals (including juveniles who will be tried as adults) for whom a federal warrant or a felony or misdemeanor warrant is outstanding.
- *National Sex Offender Registry file*—Records on individuals required to register in a jurisdiction's sex offender registry (FBI, n.d.c).

Information stored in these files comes from law enforcement agencies throughout the United States and its territories. To enter data into the NCIC, it must meet the requirements specified for each record type listed above. This does not provide for misdemeanors, state crimes, or ordinances. The NCIC stores all data meeting the above criteria.

In the early days of the NCIC, few, if any, local police agencies had been computerized. Those that were computerized tended to be the large jurisdictions, NYPD, LAPD, etc. Access to the NCIC occurred through similar state or regional criminal justice computer systems. The State provided local agencies teletype machines. Law enforcement dispatchers were able to enter a request for information through the teletype and, if a hit occurred, the information would be returned through the attached printer. The entry of these data was cryptic and difficult to use. The NCIC only provides information on serious criminal activity and offenders. The NCIC did not and still does not contain misdemeanor information and state-specific criminal information with certain exceptions. This resulted in the development of state criminal information systems.

As time progressed, this processing became more sophisticated. States interfaced their systems to the NCIC. The states then provided access to the local agencies. In many instances, large counties and large local police agencies like the New York City Police Department, Los Angeles Police Department, and Los Angeles County Sheriff's Office developed similar criminal justice databases. Today, most access occurs through the state criminal justice system. Local agencies interface with their state criminal justice system, which provides them access to state data. Through the state system, local agencies can access the NCIC. Figure 2.2 depicts typical NCIC connectivity.

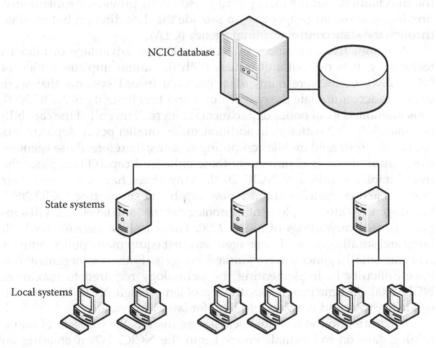

NCIC database

State systems

Local systems

Figure 2.2 Typical NCIC connectivity.

The NCIC has grown over the years to the number of transactions stated previously. In 1999, the FBI implemented a new version of the NCIC, now known as NCIC 2000. This new version of NCIC took advantage of modern digital technology. As a result, NCIC can now offer more information than it was capable of doing in the past. It is capable of working over a number of communications and data protocols such as transmission control protocol/Internet protocol (TCP/IP) (J. H. Barnes & Associates, n.d.), cellular technologies as well as radio technology, such as in the 800 MHz band, and others (Foster, 2005). Because field mobile computing is prevalent in today's law enforcement agencies, this is significant. NCIC 2000 provides officers in the field with a great deal of capability not available in the past. NCIC 2000 provides two key features to the field officers that were not available in the original NCIC single fingerprint identification, as well as imaging capability for subject photographs. NCIC 2000 also provides access to files containing persons on supervised release or convicted of a crime. Another notable feature is its ability to connect multiple records with the same criminal or the same crime.

Although the FBI operates the NCIC, it is the states that provide the data to the system. The NCIC does set standards for what information can be stored and how it must be maintained, but the state contributes the information that the local police jurisdictions provide. As mentioned previously, some large agencies do provide the data directly, but most go through the state control terminal agency (CTA).

Although these advances in NCIC 2000 take advantage of modern technology, it is not without issues. With the initial implementation of NCIC 2000, there were many state criminal record systems that were unable to accommodate the new features and functionality of NCIC 2000. This prohibited local police departments from realizing all of the capabilities that NCIC 2000 offered. In addition, many smaller police departments could not afford field mobile computing systems; therefore, these agencies were unable to take advantage of these enhanced capabilities. Since the initial implementation of NCIC 2000, many states have enhanced their criminal justice systems and are now capable of supporting NCIC 2000. Local agencies must implement technology at the local level that will support the full capabilities of NCIC 2000. This can be expensive for both large and small agencies. Large agencies must equip many police vehicles whereas small agencies have limited budgets. Both size organizations have difficulty in implementing the technology required to maximize NCIC 2000. As time progresses, these problems lessen. NCIC 2000 continues to improve and is a valuable asset for law enforcement.

In addition to the technological issues, there is the problem of maintaining data on individuals entered into the NCIC. When entering an individual into NCIC at the arrest stage, the system tracks the arrestee through each step of the criminal justice process and, at each step, his or her record must be updated. As an example, upon the arrest of a person, the officer enters the suspect into the state system, which in turn updates NCIC with the arrest information. If the district attorney files a case against the individual, the system updates to reflect that information. Likewise, if the prosecuting attorney does not file a case, the person's record requires updating to reflect that the prosecuting attorney did not file charges. When the person goes to court, the final disposition must also be updated. If they are found innocent or guilty, the system must reflect that information. If the subject serves time that must also be entered into the NCIC. It is easy to see how the system can malfunction and not always contain the most current information pertaining to an individual (Hubbard, 2008).

Uniform Crime Reports

Currently, there are two forms of crime reporting that occur in the United States. One is a manual system (summary based) that has been around since the 1920s, and the other is the National Incident-Based Reporting System (NIBRS), which is a computerized reporting system. For many years, the FBI has supported Uniform Crime Reporting (UCR).

In the traditional summary-based system, each police agency reported the number of crimes in each crime category. UCR breaks this down into two basic categories of Part 1 and Part 2 crimes. Part 1 crimes are typically felonies, which law enforcement knows as the eight major crimes. The FBI classifies 20 Part 2 crimes referred to as misdemeanors. The reporting of these crimes occurs annually in a document entitled, "Crime in the United States." The following is a breakdown of these crime categories and their associated crime types.

Part 1 crimes

1. Murder
2. Forcible rape
3. Aggravated assault
4. Robbery
5. Burglary
6. Larceny-theft
7. Motor vehicle theft
8. Arson

Human trafficking and hate crimes are also captured.

Part 2 crimes

1. Simple assaults
2. Forgery and counterfeiting
3. Fraud
4. Embezzlement
5. Stolen property: buying, receiving, possessing
6. Vandalism
7. Weapons: carrying, possessing, etc.
8. Prostitution and commercialized vice
9. Sex offenses (except forcible rape, prostitution, and commercialized vice)
10. Drug abuse violations
11. Gambling
12. Offenses against the family and children
13. Driving under the influence
14. Liquor laws
15. Drunkenness
16. Disorderly conduct
17. Vagrancy
18. All other offenses
19. Suspicion
20. Curfew and loitering laws (persons under age 18)

This version of the UCR is manual in that agencies provide a written report on a monthly basis that contains this information. The agencies submit the report to the state and the state compiles all of the information and forwards it to the FBI for inclusion in their statistics. Although this is a manual version of the report, most police record management systems (RMS) produce the printed reports and the agency sends it to the state or directly to the FBI, Uniform Crime Reporting Division.

NIBRS differs significantly from the standard summary UCR reporting in that it is an incident-based system. The system captures significant data from each crime report. There are 22 offense categories associated with the NIBRS system, made up of 46 Group A offenses. Table 2.1 displays the Group A offenses.

NIBRS also has a Group B category of crimes recorded on arrests whereas Group A records on incident. Table 2.2 depicts the NIBRS Group B offenses.

NIBRS is incident-based and requires more information pertaining to an incident. NIBRS requires that relationships be identified between suspects and the victims of crimes against persons. NIBRS requires additional information about property crimes. Additionally, NIBRS is a fully automated system that requires the submission of information to occur

Table 2.1 NIBRS Group A offenses

UCR offense	Crime against	UCR code
Arson	Property	200
Assault offenses		
Aggravated assault	Person	13A
Simple assault	Person	13B
Intimidation		13C
Bribery	Property	510
Burglary/breaking and entering	Property	220
Counterfeiting/forgery	Property	250
Destruction/damage/vandalism of property	Property	290
Drug/narcotic offenses		
Drug/narcotic violations	Society	35A
Drug equipment violations	Society	35B
Embezzlement	Property	270
Extortion/blackmail	Property	210
Fraud offenses		
False pretenses/swindle/ Confidence game	Property	26A
Credit card/automatic teller Machine fraud	Property	26B
Impersonation	Property	26C
Welfare fraud	Property	26D
Wire fraud	Property	26E
Gambling offenses		
Betting/wagering	Society	39A
Operating/promoting/assisting Gambling	Society	39B
Gambling equipment violations	Society	39C
Sports tampering	Society	39D
Homicide offenses		
Murder and nonnegligent Manslaughter	Person	09A
Negligent manslaughter	Person	09B
Justifiable homicide	Not a crime	09C
Kidnaping/abduction	Person	100
Larceny/theft offenses		
Pocket picking	Property	23A
Purse snatching	Property	23B
Shoplifting	Property	23C
Theft from building	Property	23D

(Continued)

Table 2.1 (Continued) NIBRS Group A offenses

UCR offense	Crime against	UCR code
Theft from coin-operated Machine or device	Property	23E
Theft from motor vehicle	Property	23F
Theft of motor vehicle parts or Accessories	Property	23G
All other larceny	Property	23H
Motor vehicle theft	Property	240
Pornography/obscene material	Society	370
Prostitution offenses		
Prostitution	Society	40A
Assisting or promoting Prostitution	Society	40B
Robbery	Property	120
Sex offenses, forcible		
Forcible rape	Person	11A
Forcible sodomy	Person	11B
Sexual assault with an object	Person	11C
Forcible fondling (child)	Person	11D
Sex offenses, nonforcible		
Incest	Person	36A
Statutory rape	Person	36B
Stolen property offenses	Property	280
Weapon law violations	Society	520

Table 2.2 NIBRS Group B offenses

UCR offense	Crime against	UCR code
Bad checks	Property	90A
Curfew/loitering/vagrancy violations	Society	90B
Disorderly conduct	Society	90C
Driving under the influence	Society	90D
Drunkenness	Society	90E
Family offenses, nonviolent	Person	90F
Liquor law violations	Society	90G
Peeping tom	Society	90H
Runaway	Not a crime	90I
Trespass of real property	Society	90J
All other offenses	Person, property, society	90Z

electronically. This reporting presents challenges to overcome before its use. This can also be an explanation as to why after 25 years after its development, only about 20% of criminal justice agencies were using the NIBRS method to report crime.

There are also other issues that must be overcome before NIBRS reporting becomes possible. In the early days of NIBRS, many agencies resisted going to this form of reporting because it would require a substantial revision to the crime reporting formats. As demonstrated previously, NIBRS requires a significantly larger number of data elements to be reported accurately. This meant that agencies would have to change their reporting formats. Software in use at the time needed to be modified to accommodate NIBRS reporting. Additionally, most states require that the local jurisdictions report their crime statistics to a state agency. The state makes the determination as to the method, e.g., UCR Standard or NIBRS, which they will use to report to the FBI. To this date, there are still states that report the standard UCR method. All RMS software systems on the market today have the ability to report either way.

Another factor associated with the NIBRS reporting is that some states have elected to modify NIBRS in an attempt to collect additional information. This resulted in RMS vendors developing state-specific, NIBRS versions of their software. This has also added to the slow implementation that the NIBRS has experienced. When a state elects to change from UCR Standard to NIBRS, each of the reporting jurisdictions in that the state must convert to the NIBRS format. This typically has a cost associated with the transition. Agencies must change their RMS software to accommodate this switch. The agency might be required to change the report formats to accommodate the additional data required to report NIBRS. To understand the new report formats and how the data is to be collected requires additional officer training. This typically requires that states allot the local agencies time to do this transition. States also need to provide those agencies that are not computerized a means of reporting NIBRS, which has led some states to allow these agencies to send the state their information in a manual form and the state makes the entry into the state's system for those agencies.

Although the FBI eventually would like to switch to the NIBRS format as the sole reporting format, this will clearly require additional time. The concern that is currently being raised is the validity of either UCR or NIBRS reporting because both do not track many of the modern crimes we are experiencing throughout the nation. As an example, domestic violence is a significant crime that is not tracked as domestic violence at all. There are efforts underway at this time to re-evaluate the crimes the FBI tracks and to update the types of crimes being tracked and reported.

The vendors that provide RMS systems must be capable of supporting either the Standard UCR format or NIBRS. This is challenging because these firms must also support the multitude of state variations that exist with both the Standard UCR and NIBRS. This becomes costly to these firms as they must constantly modify their systems to meet these various requirements.

Law Enforcement Online

Law Enforcement Online (LEO) as defined by the FBI is as follows: "LEO is a secure, Internet-based communications portal for law enforcement, first responders, criminal justice professionals, and anti-terrorism and intelligence agencies around the globe (FBI, n.d.b). This is a secure web site that is restricted to law enforcement personnel only. LEO provides a wealth of information to its members. It is a way for law enforcement to collaborate on a number of different issues. LEO began in 1995 as a small dial-up service and, according to the FBI, it has grown to more than 100,000 law enforcement users, and it consists of a host of features and capabilities offered through a Virtual Private Network (VPN) on the Internet (FBI, n.d.b). The following is what LEO offers law enforcement personnel:

- A national alert system directing members to the LEO site for information on emergencies (like the London bombings, for example)
- Some 1,100 Special Interest Groups (SIG) that allow members who share expertise or interests to connect with each other, including sections on terrorism, street gangs, and bombs
- Access to important and useful databases, like those run by the National Center for Missing and Exploited Children
- E-mail services, which enable members to submit fingerprints to the FBI for processing by an Integrated Automated Fingerprint Identification System
- A Virtual Command Center (VCC)—an information sharing and crisis management tool that allows the law enforcement community to use LEO at local and remote sites as an electronic command center to submit and view information and intelligence
- Distance learning, with several online learning modules on topics like terrorism response, forensic anthropology, and leadership; and
- A multimedia library of publications, documents, studies, research, technical bulletins, and other reports of interest to LEO users (FBI, n.d.b.)

LEO is an example of online forums that are available to law enforcement in today's environment. There are many others supported by law enforcement associations. Law enforcement is not unlike private sector industries in that they have organizations that maintain web sites where members can obtain information that will help them do their job better.

National Law Enforcement Telecommunication System

The National Law Enforcement Telecommunication System (Nlets) provides a number of services to local, state, and federal law enforcement agencies. Through the Nlets network, law enforcement and criminal justice agencies can access a wide range of information, from standard driver's license and vehicle queries to criminal history and Interpol information (Nlets, n.d.). Through Interpol access, officers are able to run a subject for wants in the United States, as well as other countries around the world. As with the other tools discussed in this chapter, Nlets promotes information sharing among criminal justice agencies. Nlets boasts of ninety different queries that agencies can run to obtain information on subjects and property. An example of new Nlets technological capability is Proactive Alerting (PAL). This technology allows users to set up and receive alerts on keywords queries and responses sent across the Nlets network. These "alerts" are on primary data types, such as full name, license plate, and vehicle identification number (Nlets, n.d.). Once an alert has a "hit," the system sends an e-mail to the law enforcement official notifying them of recent law enforcement contact with an individual they are seeking or tracking. To see the details of the contact made, the law enforcement official must log into the Nlets portal and look up the specified alert. The National Center for Missing and Exploited Children (NCMEC) works with Nlets to run the AMBER Alerts. They run other queries serving their organization. The officer only sees Nlets messages within a regional broadcast. Nlets plans to expand the project to provide alerting in all states and with national agencies (Nlets, n.d.).

There are many states that have developed systems similar to Nlets. With the advent of newer technologies, we are seeing more and more states developing systems that are specific to that state's requirements. California has the California Law Enforcement Telecommunication System (CLETS); in Alabama, there is the ACIC, these are two examples of state systems similar to Nlets.

Law Enforcement Information Technology Standards Council

The Law Enforcement Information Technology Standards Council (LEITSC) came to be under a grant from the U.S. Department of Justice,

Bureau of Justice Assistance in 2002. LEITSC typically works in conjunction with the International Association of Chiefs of Police (IACP), the National Sheriff's Association (NSA), National Organization of Black Law Enforcement Executives (NOBLE), and the Police Executive Research Forum (PERF) in developing and enhancing information technology standards (U.S. Department of Justice, Office of Justice Programs, Bureau of Justice Assistance, n.d.c). As we have been discussing throughout this chapter, the development of information technology standards is critical to the ability of law enforcement agencies to share information. For many years, the problem has been a lack of these standards, which made information sharing difficult and, in some instances, impossible. LEITSC has promoted information sharing through its Law Enforcement Information Sharing Program (LEISP), and the N-DEx and R-DEx programs, each of which promotes not just information sharing but also the ability to exchange data between differing information technology systems (U.S. Department of Justice, Office of Justice Programs, Bureau of Justice Assistance, n.d.c).

A significant LEITSC accomplishment was the promotion and development of a standard for RMS. In conjunction with the Integrated Justice Information Systems (IJIS) Institute, LEITSC developed a national standard for RMS functional specifications. This specification defined the needed components of a comprehensive police RMS. Later in this book, we will cover the specific functional requirements of an RMS that includes the functional requirements specified by the LEITSC RMS project. The LEITSC goals for the development of this functional specification were:

- To provide a starting point for law enforcement agencies to use when developing RMS requests for proposals (RFP)
- Streamline the process and lower the cost of implementing and maintaining and RMS
- Promote information sharing (U.S. Department of Justice, Office of Justice Programs, Bureau of Justice Assistance, n.d.c)

With these goals specified, the LEITSC formulated a functional standards committee. The committee consisted of law enforcement professionals and industry experts from around the country. They developed a functional requirement specification that law enforcement agencies use to acquire and implement a functional RMS. These systems would be capable of meeting the agency's needs and would also be capable of sharing information with other justice agencies. LEITSC tested the finished work product and validated it using a computer modeling tool and provided it to agencies for their use in acquiring and implementing a police RMS.

In addition to the RMS functional requirements, LEITSC also developed a comprehensive Computer-Aided Dispatch (CAD) functional requirement specification. This used the same approach and techniques described previously for the RMS project. This provided agencies the ability to understand the core requirements of a CAD system. As with the RMS, LEITSC tested the finished product and validated it using a computer modeling tool and provided it to agencies for their use in acquiring a quality CAD system that would support information sharing.

Another vital LEITSC contribution was the "Project Manager's Guide to RMS/CAD Systems Software Acquisition" that LEITSC developed. Project management has become a significant task for agencies in the implementation of information technology systems, particularly CAD and RMS systems because they are vital systems. This document is a high level overview for planning and managing these projects. Too often, system implementations fail because of poor planning and project management. LEITSC sought to assist agencies with this process through these documents.

LEITSC has also published Information Exchange Package Documents (IEPDs) for CAD and RMS systems using the NIEM model. The intent of these documents is for software developers to utilize the XML schema and data models in the development of a number of data exchange components for CAD and RMS systems.

Clearly, LEITSC performs a significant role in assisting with the development and implementation of key criminal justice information systems. This is a vital role for ensuring the future of these systems and their practicality for the end user.

World Wide Web

It is not the intent of this book to describe the World Wide Web (WWW) but rather to provide a general understanding of how the criminal justice system uses the WWW in today's environment. The WWW has become a significant law enforcement tool. Just about every law enforcement agency supports a web page where the agency provides information to the community in which they serve. Like all web sites, some are more sophisticated than others. Typically, a police department's web site will allow citizens to obtain valuable information. Many police departments are providing the citizens the ability to report minor crimes online. Citizens may also provide police agencies with leads about wanted persons and a variety of other things.

The uses of the web are many, some of which we have already discussed in this chapter. The web provides enormous amounts of data to the world. These data can also be valuable to criminal justice agencies for a variety of reasons. As an example, an investigator might use the Internet to help identify wanted criminals or to put out information warning citizens of potential criminals.

In addition to using the Internet as described in this way, many law enforcement agencies use the WWW to share information among other law enforcement agencies. The Internet is an excellent tool to pass information on wanted suspects, stolen property, missing persons, and other justice-related issues. Much more occurs in helping to solve crimes with the use of the Internet.

References

De Anza College. (n.d.). *Title III Monthly Progress Report*. Retrieved from http://www.deanza.edu/studentsuccess/title3/LAMonthly%20Report_5_08.doc.

FBI. (n.d.a). *How N-DEx Can Help Your Agency*. Retrieved from http://www.fbi.gov/about-us/cjis/n-dex/how-n-dex-can-help-your-agency.

FBI. (n.d.b). *Law Enforcement Online Enterprise Portal Makes Access More Convenient*. Retrieved from https://www.fbi.gov/about-us/cjis/cjis-link/december-2012/Law%20Enforcement%20Online%20Enterprise%20Portal%20Makes%20Access%20More%20Convenient

FBI. (n.d.c). *National Crime Information Center*. Retrieved from https://www.fbi.gov/about-us/cjis/ncic.

Foster, R. E. (2005). *Police technology*. Upper Saddle River, New Jersey: Pearson Prentice Hall.

Hubbard, T. E. (2008). Automatic license plate recognition: An exciting new law enforcement tool with potentially scary consequences. *Syracuse Journal of Science and Technology Law*, 8–9.

J. H. Barnes & Associates. (n.d.) *Technology Infrastructure Management Services*. Retrieved from http://jhbarnes.net/.

McCrea, E. S., & Brasseur, J. A. (2003). *The supervisory process in speech pathology and audiology*. Allyn & Bacon.

National Information Exchange Model (NIEM). (n.d.). *History*. Retrieved from https://www.niem.gov/aboutniem/Pages/history.aspx.

National Law Enforcement Telecommunication System (Nlets). (n.d.). *Transactions*. Retrieved from https://www.nlets.org/transactions.

Newton, H. and Kanareykin, S. (2007). *GJXDM implementations and network performance*. Center for Advanced Defense Studies: Defense Concepts Series 2007.

Pattavina, A. (2005). *Information technology and the criminal justice system*. Thousand Oaks, California: Sage Publications.

Semanticommunity.info. (n.d.). *Assessment Report*. Retrievied from http://semanticommunity.info/National_Information_Exchange_Model/Assessment_Report.

TuTarz.com. (n.d.). *Online Tutorials*. Retrieved from http://tutarz.com/.

United States Department of Justice. (2007). *Law Enforcement Information Sharing Program* (USDOJ LEISP Exchange Specification 3.0 rev 9). Retrieved from http://www.oasis-open.org/committees/download.php/27606/LEXS.

U.S. Department of Justice. (n.d.). Retrieved from http://www.it.ojp.gov/default.aspx?area=nationalInitiatives&page=1083.

U.S. Department of Justice, Office of Justice Programs, Bureau of Justice Assistance. (n.d.a). *History and Background*. Retrieved from http://www.it.ojp.gov/initiatives/gjxdm/background.

U.S. Department of Justice, Office of Justice Programs, Bureau of Justice Assistance. (n.d.b). *Projects of National Scale*. Retrieved from http://www.it.ojp.gov /initiatives.

U.S. Department of Justice, Office of Justice Programs, Bureau of Justice Assistance. (n.d.c). *Standard Functional Specifications for Law Enforcement Computer Aided Dispatch Systems*. Retrieved from http://www.it.ojp.gov/documents/LEITSC _Law_Enforcement_CAD_Systems.pdf.

W3C. (n.d.). *Conformance: Requirements and Recommendations*. Retrieved from http://www.w3.org/TR/html401/conform.html#deprecated.

w3schools. (n.d.a) *How Can XML Be Used?* Retrieved from http://www.w3schools .com/xml/xml_usedfor.asp.

w3schools. (n.d.b). *HTML: The Language for Building Web Pages*. Retrieved from http://www.w3schools.com.

w3schools. (n.d.c). *XML DOM Tutorial*. Retrieved from http://www.w3schools .com/xml/dom_intro.asp.

w3schools. (n.d.d). *XML Introduction—What is XML?* Retrieved from http://www .w3schools.com/XML/xml_whatis.asp.

chapter three

9-1-1: Its history, current status, and the next generation

9-1-1 is a national emergency number that has advanced over the years and has undergone and still faces many challenges.

List of definitions

ALI—automated location information

ANI—automated name information

Cellular phones—phones that communicate through the cellular network and not wired to a physical location

Enhanced 9-1-1—refers to the 9-1-1 system's ability to provide a caller's name and address

MSAG—Master Street Address Guide

NG9-1-1—represents the next generation of 9-1-1 systems

PSAP—public safety answering point

SSAP—Secondary Public Safety Answering Point

Introduction

The concept of a single number to call the police or fire has been around for many years. In the early days of the telephone, citizens would often call the operator and ask to be connected to police or fire, depending on the emergency. Frequently, the operator activated the city's fire alarm and acted as an informational clearinghouse when an emergency such as a fire occurred. When North American cities and towns began to convert to rotary dial or "automatic" telephone service, many people became concerned about the loss of the personalized service provided by local operators. Telephone companies partially solved this problem by telling people to dial "0" for the local assistance operator if they did not know the fire or police department's full number (Swihart, 1995). As telephone technology progressed, many agencies provided a distinctive seven-digit telephone number that was easy to remember, e.g., 527-1111. Of course, the use of a local phone number limits the caller to that community.

The idea of a single national emergency number is not new. Other nations, such as Great Britain, had a three-digit emergency reporting number as early as 1937 (Pivetta, 1993). It was not until 1967 that the concept emerged in the United States (Pivetta, 1993). The President's Commission on Law Enforcement recommended in 1967 that a single emergency telephone number be established (Pivetta, 1993; Swihart, 1995). In 1958, the U.S. Congress first investigated a universal emergency number for the United States and finally passed the legal mandate in 1967. The installation of the first system occurred in Haleyville, Alabama, and the first call occurred on February 16, 1968 (About.Com, n.d.). AT&T had originally planned to implement a 9-1-1 system for Huntington, Indiana; however, Alabama Telephone worked diligently to become the first telephone company to provide this service.

9-1-1 became the universal emergency number that is still in existence today. Over the years, it has evolved both in its capabilities and its integration with other emergency dispatching systems. In its beginnings, 9-1-1 was just a common number that allowed citizens to dial 9-1-1 anywhere and obtain police, fire, or EMS service. Although this technology was available, not all emergency service agencies supported 9-1-1. To this date, there are still communities that do not use 9-1-1 as their emergency number.

Since its early days, 9-1-1 has advanced significantly. In the 1980s, telephone companies expanded the 9-1-1 system's capabilities to include the name and address of the registered phone owner, known as automated name index (ANI) and automated location index (ALI). The newer version of 9-1-1 systems became known as Enhanced 9-1-1 or E9-1-1. This capability allowed call takers to identify the location of the caller and provided the potential name of the caller, which was the name of the registered phone owner. The first systems provided this information through a small terminal placed at each call taker position. When the dispatch center received a 9-1-1 call, the location of the call, the name of the registered phone owner, and the telephone number appeared on this terminal.

Public safety answering points (PSAPs) rapidly began to integrate this technology with computer-aided dispatch (CAD) systems. This significantly improved the dispatching speed of emergency calls. These early implementations of joint CAD and E9-1-1 systems quickly became integrated such that when an E9-1-1 call comes into the dispatch center, a window in the CAD system opens with the E9-1-1 information. The call taker could accept these data, in which case the call for service screen populates with the E9-1-1 data, or the call taker can modify the data as needed. The E9-1-1 interface became common place with all CAD systems.

America's 9-1-1 system has been extremely successful, but new technology is presenting many challenges that we discuss in this chapter. As an example, when 9-1-1 came to be, the caller location was easily identifiable because the telephone line was connected to a physical location. The emergence of new Internet technologies and capabilities has changed the way we use telephones. Cellular phones were the first to introduce challenges to the nation's 9-1-1 system because with the use of cell phones, the telephone became mobile. This presented significant challenges to the nation's 9-1-1 system. The countries 9-1-1 system now faces new challenges from cellular, Internet, and satellite phones as well as other forms of communication. Text messaging and other similar technologies all have had significant impacts on the 9-1-1 system, and that is why the National Emergency Number Association (NENA) is working diligently to define the future 9-1-1 system that will address all of these new challenges (Galvin, n.d.). Next Generation (NG) 9-1-1 is the new direction for the nation's 9-1-1 system.

The following sections present the three types of 9-1-1 systems in use today, Basic 9-1-1, Enhanced 9-1-1, and NG9-1-1. Each of these systems has played a significant role in what has become a nationally recognized telephone number for citizens to call whenever they have an emergency. Both Basic 9-1-1 and Enhanced 9-1-1 are quickly becoming outdated by new technologies. The NENA, the Association of Public Safety Communications Officials (APCO), and the Federal Communication Commission (FCC) are working diligently to ensure the country will always have this number for citizens to call whenever the need for emergency services arises.

Basic 9-1-1: How it works

As discussed in the previous section, Basic 9-1-1 was the first in the family of 9-1-1 systems in use today. Its intent was to have a single phone number that a citizen could call to access police, fire, or EMS services from anywhere. Basic 9-1-1 is still in use today in approximately 5% to 7% of the nation's PSAPs (Layton, 2006). Although we are all used to dialing 9-1-1 today and contacting the appropriate emergency dispatch center, the jurisdiction in which we are calling from was not easy to accomplish. How can the phone system know to which center it should direct a 9-1-1 call? As an example, the 9-1-1 system must be able to distinguish a 9-1-1 call coming from within limits so the appropriate agencies can be dispatched to the location.

Basic 9-1-1 had limitations in its ability to route a 9-1-1 call. Early 9-1-1 systems routed calls to an agency that was largely responsible for that area. The prefix of the caller's phone number determines the routing of these calls. The following is an example of basic routing: All 22X prefixes belong to Any Town Police Department. However, what if not all 22X prefixes were in Any Town Police Department's jurisdiction? This would require the call taker to contact the appropriate agency and notify that agency of the citizen's request for service (Pivetta, 1993).

Basic 9-1-1 was not a comprehensive system. It was just a phone line, like any other phone line. The phone line was only able to go to a single location, e.g., police, fire, or EMS. The entity would have to decide which agency such as police, fire, or EMS would receive the call. If the police department received the call, the call taker would transfer the call to the fire department to handle if it were a fire call, or to the EMS department if it were a medical call (Pivetta, 1993).

The use of a simple number for citizens to call when an emergency occurred was the main advantage of Basic 9-1-1. Some cities never implemented a dedicated 9-1-1 telephone line. When a citizen called 9-1-1, it routed the call to the standard dispatch center's seven-digit telephone number. This was a practice found in rural areas of the country. These agencies did this to ensure that someone traveling to their community or region used to dialing 9-1-1 for emergencies could still do so and contact an emergency services agency.

Enhanced 9-1-1

The City of Chicago claims to have implemented the first Enhanced 9-1-1 system in the United States in 1970. The major difference between Basic 9-1-1 and Enhanced 9-1-1 is that Enhanced 9-1-1 added the caller's address, ALI, and the name of the registered owner, ANI. Adding these features and functionality required significant enhancements to Basic 9-1-1. The following is a list of the components required by the new E9-1-1 system (Pivetta, 1993):

- *Automatic location identification (ALI)*—This is the location, by address, from which the 9-1-1 call initiated. When a person dials 9-1-1, the system performs what the industry terms an ALI dip. An ALI dip occurs when a person calls 9-1-1. The system uses the phone number to look up the address of the registered phone owner.
- *Automated name index (ANI)*—This is the name of the registered phone owner. Obviously, this may or may not be the actual person calling 9-1-1, and that is why the call taker must ask the caller to verify their name.
- *Master Street Address Guide (MSAG)*—The MSAG is the database that defines the geographic area of the 9-1-1 service. It is a list of each street within the jurisdiction. It typically provides the street name, the low and high ranges of the address numbers on each street, the community name, the emergency service number (ESN), and the PSAP identification. The MSAG is essential to E9-1-1 because it serves to validate the caller's address.
- *Emergency service number (ESN)*—The ESN is a three-digit number with one digit identifying the responsible police department, another digit identifying the fire department, and another digit identifying the EMS agency for that address. The ESN number links

to the MSAG to ensure the dispatching of the appropriate unit to the correct address. When the dispatch center receives an E9-1-1 call, the system looks up the address in the MSAG and obtains the appropriate emergency agencies to send to the call based on the ESN.

- *Emergency service zone (ESZ)*—The ESZ is a geographical area having the same police, fire, and EMS jurisdictions and common PSAP. This directly links to the ESN.
- *Selective router*—The selective router is a tool used to route calls to the appropriate PSAP (Pivetta, 1993). The MSAG tables determine the routing that show the exact location of the call and determines the appropriate PSAP to handle the call. The selective router includes the following features:
  - *Alternate routing*—If a PSAP is unable to answer a call, the alternate router routes the call to another PSAP. Issues surround this capability that local agencies must address. As an example, it is not feasible for a large agency to route its calls to a smaller agency because the smaller agency is most likely unable to handle the larger volume of workload.
  - *Default routing*—In the event the selective router loses its memory switch, the selective router will route according to a hardwired routing instruction that will route to a PSAP, although that PSAP may not be the one responsible for the caller's location. Default routing requires caution because of similar issues as associated with agency size that face alternate routing.
  - *Time of day routing*—The selective router can be programmed to route calls to a different PSAP based on a time of day and day of week (Pivetta, 1993). This occurs mainly in rural areas of the country. A small city maintains emergency services during a normal week day operations. After hours, the emergency services' responsibilities switch to a 24-hour emergency service operation. As an example, Country Town USA accepts emergency calls from 8:00 a.m. to 5:00 p.m. Monday through Friday; all other times, they route calls to the county Sheriff's dispatch center.
  - *Call transferring*—From time to time, it becomes necessary to transfer an E9-1-1 call to another PSAP (Pivetta, 1993). Most quality selective routers have the ability to transfer the entire 9-1-1 call (ANI and ALI) to another PSAP. Often, two jurisdictions share a 9-1-1 call. As an example, one PSAP may be responsible to dispatch police services to their community, but the county dispatches fire services from their PSAP. Each must be capable of sharing the 9-1-1 data. Call Transfer also becomes necessary in jurisdictions that answer cellular calls for an entire region. That information must be shared with the appropriate responding agency.

- Ring down to secondary PSAP (SSAP)—In some jurisdictions, there is a single PSAP that answers all 9-1-1 calls. The call taker verifies the location of the call and then performs a "ring down" to the right responder(s), passing the caller and the E9-1-1 call information to the responsible dispatch agency. As an example, in the state of New Hampshire, all 9-1-1 calls get routed to a central call answering center. Call takers at that location verify the caller information and then "ring down" the appropriate emergency responder(s), passing the appropriate call information to the responding agency(s) SSAP.

In addition to the previously mentioned components added to the Basic 9-1-1 system, a significant software component had to be developed to handle an E9-1-1 call. When an E9-1-1 call occurs, it goes from the caller's location to the telephone company's central office (CO). The computers at the CO perform an ANI/ALI dip, which is just a database lookup, based on the phone number that generated the call. The system obtains the address and the name of the owner of the phone. During this lookup, the system determines the appropriate PSAP based on the address of the phone location. This address comes from the MSAG. Unlike Basic 9-1-1, the E9-1-1 system can determine the appropriate responding agency even if the prefix overlaps jurisdictions. The ANI/ALI lookup provides the ESN number, which determines the appropriate PSAP responsible for handling the call. This technology provides the ability to distinguish between two separate PSAPs even if the calls come from the same prefix. Figure 3.1 depicts the Central Office E9-1-1 call processing previously described.

Early E9-1-1 systems provided a small terminal to display the ANI/ALI information of a call. Not all E9-1-1 systems then or now interface to a CAD system. This requires a separate terminal or workstation to display the E9-1-1 information/recommendation. E9-1-1 systems provide the ANI/ALI data to a dumb terminal or to an intelligent workstation. Modern systems incorporate the E9-1-1 information with CAD.

Challenges faced by the 9-1-1 system

Advances in technology over the years presented challenges to the 9-1-1 system. Cellular phones were the first new challenge faced by the 9-1-1 system, particularly the E9-1-1 systems. At the time, Basic and Enhanced 9-1-1 came into being when cellular phones did not exist. This made tracking the call location easy. Upon receipt of a 9-1-1 call, the system performed an MSAG lookup, and the information was forwarded to the PSAP responsible for handling that emergency. The rest was up to the call taker and dispatcher to handle.

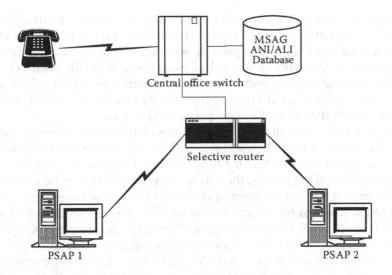

Figure 3.1 Central office E9-1-1 call processing.

Private branch exchange systems

There are challenges for this technology with calls coming from private branch exchange (PBX) systems. PBX systems are common in business environments. Large business complexes, government buildings, and college and university campuses all use PBX systems. The problem that this creates for the 9-1-1 system is identifying the location of the 9-1-1 call. When a caller dials 9-1-1 from his or her desk or other location, the call goes through the PBX. The 9-1-1 system will recognize this call as coming from the central location but not the specific location of the caller. It is also most likely that the ANI information will be wrong, displaying the name of the company and not the caller. As an example, in a large complex with buildings spread out over a large area but the system routes calls to the central PBX, located a long distance from where the call is coming, it can be difficult to route the emergency unit to the precise location of the call. In some instances, where the person is calling from and the location of the incident could be in different emergency jurisdictions. This may cause the wrong emergency agency to be dispatched, which could cause serious response delays. This problem has been challenging to overcome.

Several options designed to deal with the PBX issue have emerged. The older analog PBX systems do not have a lot of options. The most common method of dealing with this PBX occurs with the use of dedicated circuits that operate with the centralized automated message accounting (CAMA) signal protocol (National Emergency Number Association, 2003). For PBX systems that use analog trunks, there are a couple of ways that this problem might be addressed. The way recommended by the NENA is by using dedicated circuits that operate with the CAMA signaling protocol (NENA, n.d.-b). Another method might be to provide software that allows PBX owners to input address data. This approach has many obvious pitfalls, such as keeping the data up to date, and other issues. Another popular method is to provide the local ANI/ALI data to the security officer. The security officer then forwards the call to the appropriate PSAP (Pivetta, 1993).

Fortunately, the digital age has assisted with this problem to some extent with the development of Private Switch (PS) 9-1-1 systems. For PBX systems that use digital trunks, Primary Rate Interface Integrated Services Digital Network (PRI-ISDN) trunks, the provisioning of PS/911 may be accommodated without the requirement of dedicated trunks for transporting 9-1-1 calls (NENA, n.d.-b). NENA conducted significant research in this area, and they claim successful provisioning of "PS/911 for sites using PBX systems equipped with PRI-ISDN trunks without having to use dedicated CAMA-type circuits. The system passes the 9-1-1 calls to the local service provider's serving CO over the PRI-ISDN trunks like a regular local call. The system then routes the call to the 9-1-1 selective router via the 9-1-1 trunk group that connects the CO switch to the 9-1-1 selective router. This represents a clear advantage over the use of dedicated circuits from each PBX to the 9-1-1 selective router" (Trunking for Private Switch 9-1-1 Service, 2003).

TTY/TDD communications

In today's society, many disabled people cannot communicate orally or hear well enough to communicate with PSAPs. The Americans with Disabilities Act requires telephone emergency services to include 9-1-1 services to provide direct services to people who use Text Telephone (TTY) or Telecommunications Device for the Deaf (TDD). Prior to computerization, emergency dispatch centers operated in a manual mode; they typically supported manual TTY/TDD devices. These devises alert the call taker/dispatcher with a distinct tone that a TTY/TDD call was incoming. The call taker/dispatcher would put the phone on the TTY/TDD device through the acoustic coupler to start communicating with the caller by typing what they want to say. The system sends the message to the person's device and displays it on a screen. The citizen and the call taker/dispatcher communicate back and forth using these devices and this methodology. Figure 3.2 depicts a typical TTY/TDD device (NENA, 2005).

In emergency communication centers, we often find preformatted messages that assist the call taker/dispatcher with quickly responding to a TTY/TDD caller. When answering a call, a typical message might be "Simi Valley 9-1-1 Center what is the nature of your emergency?" There can be many similar messages created that will help speed up the communication process.

Figure 3.2 TTY/TDD.

Handicapped individuals may differ in their communications needs. Some people can talk but require TTY/TTD help because they cannot hear. The industry refers to this as *voice carry over*. Still others require TTY/TDD help because they cannot speak, but they can hear. The industry refers to this as *hearing carry over*. PSAPs must be capable of handling both types of situations.

As technology is changing, new issues arise for disabled communications. Cellular technology, smart phones, voice over Internet protocol (VoIP), and other technologies impact handicapped people's ability to access the 9-1-1 system. Earlier analog phones were perfectly capable of accessing the TTY/TTD devices at a PSAP. Digital cellular phones require that capabilities be incorporated to allow these phones to access 9-1-1 TTY/TDD. VoIP phones are not able to access the TTY/TDD. Many models of cell "smart phones" have a TTY software application, such as the Sidekick from T-Mobile. The user can text from the cell phone keypad, and the cell carrier network server converts to TTY modem tones for a PSTN call to the legacy TTY device (RIT NTID 911 Briefing, 2011).

Cellular phone technology

Although there are challenges with the traditional wired phones as discussed earlier, cellular phone technology presented a whole new set of challenges to the 9-1-1 system. With cellular phones, there is no wire. Someone can call 9-1-1 from anywhere, and the call may not go through the appropriate selective router. In the early days of cellular technology, callers would call 9-1-1 while in a location outside of where they lived, and the ALI information would reflect the address of the phone owner, similar to how it does with a wired phone. The difference is the ALI information is not correct because the caller was miles from their home location at the time they called 9-1-1. This created obvious difficulties for the PSAP. This severely hampered the nation's E9-1-1 system, and it threatened the entire E9-1-1 system as we know it.

The FCC recognized this problem and involved both NENA and APCO and developed a three-phased approach to resolving this problem (Dispatch Magazine On-line, n.d.). The FCC mandated that the telephone companies fix this problem and laid out a three-phased approach.

- *Phase 0*

  This phase simply requires that when a person dials 9-1-1 from their cell phone, a call taker at a PSAP answers the call. All 9-1-1 calls must be relayed to a call center, regardless of whether the mobile phone user is a customer of the network in use (FCC, n.d., http://www.fcc.gov/encyclopedia/enhanced-9-1-1-wireless-services). This allotted time to telephone companies and PSAPs to enhance the 9-1-1 system to accommodate cellular phones.
- *Phase 1*

  Wireless network operators must verify the phone number and cell phone tower used by callers, within 6 minutes of a request by a PSAP.
- *Phase 2*

  To be considered Phase 2 compliant, both the PSAP and the telephone company must be capable of the following:
  - Ninety-five percent of a network operator's in-service phones must be E9-1-1 compliant ("location capable") by December 31, 2005. (Several carriers missed this deadline and received fines from the FCC.)
  - Wireless network operators must provide the latitude and longitude of callers within 300 meters, within 6 minutes of a request by a PSAP. Accuracy rates must meet FCC standards on average within any given participating PSAP service area by September 11, 2012 (deferred from September 11, 2008) (NENA, n.d.-a).

The implementation of these three phases occurred over time, and although the FCC slated December 31, 2005, many agencies were unable to meet this deadline. To meet these requirements, mapping became necessary. With a map integrated with the CAD system and/or the E9-1-1 system, the location of the call can be plotted on the map using the X, Y coordinates.

The challenge for cellular companies was how to get the X, Y coordinates and send them to the PSAP. The solution was to install a global positioning system (GPS) chip in all cell phones. This solution did meet with some early resistance. Many people did not believe it was appropriate for the government to know their location. They did not like the idea that they could be tracked using the GPS chip in their phone. To address this, all PSAPs have a ten-digit phone number for citizens to call the PSAP, which would not invoke a GPS chip. The only time the GPS chip activates is if the caller dialed 9-1-1. This is similar to how fixed position 9-1-1 functions. In the traditional system, if the caller dials 9-1-1, he or she understands that they are giving up their right to privacy. If the citizen wants to maintain their privacy, the citizen calls the regular ten-digit emergency number. Figure 3.3 is a sample CAD map that is displaying the location of 9-1-1 calls provided through the cellular phone GPS chip.

The integration of the 9-1-1 system as described in this section overcomes the problem with cellular call location.

GPS technology, in addition to X, Y coordinates, also provides Z coordinates. The Z coordinate is the height of the caller location. Height is essential for tall buildings that have many stories. Major cities have tall buildings and a 9-1-1 call from the 10th story may be difficult to locate. The use of the Z coordinate provides the height, and the 9-1-1 system and/or the CAD system convert the Z coordinate to the precise floor from which the call is coming from.

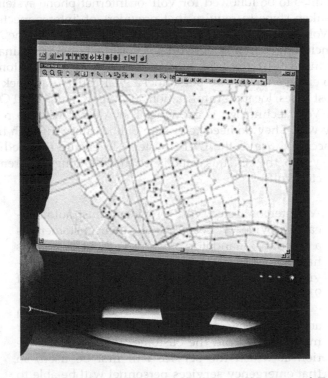

Figure 3.3 CAD mapping and phase 2 compliance. (Courtesy of Zana, A. P., Intergraph Public Safety, ICAD, Computer software, Huntsville, AL: Intergraph Corporation, 2015.)

Voice over Internet protocol

Shortly after resolving the cellular problem, another problem for the 9-1-1 system arose that presented new challenges to the E9-1-1 system, the voice over Internet protocol (VoIP). VoIP provides end users with the ability to make phone calls using the Internet. This eliminates going through the commercial telephone system. Although this technology is an advancement, it presents many new challenges. When someone makes a phone call over the Internet, it bypasses the E9-1-1 system entirely. This means that there is no ANI or ALI information forwarded to the PSAP. The call taker will see a blank screen, which they refer to as a "ghost" caller. "Ghost" callers also occur when a standard cell phone user makes a 9-1-1 call from out of the cell phones home area. In some instances, the call gets diverted to a PSAP business number. As an example, a person with a VoIP-based phone dials 9-1-1, and the system connects them to an administrative line instead of reaching the PSAP. Obviously, this could be a life-threatening situation.

Once again, the FCC has become involved and established standards and guidelines to be followed for VoIP or Internet phone systems. "The FCC has taken steps to require that providers of 'interconnected' VoIP services (VoIP services that use the Public Switched Telephone Network (PSTN), including wireless networks, to originate and terminate calls) meet Enhanced 9-1-1 (E9-1-1) obligations. E9-1-1 systems automatically provide to emergency service personnel a 9-1-1 caller's call back number and in most cases, location information" (FCC.gov., n.d.). The FCC recognizes that VoIP technology is growing. They do not want to restrict its use in any way. They do need to ensure public safety through the effective and accurate use of the E9-1-1 system. To ensure the credibility of the E9-1-1 system, the FCC has established the following requirements for interconnected VoIP:

> All interconnected VoIP providers must automatically provide 911 service to all their customers as a standard, mandatory feature without customers having to specifically request this service. VoIP providers may not allow their customers to 'opt-out' of 911 service.
>
> Before an interconnected VoIP provider can activate a new customer's service, the provider must obtain from the customer the physical location at which the service will first be used, so that emergency services personnel will be able to locate any customer dialing 911. Interconnected VoIP providers must also provide one or more easy

ways for their customers to update the physical location they have registered with the provider if it changes.

Interconnected VoIP providers must transmit all 911 calls, as well as a callback number and the caller's registered physical location, to the appropriate emergency services call center or local emergency authority.

Interconnected VoIP providers must take appropriate action to ensure that their customers have a clear understanding of the limitations, if any, of their 911 service. All providers must specifically advise new and existing customers, prominently and in plain language, of the circumstances under which 911 service may not be available through the interconnected VoIP service or may in some way be limited in comparison to traditional 911 service. They must distribute labels to all customers warning them if 911 service may be limited or not available and instructing them to place the labels on and/or near the equipment used in conjunction with the interconnected VoIP service.

Interconnected VoIP providers must obtain affirmative acknowledgement from all existing customers that they are aware of and understand the limitations of their 911 service.

In some areas, emergency service providers are not capable of receiving or processing the location information or call back number that is automatically transmitted with 911 calls. In those areas, interconnected VoIP providers must ensure that a 911 call is routed to the appropriate PSAP. (FCC.gov., n.d.)

Although these requirements are good, there are still issues with VoIP technology that can cause difficulties for the E9-1-1 system. The FCC does not require all Internet services be compliant with the previously mentioned requirements, only interconnected VoIP services must comply. It is possible for callers to be out of their general area, which would present a problem in establishing caller location. The problem is that the end user can connect to the Internet in several different ways. Because of this capability, Internet 9-1-1 contact continues to be problematic. Residential VoIP phone providers do provide E9-1-1 services from the home. Another threat to VoIP users is that a power outage can cause the Internet to go down. The FCC recommends that a traditional landline phone be kept if the caller uses VoIP phones (FCC.gov., n.d.). Many of these problems have still not been overcome by VoIP technology.

Next generation 9-1-1

The era of wireless communication is upon us. Although this is a benefit to individuals and society in many ways, it also presents many challenges in the emergency communications environment. As technology changes, the 9-1-1 paradigm needs to evolve to maintain its effectiveness. With wireless communications, the mode of communication can occur in several ways. Wireless communications can include telephonic, text messaging, e-mail, and photo and video communication. Gone are the days when the only form of communication with the PSAP was through the wire-line telephone. These multiple ways of communicating with the PSAP have created significant challenges in the public safety communications environment. There was clearly a need to improve 9-1-1 technology once again to meet with modern technology and social trends.

Next Generation 9-1-1 will accommodate many new Internet Protocol based devices. The goal of NG9-1-1 is for the PSAP to be able to communicate with these devices. With the implementation of NG9-1-1, citizens will still be able to contact the PSAP through the standard devices that it is capable of using today such as wired telephones and cellular phones. In addition to the new technologies discussed, NG9-1-1 allows PSAPs and citizens to communicate through other wireless technologies. "The PSAP of the future will also be able to receive information from personal safety devices such as Advanced Automatic Collision Notification systems, medical alert systems, and sensors of various types. The new infrastructure envisioned by the NG9-1-1 project will support 'long distance' 9-1-1 services, as well as transfer of emergency calls, to other PSAPs—including any accompanying data. In addition, the PSAP will be able to issue emergency alerts to wireless devices in an area via voice or text message, and to highway alert systems" (NextGeneration 911, n.d.).

In the TTY/TDD section of this chapter, we discussed issues with this technology and how it communicates with the PSAP under normal E9-1-1 conditions. As indicated, there are issues with digital E9-1-1 systems that negatively impact TTY/TDD systems. Under the NG9-1-1, these problems no longer exist. Handicapped people will be able to text message, sending and receiving messages between the NG9-1-1 center and their computer or their Smart Phone. They will also be able to send pictures or video when needed.

Another noteworthy feature that is a part of NG9-1-1 is the ability to identify everyone in the vicinity with an Internet-connected device and automatically notify them to avoid the area (Next_Generation_9-1-1, n.d.). This aspect of the NG9-1-1 system helps to reduce the number of calls received by the PSAP for the same incident. The system can also integrate with the Amber Alert System, which sends information to the public as required. It can also be used to send other information as might be required. Another significant capability closely related is the NG9-1-1 system's ability to be interfaced to an Advanced Automatic Collision Notification system. These systems, like OnStar and others, have the capability of making notification when a vehicle is in a collision, even if the driver of the vehicle is unable to make such a notification. These vehicles can also be tracked because of the GPS chip installed. On the basis of the seriousness of the collision, the PSAP can dispatch the appropriate emergency agency to the scene.

As we have seen throughout this chapter, 9-1-1 has faced many challenges over the years. The implementation of NG9-1-1 is not without its issues. Intelligent transportation systems have done a good analysis of the issues that NG9-1-1 faces. They have identified ten issues that needed to be considered and addressed. The issues are as follows.

- Current funding, budgeting, and cost recovery policies may not be able to support the implementation and sustainment of NG9-1-1 (NG9-1-1 Transition Issues Report, 2008).

  Funding for NG9-1-1 is an issue. Typically, PSAPs receive funds to implement and maintain the 9-1-1 system. Landlines are the basis for these charges, but most phones today are wireless. Many jurisdictions have not transitioned to charging for wireless technology, and where they have, they cannot track out of jurisdiction cell phones that also access the E9-1-1 system. The more affluent communities are likely to be able to implement the NG9-1-1 system. Those less affluent areas may not be able to afford to implement NG9-1-1 for some time.

- Security controls for the NG9-1-1 system and emergency data need to be defined and properly managed and maintained (NG9-1-1 Transition Issues Report, 2008).

  Whenever operating over an IP network, there are security issues that must be addressed. This report recognizes that there are issues that need to be addressed to insure the proper security of an NG9-1-1 system.

- Responsibility for the acquisition and delivery of location information and the mechanism to obtain and verify the location data needs to be defined (NG9-1-1 Transition Issues Report, 2008).

  ITS contends "the analysis of this issue assumes that PSAPs will be able to receive 9-1-1 calls from IP-based devices that ultimately connect to an emergency communication network. There may be a variety of 9-1-1 call originating sources public or private that may connect to NG9-1-1 (such as, WiFi Hotspot, enterprise local area network).

This issue also assumes that E9-1-1 is the baseline of 9-1-1 services available at many PSAPs" (NG9-1-1 Transition Issues Report, 2008).

• With the increase of personally identifiable information available with an NG9-1-1 call, existing laws may not be sufficient to protect the privacy of a 9-1-1 caller (NG9-1-1 Transition Issues Report, 2008).

> For public safety to respond to 9-1-1 calls, personal and identifiable information must be obtained both automatically (such as, location and telephone number) and directly from the caller or the call stream data. Positive identification of the location of a caller, coupled with the ability to identify other personal information that may contribute to effective emergency response, but poses privacy concerns that are certainly present today, and will increase in the NG9-1-1 environment. To further compound privacy concerns, NG9-1-1 offers the ability to interconnect other systems or databases to provide supplemental information such as medical and health data that are currently not widely available to PSAPs and public safety agencies in an automated or electronic fashion. This raises issues of legal privacy and the need for NG systems to address user access and data rights management and the ability to respond to compromised access.

NG9-1-1 Transition Issues Report, 2008

• Routing and prioritization in the NG9-1-1 environment is more complex and includes the ability to dynamically route calls based on factors beyond location of the caller (NG9-1-1 Transition Issues Report, 2008).

In many respects, this issue is self-explanatory. The NG9-1-1 system is diverse and affords a superb deal of flexibility. That flexibility can lead to complex call routing issues. With the IP open architecture, the NG9-1-1 system will enable the ability to route 9-1-1 calls throughout the nation. There are no location limitations as in today's 9-1-1. Location-to-service translation servers and a national PSAP uniform resource locator (URL) registry must be developed to support the ability to route NG9-1-1 calls at a national level (NG9-1-1 Transition Issues Report, 2008). Obviously, call routing is crucial and can be lost without the proper routing calls. This will have to be addressed to maintain appropriate routing of NG9-1-1 calls.

- Mechanisms need to be developed to certify and authenticate service and infrastructure providers to allow access to NG9-1-1 (NG9-1-1 Transition Issues Report, 2008).

> Telecommunications services, and access to 9-1-1 by such services are more complex in the NG environment. The actual services themselves, whether they are the delivery of a 9-1-1 call, or an enhancement to the treatment of that call, could be provided by a third party service provider separate from those that provide access to such services. Consequently, mechanisms to regulate, certify, and authenticate service providers of all types critical to emergency communications, to ensure consistency, must be defined. They require authorization and standard contributions to the process so NG9-1-1 PSAPs can receive data related to 9-1-1 calls.
>
> **NG9-1-1 Transition Issues Report, 2008**

- NG9-1-1 allows for a level of coordination and resource sharing that does not currently exist in today's 9-1-1 environment (NG9-1-1 Transition Issues Report, 2008).

> The nature of NG9-1-1 system allows for the sharing of services and resources, including infrastructure and applications. Without establishing an agreed upon framework (institutional arrangement) among PSAPs, 9-1-1 Authorities, and other entities (e.g., Public Safety Dispatch and other service providers), the benefits of sharing resources and services will not be fully realized. This may prevent the realization of potential cost savings by a region or state that has multiple PSAPs and other entities.
>
> **NG9-1-1 Transition Issues Report, 2008**

- Industry may be reluctant to develop and adopt open standards, which could limit the availability of interoperable NG9-1-1 services and equipment (NG9-1-1 Transition Issues Report, 2008).

> Lack of support from service providers and equipment manufacturers in developing and adopting open standards will limit the availability of interoperable services and equipment. This will have an

impact on the ability of the NG9-1-1 system to inter-
connect and achieve the NG9-1-1 vision to provide
ubiquitous, interconnected NG9-1-1 services across
the Nation.

NG9-1-1 Transition Issues Report, 2008

• Liability protection or parity needs to be extended to protect stake-
holders involved in NG9-1-1 (NG9-1-1 Transition Issues Report, 2008).

Experience in the deployment of E9-1-1 has shown
that a lack of legal clarity on the issue of liability
parity can lead to delays in the provisioning of
E9-1-1 service. NG9-1-1 will potentially promote a
more complex service delivery environment, which
will further complicate liability protection for new
and future services.

NG9-1-1 Transition Issues Report, 2008

• New capabilities and services enabled by NG9-1-1 could impact
PSAP operations and training for both PSAP administrators and call
takers (NG9-1-1 Transition Issues Report, 2008).

As implementation of the NG9-1-1 occurs, 9-1-1
Authorities and PSAP directors will have to deter-
mine how to modify existing PSAP practices and
procedures (e.g., Standard Operating Procedures
[SOP] and training) and resources (e.g., Human
Machine Interface [HMI] solutions for existing cus-
tomer premises equipment [CPE]) to accommodate
NG9-1-1 services. Currently, neither nationwide
SOPs nor a training curriculum fully exist NG9-1-
1system operation.

NG9-1-1 Transition Issues Report, 2008

NG9-1-1 is certainly the wave of the future, but it will require
some significant adaptation. Although the ten items discussed previously pertain to the 9-1-1 system, there are also issues with CAD
systems. CAD systems typically integrate the E9-1-1 system into the
CAD. With NG9-1-1, there will be the standard interfaces. To accommodate all other forms of data entry that will occur under NG9-1-1
requires substantial modifications to most existing CAD systems.

In Chapter 4, we will discuss the integration of 9-1-1 into the typical CAD system installed in many of the current PSAPs.

References

About.Com. (n.d.). *The history of 9-1-1 emergency calls.* Retrieved from http://inventors.about.com/library/inventors/bl911.htm.

Dispatch Magazine On-line. (n.d.). *The history of 911 emergency calls—Inventors.* Retrieved from http://www.911dispatch.com/.

FCC.gov. (n.d.). *VoIP and 911 service.* Retrieved from http://www.fcc.gov/guides/voip-and-911-services.

Galvin, B. (n.d.). Benefits *of* integrating CAD and RMS. *9-1-1 Magazine.* Retrieved from http://www.9-1-1magazine.com/Galvin-CAD-and-RMS.

Layton, J. (2006, July). *How 9-1-1 works.* HowStuffWorks.com. Retrieved from http://people.howstuffworks.com/9-1-1.htm.

National Emergency Number Association (2003, April). *Trunking for Private Switch 9-1-1 Service.* (Issue NENA 03-502). Alexandria, VA: Author

National Emergency Number Association (2005, June 25). *TTY/TDD Communications Standard Operating Procedure Model Recommendation.* Alexandria, VA: Author.

National Emergency Number Association. (n.d., a). Cell phones and 9-1-1. Retrieved from http://www.nena.org/?page=911Cellphones.

National Emergency Number Association. (n.d., b). *MLTS & PBX Project.* Retrieved from http://www.nena.org/?page=MLTS_PBX.

NextGeneration 911 (n.d.). NG 9-1-1 Overview. Retrieved from http://ng9-1-1.org.

NG9-1-1 Transition Issues Report. (2008). Retrieved from http://www.itsdocs.fhwa.dot.gov/ng911/pdf/NG911_TransitionIssuesReport_FINAL_v1.

Pivetta, S. (1993). *The 9-1-1 Puzzle: Putting the Pieces Together.* The National Emergency Number Association.

Swihart, S. (1995, Spring). Telecom history. *Journal of the Telephone History Institute, 2.*

Telcom Digest (1997). *Misdialing 9-1-1 from Hotels.* Retrieved from http://massis.lcs.mit.edu/archives/back.issues/1997.volume.17/vol17.iss351-365

chapter four

Police computer-aided dispatch systems

Command and control of police resources is critical to service delivery in a timely and efficient manner; computer-aided dispatch systems fulfill this role.

List of definitions

CAD—computer-aided dispatch
NCIC (2000)—National Crime Information Center
RMS—record management system
Telecommunicators—dispatchers and call takers

Introduction

Communication centers are the central nerve center of a police department. A standard dispatch center employs people to take calls from citizens and to dispatch police, fire, and Emergency Medical Services (EMS) units to the call location. Most citizen calls for service originate either in the dispatch center or through the officer in the field. The officer generates an event and reports the activity to the dispatcher. The dispatcher tracks the call for the remainder of its life cycle. Before automating the dispatch center, call taker/dispatchers processed all data manually. When a resident called the dispatch center, a call taker/dispatcher would answer the phone and examine the caller to understand the nature of the call and the location. If the call taker determined it was necessary to send a patrol car to the scene, he or she would collect additional information such as location of the incident, name of the complainant, and as much information about the event as they can get. The call taker/dispatcher would stamp the critical times associated with the call. These include the time the dispatch was received, the time the unit arrived on the scene, and the time the officer completed the call. At the completion of the call, the call taker/dispatcher types the predefined information onto a radio log. The radio log is a synchronous record of activities for a span of time (Chu, 2001).

Call takers and dispatchers also track police officer's field activities. They capture and record officer generated activities, such as traffic stops, suspicious persons, and other activities officers engage in during a shift. In a manual system, the call taker/dispatcher manually records the time and location of the officer generated activity. The call taker/ dispatcher also has the responsibility to perform inquiries into external systems such as the National Crime Information Center (NCIC) 2000, state criminal databases, Department of Motor Vehicles, and other external systems. Call takers and dispatchers also have the ancillary responsibilities of accessing a variety of manuals and making contact with external agencies.

Without any form of automation, the workload on call takers and dispatchers became increasingly intense. There were many manual systems developed to handle communication center workload. As an example, a large communication center split the call-taking and dispatching functions. Call takers captured the initial call information from the citizen and passed the call to the dispatcher via a conveyor belt. The call taker would place the completed call certificate on a conveyor belt that sent the call to the dispatchers. The dispatchers would take the card off the conveyor belt as it passed them. The dispatcher then dispatched the appropriate unit to the call and took responsibility for that call to its completion.

Information technology–advanced agencies automated the call-taking and dispatching process with the development of computer-aided dispatch (CAD) systems. CAD systems came into their own right in circa 1968, with the development of the nation's first CAD system.

System performance requirements

CAD systems are real-time systems. They are command and control systems in that CAD systems require the ability to process all CAD transactions in less than 1 second. CAD transactions include routing a call to the dispatch queue, map display device, validating an address (unless an exact match occurs, in which case the display of alternatives shall not exceed 2 seconds), displaying indicators of hazards or other premise information, and displaying or updating a call record. Measuring the successful processing of a transaction is the elapsed time between the completion of the request by the operator (such as pressing the enter key after an entry on the command line, a mouse button clicked) and the appearance of the requested information or verification of an executed function on the requester's screen (Ackroyd et al., 1992).

Today's CAD systems are sophisticated command and control systems that integrate numerous technologies, such as telephony, voice over Internet protocol, geographic information systems, mobile computing, automated vehicle location (AVL) systems, and other ancillary systems. Modern CAD systems can be broken down into six basic components:

1. Administrative
2. CAD system baseline functions
3. Call-taking functions
4. Dispatching functions
5. Supervisory functions
6. External interfaces

The following subsection defines these six CAD components.

Administrative functions

Administrative functions are part of all CAD systems. CAD vendors develop these systems so they can easily modify them to meet an individual agency's dispatching needs without having to modify the core software. In addition to customizing a CAD system to meet individual agency's needs, administrative functions provide a vehicle for performing all levels of application maintenance, including the following:

- Operator-level configuration, which includes the ability to add and delete users, change user IDs, modify command areas and command zones, change passwords, and manage workstation configurations
- Ability to create and revise squad and shift data from multiple sources
- Ability to define and modify group configuration parameters
- Code table management
- Ability to configure workstation and other hardware devices, including status monitor and function key assignment
- Ability to set database management parameters, such as date and time, system parameters, and frequency of data purges and password change

Specific administrative functions vary from one vendor product to another. These are the basic functions found in leading products of CAD system providers.

Window configurations

Current windowing technologies provide flexibility in the presentation of data. Modern CAD systems make maximum use of this technology. Windowing technology allows the operator to configure the presentation of the standard CAD system windows according to the operator's preference. Once arranged to the operator's satisfaction, the operator can save the configuration under his or her login. This flexibility aids operators in providing increased productivity and job satisfaction. Included in windowing technology are features associated with graphical user interfaces (GUIs), such as cut, copy, and paste routines that allow users to copy or cut information from other program screens and paste that data into a CAD screen. Drop-down windows are also a part of the standard Windows features. These systems use drop-down windows to display code tables, unit identification, and other similar data elements where multiple choices are available for selection.

Most modern CAD systems require a minimum of two and often three workstations to display all of the necessary windows. The windows are sizable, and it is common to find multiple windows open at any given time. Some CAD systems allow the end user to save the configuration to their login ID. This allows them to reuse the window configuration the next time they log-in.

Squad or shift activation

CAD systems have the ability to preload information pertaining to squads or shifts. A squad or a shift consists of personnel assigned to a function or unit. Supervisors can preload a shift with all of the appropriate personnel and units. When the shift comes on duty, the dispatcher activates the squad or shift through a simple command. The system recommends the recently activated units, upon activating a squad or shift. The dispatcher still controls the individual units left on from the previous squad until they log off at the end of shift. This function typically includes a command that shows an officer is no longer available for calls but is on an overtime activity such as report writing. Agencies also need to activate distinctive alert conditions, which result in differing levels of preparedness in anticipation of an unusual or critical situation. For example, the police department may "squad up" before an expected demonstration. Assignments to vehicles, equipment issuance, and supervisory monitoring and proximity to squad members will change according to the level of alert. The use of a basic preset command or function call makes it possible to broadcast such alerts to the appropriate operational level (sector, district, and citywide).

Code table management

A CAD system must support the use of code tables. Code tables provide the agency with the ability to customize various features and functions. Often code tables allow the agency to establish acceptable responses to fields. As an example, "call type" is a field that signifies the type of call received such as "burglary in progress." A call table allows the end user

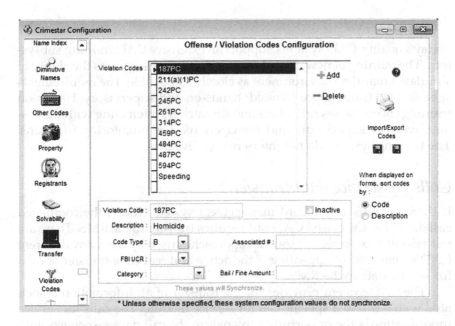

Figure 4.1 Code table list and sample code table. (From Gagne, A., CrimeStar, Version 10.6, Computer software, San Jose, CA: CrimeStar Corporation, 2015.)

to specify the call types acceptable to the system. In today's modern CAD systems, combo and list boxes provide the end users the ability to display the code tables, allowing the end user to select the appropriate call type.

Code tables vary in sophistication depending on the system and the purpose of the code table. Figure 4.1 depicts a typical list of code tables and the use of a code table.

Unit recommendation and validation tables

A critical component of a CAD system is an emergency service, unit recommendation, and validation. The basis of unit recommendation is the type of unit required to respond to a call. As an example, a priority one in-progress felony call requires two units, whereas a "cold" burglary report call only requires a single unit. In addition, public safety agencies typically respond units to a call based on the unit's capability and service responsibility. As an example, agencies assign specific units to a particular geographic area, usually known as a beat. The CAD system administrator must be able to maintain a unit recommendation and validation table. This table defines specific police, fire, and EMS units. Included in their definitions are the unit designators and a definition of the unit's capabilities such as patrol, detective, or traffic accident investigation unit. The system only recommends valid units for the type of call.

Training support

Today's quality CAD systems support an extensive CAD training subsystem. The training of new call takers and dispatchers requires the ability to simulate a real-time environment as closely as possible. The requirements specified for training are twofold: hands-on and supervisory. Hands-on training encompasses call takers and dispatchers interacting with the system, whereas supervisors and managers require monitoring functions. The training systems do not interfere with live data.

Calls for service data transfer

If there is a link to a record management system (RMS), the completed call data from the closed CAD call requires transfer to the RMS. There are varieties of acceptable call transfer approaches used by the many different CAD systems. Most appealing is the active and real-time transfer of calls for service data to the RMS.

The CAD system provides for the transfer of all information associated with a call to a specific call for service module. The calls for service module affords the opportunity to analyze the call data associated with the call in an offline mode. The data also serve as the beginning of an incident report within the RMS. Figure 4.2 presents a sample call for service module.

The data from the calls typically remain on the CAD system for a user-definable period. Any changes to the call record must also update the call for service module on the RMS. In the real world, agencies that have RMS systems linked to the CAD system usually delete the data off the CAD system approximately every 3 months. The data on the RMS system serve the necessary purposes for management reports and archival references. If the CAD system is a standalone system, the data usually remain on the CAD system and are accessible through the management information component of the CAD system for management reporting and call history purposes.

CAD system baseline functions

There are certain functions that are pertinent to both call-taking and dispatching functions. In the following sections, we describe these baseline functions and the tasks that they perform in a CAD environment.

Activity logging

Activity logging is a critical function in a CAD system. Logging all activities guarantees the ability to rebuild the system in the event of a

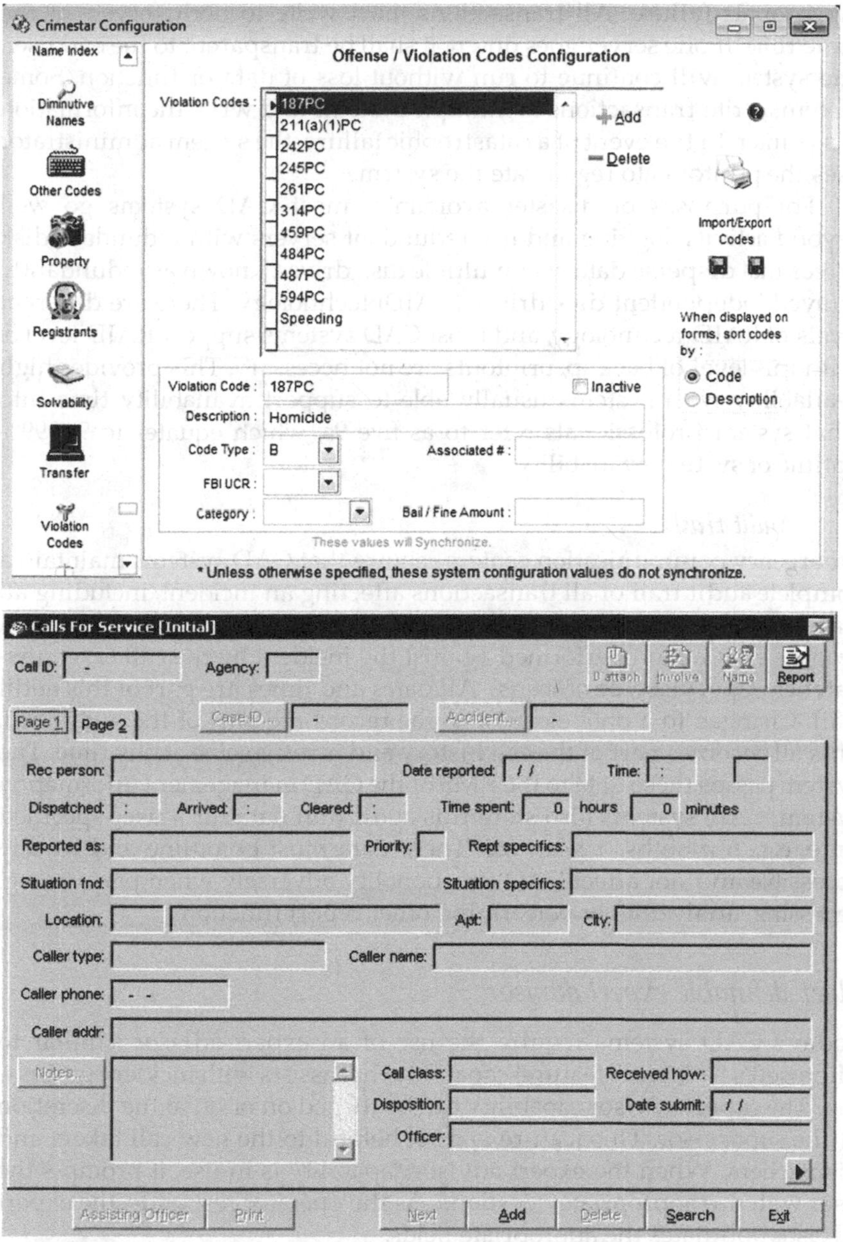

Figure 4.2 Call for service module. (From Gagne, A., CrimeStar, Version 10.6, Computer software, San Jose, CA: CrimeStar Corporation, 2015.)

catastrophic failure. All transactions must write to both servers at the same time. If one server goes down, it shall be transparent to the end user. The system will continue to run without loss of data or function. Some systems write transactions to multiple systems and write the information to a printer. In the event of a catastrophic failure, the system administrator uses the printouts to regenerate the system.

For purposes of disaster avoidance, most CAD systems go well beyond activity logging and use redundant servers with redundant disk drives that disperse data over multiple disk drives, known as redundantly arrayed independent disk drives (RAID) technology. There are different levels of RAID technology, and most CAD systems support RAID level 5. With this level of backup, printouts are not necessary. This provides high availability with systems usually able to support availability time into what system professionals refer to as five 9s, which equates to 99.999% uptime or system availability.

Audit trail

Emergency communication centers require that CAD systems maintain a complete audit trail of all transactions affecting an incident, including all transactions and messages from the mobile computing units. The system records each action performed against the incident by the call taker, dispatcher, supervisor, or officer(s). All dates and times are part of this audit trail. Changes to a data element in the record are part of the audit trail. This all becomes part of the call history and is retrievable at any time. The system passes these data to the RMS or the CAD management information system. CAD systems also store this audit trail data for a user-specified time, e.g., 6 months, 1 year, etc. These data must be online and readily accessible and not affect CAD functionality adversely when performing, accessing, analyzing, or performing other report functions.

User-definable expert advisor

Today's CAD systems require the use of an expert advisor (similar to Microsoft's "Wizard" feature) capability that assists with incident processing. The expert advisor capability can be turned on or off at the discretion of the supervisor. This feature is most helpful to the new call takers and dispatchers. When the expert advisor capability is in use, it prompts the user with the appropriate questions. As the operator responds, the expert advisor populates the appropriate fields.

Library function

Another powerful feature found on modern CAD systems is what agencies refer to as a library function. Communications personnel are always in need of accessing information. In the days of the old manual systems, communication centers maintained this ancillary information in three ring binders and card catalog files. With the advent of CAD, communication centers computerized this information in what the industry refers to as a CAD Library.

A library function provides the ability to create information and reference files. Files contained within the library are user defined and can relate to any topic deemed appropriate by the department. Topics can have subtopics further describing the main topic or to provide additional information. As an example, a department can place their entire policy and procedure manual online. The topic is policy and procedures. Contained within the policy and procedure manual are subtopics such as alarm response and deployment procedures. With the library function, they can drill down further into these other areas and obtain the necessary information.

In addition to the ability to access this information in a window, agencies can link library topics to a specific call type. The call taker enters the call type, such as robbery with hostages, whereupon an icon illuminates signifying library information is available. The call taker or dispatcher can then click on the icon and view information and instructions pertaining to that call type. An example and the significant use for this feature are the ability to enter prearrival medical instructions and link them to a call type. Figure 4.3 shows a sample of medical dispatch protocol.

The library function must include the ability to search on specific key words or hypertext. Hypertext capability allows the operator to access information without knowing a specific topic or coded information. Access occurs based on the text entered. The system searches the library database for the specific information based on the text entered.

Card file

Communications personnel require access to phone numbers. In the old manual systems, access to phone numbers occurred using an ordinary telephone card file or "Rolodex" system. It provides a means of storing names, addresses, and telephone numbers of key people and organizations. Contained within the card file are notification lists, referral lists, and other relevant contacts. CAD systems provide automated card file subsystems. These modules have the ability to catalog the data by topic and subtopic. As an example, if a dispatcher needs a veterinarian at an incident, the dispatcher accesses the card file and enters the topic of "veterinarian." The system then displays two subcategories of large animal or small. When the dispatcher selects small animal, a list of all small animal veterinarians appears, displaying names, addresses, telephone numbers, and the veterinarian's specialty. The dispatcher selects the appropriate veterinarian to call for the situation at hand.

KB #	Error message	Solution
KB0135	Cannot load AMPDS32 because #0 system is out of memory	Use Unwise.exe (C:\Proqa.win\) to uninstall the pr more...
KB0134	GLBSSTUB has called an access violation in...	Browse to the ProQA CD manually, and run Lang.exe more...
KB0133	Create: AmpdsRetrvBinvers: cannot read PROQA version (48).	Ensure everyone is logged off ProQA. Back up your more...
KB0123	Cannot focus on a disabled or invisible window...	Delete the CEWIN.INI File from the Windows or Winn more...
KB0106	The database information could not be found.	Use the following steps to create the CBRN surv more...
KB0100	ProQA version information window shows open Err over and over	Please choose from the following two options: more...
KB0099	Missing files warning message when starting ProQA configuration utility	Open the lang.dat file in the C:\ProQA.Win\Data di more...
KB0084	Shunt from card 18 to 17-KQ 5 additional info. tab has wrong axioms	Click the "Det. Codes" tab to the left of the "Add more..."

Figure 4.3 Sample medical dispatch.   (*Continued*)

KB0058	I receive an error 'Susp. Workable Arrest STOMA' when opening ProQA	To resolve this issue, use the following procedure more...
KB0013	Cases won't close in ProQA	The case was not opened on the workstation where t more...
KB0010	Card 24 is shunting to card 26	*Critical Update Available* more...

Figure 4.3 (Continued) Sample medical dispatch.

Command line

Emerging technologies simplify the CAD command entry process. In the early CAD systems, the command line was where the dispatchers controlled the CAD system. Commands typically consisted of a two- or three-letter command followed by qualifying or defining information. As an example, when a field officer makes a traffic stop and notifies the dispatcher, the dispatch enters a command that might look like this: "TS 1A12, First and Broadway, 123 ABC." This command signifies that unit 1A12 is out on a traffic stop at First and Broadway on a vehicle with the license plate 123 ABC. Because dispatchers relied so heavily on the command line to perform CAD functions, the command line became a focal tool that dispatchers were not easily persuaded to relinquish. However, many of the new systems employ drag-and-drop and point-and-click technologies instead of commands that accomplish the same tasks. Because the command line is such a critical tool used by dispatchers, eliminating the command line from modern CAD systems is not possible at this time. Experience shows that as dispatchers become more comfortable with modern computing technologies such as drag and drop, the command line becomes less significant.

The following is a sample command line. As is evident, this is not really sophisticated, but it includes a drop-down capability that allows the end user either to review previous commands or to reissue a previous command. Figure 4.4 depicts a sample command line.

Figure 4.4 Command line. (From Gagne, A., CrimeStar, Version 10.6, Computer software, San Jose, CA: CrimeStar Corporation, 2015.)

Online messaging/conferencing

This feature provides call takers, dispatchers, field personnel with mobile computers, and other authorized users the ability to send and receive messages. Unlike e-mail, online messaging occurs in a near real-time mode. CAD systems require the ability to send a message to a specific individual, a group of individuals, or all logged on users. The receipt of a message results in the illumination of an icon signifying a message has arrived. In addition to illuminating the icon, an audible tone (with the ability to adjust or remove such tone) signifies to the operator a message has arrived. The operator views the message by clicking the icon. The message immediately displays if no other messages exist. If multiple messages exist, the system provides a selection list with the most recent message at the top. Messages are time-stamped. The operator selects the desired message, and the system displays it in a window. Once read, the operator then date- and time-stamps it. This same messaging capability is available to the officers in the field on their laptop computers.

Call entry process

Call entry is a fundamental process required of any CAD system. There are basic call entry processes required by every police department. In smaller police agencies, call taking and dispatching are a combined process. Large agencies separate these two processes. Regardless of the approach, the call entry process is the same. Within the call entry process, several requirements are unique to each type of call. During the call entry process, the call taker captures pertinent information in a preformatted screen such as the one below. Figure 4.5 depicts a call entry screen.

In this section, we describe these call-taking functions.

Basic required data elements

The CAD system must have the ability to capture basic information pertaining to the person reporting an incident, the location of the call, and the nature of the call. To the extent possible, the system must automatically capture information. The information captured becomes a part of the call record. A variety of sources feed data to the call record. A typical CAD system captures a variety of data elements. The following depicts a typical call entry screen.

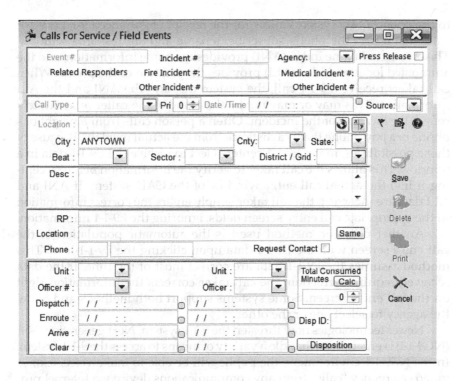

Figure 4.5 Call entry screen. (From Gagne, A., CrimeStar, Version 10.6, Computer software, San Jose, CA: CrimeStar Corporation, 2015.)

Call receipt methodologies

Call receipt in a dispatch center occurs through one of the following means:

- E9-1-1/NG9-1-1
- Ten-digit telephone lines
- Mobile computer transmissions
- Radio transmission
- Building alarm
- Alarm companies
- Text messages

Receipt of 9-1-1 calls

Today, citizens in the United States dial 9-1-1 whenever and wherever they need assistance from police, fire, or EMS. Although 9-1-1 began as a standard number used to contact the emergency service agencies, 9-1-1 significantly advanced to provide additional information. It included information pertaining to the location of the call and the person registered to the phone. CAD systems allow for the receipt of enhanced 9-1-1 (E9-1-1) calls that reflect the phone subscriber's name and address in a window. The automated name index (ANI) provides the name information, and the automated location index (ALI) provides the location of the phone. When call takers receive a 9-1-1 call, the system displays the ANI and the ALI information. This may or may not be the name of the caller or accurately reflect the location of the incident. Often a person calls from a neighbor's phone or a pay phone that is a distance from the actual incident. Because of these possibilities, many E9-1-1 centers elect to receive the E9-1-1 data in a window. This allows the call taker to verify the information before accepting it into the actual call entry window of the CAD system. If ANI and ALI data are incorrect, the call taker simply enters the correct information in the appropriate call entry screen fields, ignoring the E9-1-1 information.

Another common method used is the automatic population of the call entry screen with the E9-1-1 data upon clicking the E9-1-1 icon. This method assumes the E9-1-1 data are correct most of the time. If the data received require correction, the call taker corrects the information right on the call entry screen. Some systems support both methods and allow the agency to select one or the other.

Newer technologies now threaten the 9-1-1 system. Next generation 9-1-1 (NG9-1-1) is emerging to handle a variety of means to access the 9-1-1 system. In the NG9-1-1 environment, the public will be able to make voice, text, or video emergency "calls" from any communications device via Internet protocol networks. The public safety answering point (PSAP) of the future will also be able to receive data from personal safety devices such as advanced automatic collision notification systems, medical alert systems, and sensors of various types. The new infrastructure envisioned by the NG9-1-1 project will support "long distance" 9-1-1 services as well as transfer of emergency calls to other PSAPs—including any accompanying data. In addition, the PSAP will be able to issue emergency alerts to wireless devices in an area via voice or text message and to highway alert systems (Intelligent Transportation Systems, http://www.its.dot.gov/ng911/index.htm).

Receipt of calls on 7/10-digit phone lines

Many calls for service come into the center through the standard 7/10-digit telephone lines. When the call taker receives a 7/10-digit call, he or she must interrogate the caller to obtain the necessary information. As the caller provides this information, the call taker enters it in the call entry window. Windows technologies assist this process by allowing the call taker to move to fields by tabbing or clicking. This provides the call taker the ability to enter the call information in the order the caller needs the data.

The integration of voice and data truly is the wave of the future in telephony. The capability currently exists to tie the telephone system directly to the CAD system. When the call taker receives a 7/10-digit call, an icon illuminates, informing the call taker of the pending call. The call taker clicks on the icon that automatically opens a call entry window, allowing the dispatcher to enter the required information. Computer–telephony integration further provides the dispatcher or call taker the ability to call a complainant back simply by clicking on the telephone number field. When the CAD system integrates the telephone system's caller ID, the interface provides the caller's name and telephone number and populates the call entry screen with these data, providing the call permits its ID.

Call receipt through mobile computers (on-view events)

Most police departments use mobile computers in the field units. Citizens often stop police units to report an incident. Field units also observe incidents that require the creation of a call for service. The system must provide the ability to enter call information from the field. When a field unit initiates a call, that unit enters the data in a similar call entry screen as the one used by the call taker. The field unit transmits these data to dispatch. The system creates the call and shows the unit on scene. From that point forward, controlling the unit and managing the call is identical to the normal process for handling calls. In essence, the field unit acts like a call taker. The call appears on the dispatcher's unit and calls status monitor as a regular call. The field unit can also add notes and close the call.

Call receipt through voice radio

Field personnel often notify dispatchers over the radio whenever they observe an event. They also notify dispatchers whenever they become involved in an activity that results in the creation of an incident or traffic accident report. The system must provide the capability of entering a call for service reported by a field unit. Once received, incident tracking occurs as any other call received from E9-1-1 or 7/10-digit lines. The most efficient way of entering this type of call is through the command line.

Minimum required data elements

Call takers must be able to rapidly forward a call to the dispatchers with only the call type and location of the event as required fields. As call takers capture additional information, the call taker shall have the ability to enter this information and have it forwarded to the appropriate dispatcher with a notification to the dispatcher that additional information is available on that call.

Call priority

CAD systems require the ability to establish priorities for each call type. In sophisticated systems, the call priority is user-definable and flexible to user needs. The system automatically assigns the priority based on the priority level in the call-type code table. CAD systems allow call takers to change that priority either by increasing or by lowering the priority level throughout the life of the call. Call takers routinely receive call-backs pertaining to a call that changes the call priority. As an example, a citizen calls to report a loud argument occurring at a neighbor's home. The call taker transfers the dispatchers with the system-recommended priority level. Fifteen minutes later, the caller recontacts the call taker reporting shots fired. This requires the call taker to recall the incident and up the priority level as appropriate. Dispatch requires the ability to change the general status of a call at any time. The response algorithm must accommodate a graduated response level. Dispatch requires there be an emergency priority level that a call taker assigns to a call requiring immediate attention. Assignment of this priority immediately places the call at the top of the pending queue regardless of time received.

Ability to add or modify information to a call in progress

Call takers commonly receive additional information from a variety of sources. Dispatchers require that the system supports the ability to add information to a call regardless of its status. The dispatcher recognizes new information as it arrives because the call status monitor alerts the dispatcher by a color change, a reverse video, or other technique to signify the arrival of additional information for a specific call. New information also updates the field mobile computers and alerts the field officer to the availability of new data.

Duplicate call detection

A common occurrence in most dispatch centers is the receipt of multiple phone calls reporting the same incident. As an example, when a traffic accident occurs, communication centers often receive multiple calls reporting the incident. The problem occurs in discerning which calls are duplicates and which ones are separate incidents. Communications requires the CAD system be capable of detecting possible duplicate calls. The parameters for the identification of duplicate calls must be agency definable. Typically, the CAD system performs a radius search of the area immediately surrounding the call for service. The agency defines the size of the radius. Most of the advanced CAD systems allow the call taker to use the map and box the area of the potential duplicate call and see all calls in the area that might be duplicates. A parameter for the detection of a possible duplicate call includes the call type and, in some instances, similar calls. Immediately upon entering a call, the system notifies the

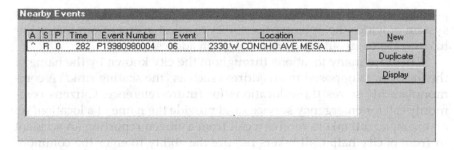

Figure 4.6 Duplicate call screen. (From Gagne, A., CrimeStar, Version 10.6, Computer software, San Jose, CA: CrimeStar Corporation, 2015.)

operator of possible duplicate calls and displays a listing of these calls, which often appear as shown in Figure 4.6.

By selecting an event from this form then selecting the display button, the "display event" form appears, allowing the operator to review the details of the event to determine whether the current call is new or a duplicate of an existing call.

Upon detection of a duplicate call, the operator must reconcile both calls. If the operator determines the calls are duplicates, the system provides the following possible resolutions:

- The call taker or dispatcher deletes the latest call and stores information about the duplicate call in the system's transaction logs.
- The call taker or dispatcher may merge the information obtained from the latest call with the previously entered call.
- The call taker or dispatcher overrides the duplicate call alert and accepts the call as an original call.

CAD geofile processing

When a call taker enters the call into the system, the CAD system verifies the location through the geofile. Geofile processing includes the ability to verify addresses through one or more of the following:

- Exact address
- Intersection
- Common place name or alias (e.g., city hall)
- Street name
- Block range
- x–y–z coordinates

An exact address match requires no further geofile processing. Unverifiable street name entries cause the system to display a list of possible streets with the most likely street being at the top of the list. The system provides the operator the ability to select a street from that list or to override the geofile and enter the given address.

There are many locations throughout the city known by the name of the location, as opposed to an address such as "the skating rink." A commonplace file stores these locations for future reference. Citizens commonly call for emergency services and provide the name of a location. As an example, call takers receive a call from a citizen reporting an accident in front of city hall. Call takers require the ability to enter the commonplace name to which the system provides the precise address. The possibility exists to have multiple commonplace names. As an example, if citizen reports an incident at a 7-11 store, obviously there are many 7-11's to choose from. The system provides a list of all 7-11 stores from which the call taker can question the caller for the precise location. The commonplace file includes a Soundex capability to allow for the misspelling of a commonplace name.

Hazard information file

Public safety agencies require hazard information be attached to a specific location. Upon entry of an address, the system accesses this file or files. The system notifies the call taker of hazards at that location or within an agency-definable radius from the address of the call. Typically, an icon illuminates signifying hazardous information exists. The call taker clicks on the icon, and a window opens displaying the hazard details. Quality CAD systems display multiple hazards for one location listed in the order of the most threatening first. The system also logs the date, time, and user ID of all persons viewing the information. This same process reoccurs for the dispatchers when they call up the incident. Upon the dispatching of a call, the CAD system sends all hazard information to the field unit's mobile computer.

CAD systems provide the ability to enter and retrieve temporary hazards. Temporary hazards include an expiration date and time. The system automatically deletes the hazard upon reaching the specified date and time. The uses of temporary hazard flags occur for such things as temporary street closures, temporary storage of volatile chemicals, transportation of hazardous materials along a predefined route, issuance of restraining orders, etc.

Premise information file

The maintenance of premise information occurs for a variety of reasons for each department. CAD systems include a premise information file that functions similar to the hazard information file discussed previously.

Typical premise information files capture information on alarms. It includes contact information and owner information to allow call takers and dispatchers to contact responsible parties. In addition, the premise file stores information on specific apartments and business suite numbers. The premise file stores graphic files such as the department's tactical response guides for schools, apartment complexes, and businesses.

The premise information file typically stores nonhazard information. The typical use of a premise file occurs when the department wants to record the fact that a patient with Alzheimer's lives at a particular address. Modern CAD systems illuminate icon signifying premise information exists. The call taker clicks on the icon, and a window opens displaying the premise details. If there is known information but not available to the dispatcher, a flag will notify the dispatcher to contact the supervisor. This same process occurs for the dispatchers when they call up the incident. CAD systems can also send this information to the field unit's mobile computer.

Premise history file

Modern CAD systems track the history of calls for service at a specific location. The length of retention of these data typically is user definable. The premise history includes the type of call, the departments responding, and the final dispositions. Field units have the ability to access the premise history file from their mobile computer.

Call scheduling

Dispatchers require the capability of scheduling the dispatching of a call for a specific day and time. As an example, a call taker may receive a call from a victim of a malicious mischief. Because of prior commitments, the victim cannot wait for an officer to arrive and take a report. Using the call scheduling feature, the call taker establishes an appointment with the victim. When the call taker enters the call, it does not appear on the dispatcher's call pending queue until a user-defined time before the scheduled appointment.

Dispatch process

The dispatching process is a separate function from that of call taking. In some environments, the call taker and the dispatcher are one and the same person. The tasks of dispatching are unique. Dispatchers control and monitor the field officer's activities. This is a highly interactive process. In busy environments, it is an intense process. Dispatchers must ensure the timely dispatching of calls for service. They must also track, monitor, and provide support to field officers. This support includes accessing information through local, state, and federal databases.

The following subsection define the functions performed by typical CAD systems in support of the dispatch process.

Basic data elements

CAD systems capture data elements germane to the command and control of field units. The data elements captured by the dispatchers append to the call record initiated by the call takers. In addition, there are other data elements captured by the dispatchers typically associated with field-generated activity. The following is a listing of those data elements typically found in CAD systems:

- a. Command area
- b. Unit ID
- c. Disposition of event (minimum of four multiple disposition fields required)
- d. Other agency event number
- e. Multiple unit response flag
- f. Data reject flag
- g. Data reject time correction
- h. En route priority
- i. Dispatch comments or narrative
- j. Time unit was dispatched
- k. Time unit went en route
- l. Time unit arrived
- m. Time unit en route to destination
- n. Time situation under control
- o. Time unit clears destination
- p. Time unit available for call
- q. Dispatcher ID
- r. User-definable fields (minimum of three)

The following subsections define the functions and processes typically found as part of a CAD system.

Command area dispatch

A CAD system must be able to track police activity by geographical areas. Command areas are composed of smaller command zones such as beats and police reporting districts. Police departments require the ability to establish as many command areas as desired. Also required is the ability to save these different command area definitions for future use. A dispatcher typically handles one or more command areas. CAD systems route calls to dispatchers based on the command area for which they are responsible. A command area can be the entire city as typically is the case in the small agency environments. Larger cities often include multiple command areas, associated with precincts. Some systems require the ability to establish temporary user-definable command areas. Information captured must be maintained as part of the system history files.

Call pending queue

Communication centers receive more calls from citizens than they are capable of dispatching at one time. In a CAD system, these excess calls display in a call pending queue. The call pending queue is a user-sizable window that displays calls awaiting dispatch. The ideal system provides the agency with the ability to define the data elements, including the order or placement in a given window. Some CAD systems provide the agencies with the ability to color code pending calls to highlight for the dispatcher certain characteristics about the pending call. Figure 4.7 depicts a call pending queue.

CAD systems prioritize calls awaiting dispatch by call type and by the time the communication center received the call. Because each agency prioritizes calls by their own standards, most CAD systems allow the agency to specify the priority of a call using code tables. The code table specifies the call type and the assumed priority level of the call. Upon entering the call type into the CAD system, the system prioritizes that call and places it in the pending queue based on the type of call and the time received. The system provides the call takers and dispatchers the ability to raise or lower the recommended priority as necessary. Normally, dispatchers dispatch calls by selecting the call at the top of the queue. There are times when it becomes necessary to dispatch a call out of order. A quality CAD system allows dispatchers to select a call to dispatch regardless of its placement in the call pending queue. Once selected, the dispatcher presses a single function key to dispatch the call. This function will change the status of the call to "dispatched" and, in some systems, move the call to an active call window. The active call window reflects all future status changes.

Unit status monitoring

In addition to call monitoring, CAD systems monitor the status of all active field units. Modern CAD systems display unit status in a user-sizable window. Unit status monitoring is a real-time function. Status changes occur either by the dispatcher entering a command reflecting a unit status change or by field units entering a status change from the mobile computing device. CAD systems provide the user the ability to define the data

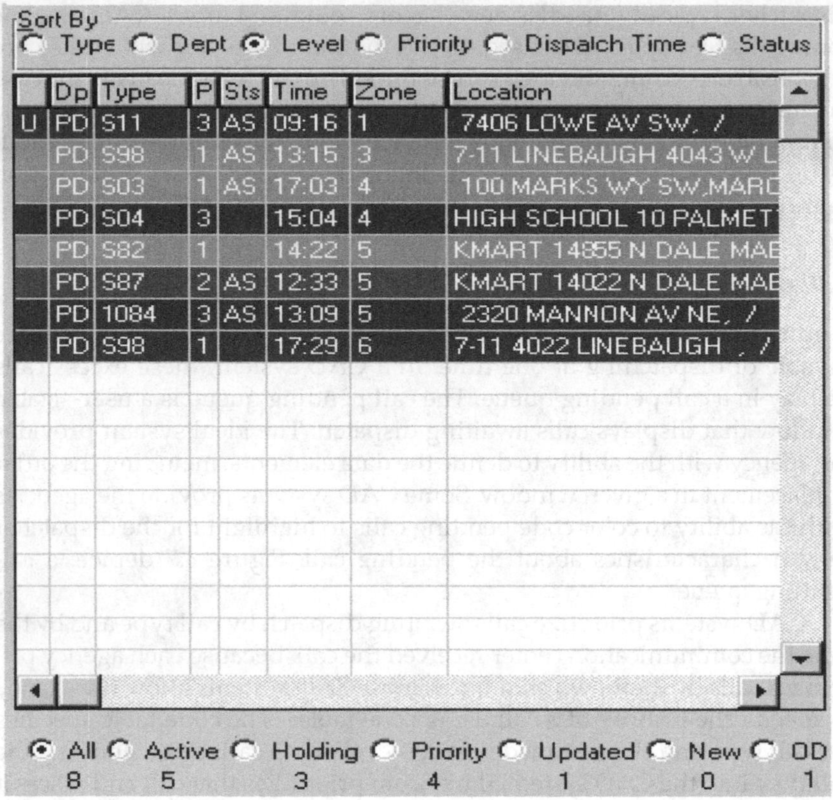

Sort By
( ) Type ( ) Dept (●) Level ( ) Priority ( ) Dispatch Time ( ) Status

	Dp	Type	P	Sts	Time	Zone	Location
U	PD	S11	3	AS	09:16	1	7406 LOWE AV SW, /
	PD	S98	1	AS	13:15	3	7-11 LINEBAUGH 4043 W L
	PD	S03	1	AS	17:03	4	100 MARKS WY SW,MARD
	PD	S04	3		15:04	4	HIGH SCHOOL 10 PALMET
	PD	S82	1		14:22	5	KMART 14855 N DALE MAE
	PD	S87	2	AS	12:33	5	KMART 14022 N DALE MAE
	PD	1084	3	AS	13:09	5	2320 MANNON AV NE, /
	PD	S98	1		17:29	6	7-11 4022 LINEBAUGH , /

(●) All ( ) Active ( ) Holding ( ) Priority ( ) Updated ( ) New ( ) OD
   8   5   3   4   1   0   1

Figure 4.7 Pending queue.

elements and their order or placement in the status window. Most CAD systems provide the user agency with the ability to specify color for the various unit statuses. They also provide the ability to establish alarms for various conditions to alert the dispatcher of potential hazardous conditions. Figure 4.8 shows a sample unit/event status window.

Most CAD systems use color to define the various unit statuses. The use of color makes it easier for the dispatcher to identify the status of any given unit under their control.

Status timers

In addition to reflecting status changes, the unit status monitor tracks the unit time in each status. Systems provide the ability to set timers by specific call type. The primary purpose of the timer is officer safety and quality control. For example, if a police unit is on a traffic stop and there is no

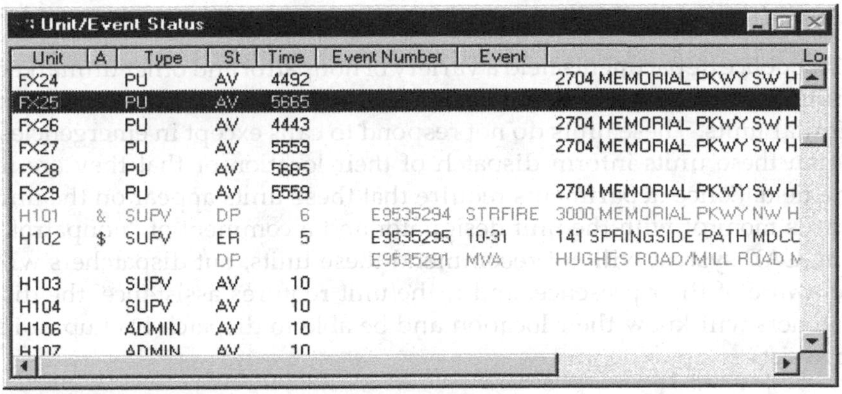

Unit	A	Type	St	Time	Event Number	Event	Lo
FX24		PU	AV	4492			2704 MEMORIAL PKWY SW H
FX25		PU	AV	5665			
FX26		PU	AV	4443			2704 MEMORIAL PKWY SW H
FX27		PU	AV	5559			2704 MEMORIAL PKWY SW H
FX28		PU	AV	5665			
FX29		PU	AV	5559			2704 MEMORIAL PKWY SW H
H101	&	SUPV	DP	6	E9535294	STRFIRE	3000 MEMORIAL PKWY NW H
H102	$	SUPV	ER	5	E9535295	10-31	141 SPRINGSIDE PATH MDCC
			DP		E9535291	MVA	HUGHES ROAD/MILL ROAD M
H103		SUPV	AV	10			
H104		SUPV	AV	10			
H106		ADMIN	AV	10			
H107		ADMIN	AV	10			

Figure 4.8 Unit/event status window. (From Gagne, A., CrimeStar, Version 10.6, Computer software, San Jose, CA: CrimeStar Corporation, 2015.)

contact with the officer for a specified length of time either electronically or by radio, the system notifies the dispatcher. Typically, this notification occurs by means of an alarm and a visual flag notifying the dispatcher of the lack of updated information. When this occurs, the dispatcher must click on the incident. This resets the timer. There are times when an officer takes more than the average amount of time with a situation. The officer notifies the dispatcher they intend to be on this call longer than usual, and there is no need to further check on their status. These instances require the ability to turn off the timer.

Available units window

The dispatch component of the CAD system must include an available unit's window. This window displays units available for dispatch. These are unassigned units or units not on any officer-generated activity. Available unit displays depict the units available to that specific dispatcher. Definition occurs by command areas or other user-definable criteria.

Event history

CAD systems provide a complete history of an event. Event history contains all units associated with the event and indicates the primary unit. Dispatchers also require the event history to capture all commands issued against units working the event, showing what happened and when. Lastly, it must list all officer IDs and names to be able to identify personnel assigned to the event.

Nonpatrol units

Most police departments field a variety of nonpatrol and other unmarked units. Such units include detective units, administrative units, and other similar units. These units do not respond to calls except in emergencies. Often these units inform dispatch of their location or that they are in the field. Police departments require that these units appear on the unit status monitor with the unit designator and a comment of "nonpatrol." The CAD system will not recommend these units, but dispatchers will be aware of their presence, and if the unit requires assistance, the dispatchers will know their location and be able to dispatch backup units to assist.

Unit history

This required function displays the history of a unit's activity in reverse chronological order, with the most recent activity at the top. The selection of a call for service responded to by the unit displays the event. Unit history must also log every time an officer does an inquiry on a vehicle license or a person.

Unit recommendation

Today's CAD systems also support dynamic unit assignment based on actual coordinates and routes. These systems select units based on minimum travel time to the incident. It calculates the travel time required using actual routes. It also takes into consideration factors such as time of day, traffic patterns, closed or blocked streets, and other impedance criteria. Geographic information systems (GIS) make it possible to graphically display the location of calls and the available units capable of responding to these calls. The system should be capable of graphically displaying in real-time mode and updating the master geofile. Upon the next initiation of an incident, the unit selection algorithm considers this new information in making a dispatch recommendation.

Officer history

CAD systems capture and record all officer activities. This includes calls for service that they handle and officer-generated activities. This requirement is similar to that of unit history. The police department requires the system attach to each officer assigned to a unit the activity of that unit. This required function displays the history of an officer's activity in reverse chronological order, with the most recent activity at the top. The selection of a call for service responded to by the officer displays the event.

The system allows agencies to save officer history indefinitely for future use. As an example, if an officer's activity comes under question through a citizen complaint, the agency can use the saved history to determine facts surrounding the issue in question.

System status management

Many of today's new CAD systems incorporate a system status management (SSM) component for its CAD system. SSM augments a CAD system's performance by enhancing dispatch and resource deployment strategies. This allows an agency to make maximum utilization of its resources and achieve the lowest possible response times.

The SSM component of a CAD system enhances usage and deployment of resources through the following mechanisms:

- Enhanced and expanded unit status keeping
- Enhanced dispatching algorithms
- Interfacing with automatic vehicle location system
- Using nonlinear distance and/or response time calculations
- Improved resource deployment and staging

Enhanced dispatching algorithms allow dispatching on the basis of closest appropriate unit by station, post, or AVL location. SSM also allows dispatching on the basis of the closest available unit by fastest estimated response time and scheduled (or anticipated) availability. The system chooses available units for dispatch based on how quickly they can respond to the scene. In addition, SSM is capable of selecting a unit already occupied on a call if in-service time will allow that unit to respond and arrive sooner than the next closest available unit. Considering roadway conditions, time of day, traffic patterns, and roadway impedance makes response time calculations much more accurate. Distance and response time calculations occur through estimated roadway mileage and not linear distances or "as the crow flies."

Management information derived from an SSM package can be used to determine and prestage units based on predictable, scheduled, and dynamic conditions. Historical analysis of unit coverage and response times allows the agency to determine a set of deployment strategies. These strategies afford maximum coverage and fastest possible response times. If an agency implements AVL, the agency can sample actual AVL location data to refine the day-of-the-week and the time-of-the-day driving patterns used in SSM.

SSM is an integral component of the CAD system and not a separate interfaced module. The SSM component drives the dispatch algorithm, monitors resource status, and makes a recommendation for unit deployment, develops and provides analysis of historical data, and provides flexibility in design to accommodate future changes to agency operations.

Supervisory function

Supervisory functions pertain to the day-to-day management of call-taking and dispatching operations within a CAD system. They differ from administrative functions discussed below. Supervisory functions include managing workload distribution for both the communications center and the field units. It also includes monitoring the work activities of individual call takers and dispatchers. These functions are necessary to ensure a CAD system functions appropriately and provides the necessary communication center support.

The following subsections describe typical supervisory functions required of a CAD system.

Supervisory workstation

CAD system supervisory capabilities link to the user ID and password as opposed to a workstation. A supervisor can log on to any position and perform supervisory functions. The supervisor capabilities include all call-taking and dispatching processes as well as functions unique to the supervisor.

Supervisor monitoring capability

CAD systems require the supervisor be capable of monitoring the activities of any call taker or dispatcher. Supervisors must have the ability to increase the priority level of a call from their workstation. As an example, if a call comes in that only requires a normal response and the supervisor determines it to be more urgent, the supervisor can up the level of priority to a higher level causing the incident to move up in the pending queue.

Emergency alert

There are times when a dispatcher or call taker may encounter a significant emergency. Modern CAD systems include an emergency alert feature. This feature allows the call taker or dispatcher to notify all others that this is a significant emergency. Usually, this alert is triggered in one of two ways, automatically by call type or manually by call taker or dispatcher activation. The system requires an emergency alert function that notifies the supervisor by illuminating a distinct emergency alert icon and by sounding an audible alarm. This requires the supervisor to click on the icon before it turns off. When the supervisor clicks the icon, a window opens displaying the following information:

- Call taker or dispatcher workstation triggering the alert
- All known information about the call
- Field personnel assigned to the call
- Field supervisor's name and unit ID responsible for the incident

The emergency alert can also causes an emergency notification to be sent to the field supervisor's mobile computing terminal.

Administrative function

Quality CAD systems provide the agency with the ability to perform a variety of administrative functions. Administrative functions provide a vehicle for performing all levels of application maintenance, including the following:

- Operator-level configuration, including the ability to add and delete users, change user IDs, modify command areas and command zones, change passwords, and manager workstation configurations
- Ability to create and revise squad and shift data from multiple sources
- Ability to define and modify group configuration parameters
- Code table management
- Ability to configure workstation and other hardware devices, including status monitor and function key assignment
- Ability to set database management parameters, such as date and time, system parameters, and frequency of data purges and password changes

The administrative functions typically provide a complete subsystem of the CAD system.

Code table management

CAD systems support the use of code tables. Code tables provide the agency with the ability to customize various features and functions. Often code tables allow the agency to establish acceptable responses to specific fields. In a GUI system, vendors use combo and list boxes to display and access code tables. Code tables provide customization without affecting the actual software code.

Unit validation and recommendation tables

CAD systems provide the system administrator with the ability to maintain a unit validation table. This table defines specific units. Included in their definitions are the unit designators and a definition of the unit's capabilities, i.e., patrol unit, or traffic accident investigation unit, etc. The system only recommends valid units for call responses.

The basis of unit recommendation is the unit type required to respond to a call. As an example, a priority one in-progress felony call requires two units, whereas a "cold" burglary only requires one. Unit recommendations are table driven and user definable. The system administrator typically maintains these tables.

CAD mapping

CAD systems integrated with a high-speed mapping system are today's standard. The CAD mapping system display maps showing street centerlines and premise or organizational boundaries. Generically, the map displays streets and detailed information on buildings and other locations. Tactically, the map provides a means of geographically displaying a call and unit locations. It displays the area for which the call taker or dispatcher is responsible. The map requires full integration with the CAD system. When a call taker enters a call, the system displays the geographic area immediately surrounding the call and marks the call with a symbol. The system uses color codes to denote the call status, such as white pending indicating dispatch, green in route, blue on scene. Typical of modern CAD systems, the user can define both the symbols and the color codes. Figure 4.9 depicts a sample CAD map.

These maps have the ability to display all possible duplicate calls. The CAD system allows the call taker to click on an incident and display all the information about that call. Standard mapping functions allow the call taker to zoom in on a user-definable area and to zoom out to see a broader area of activity and to see more detailed information. Included in this display are other calls in the area, units in the area, and other vital information.

Integrated CAD maps have the capability of providing a visual routing display from any point of reference on the map to any other point of reference. The CAD system routes the calls based on time-of-the-day and day-of-the-week traffic impedance data.

The CAD maps visually display premise and hazard information pertaining to specific locations. A window opens when the operator clicks on the premise or hazard icon. Figure 4.10 depicts a sample map that displays geographical information related to locations.

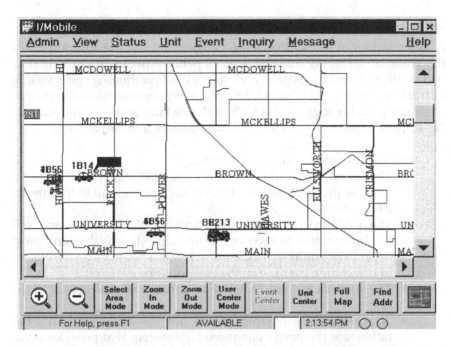

Figure 4.9 Sample CAD map. (Courtesy of Zana, A. P., Intergraph Public Safety, ICAD, Computer software, Huntsville, AL: Intergraph Corporation, 2015.)

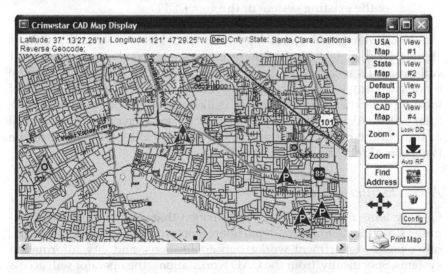

Figure 4.10 CAD map and narrative. (From Gagne, A., CrimeStar, Version 10.6, Computer software, San Jose, CA: CrimeStar Corporation, 2015.)

GPS/AVL requirements

A key component of the dispatching environment is the ability to track the real-time locations and status of all police units within jurisdiction. AVL systems achieve this goal. AVL uses global positioning system (GPS) to track emergency vehicles. A GPS/AVL subsystem combines the precise positioning technology of the GPS with tracking and communications capabilities to provide tools for unit management and dispatching.

GPS/AVL subsystem functional summary
- The subsystem would be closely integrated with the CAD system to show the location and status of each police unit in the city on a map display.
- The CAD system would use the GPS/AVL location and status information to recommend the closest, available, and most appropriate units to incidents. "Closest" should mean the closest in travel time over the city's transportation network.
- The subsystem would track the estimated all police units in the city.
- The proposed subsystem would not use differential GPS but rather use the newly enhanced GPS system that provides accuracy of 10 meters.
- The proposed subsystem could operate over the city's current 800-MHz communication network using nontrunked channels of the existing system or through CDPD.

As cellular phone technology advances, there are several problems created for dispatch. Most of these issues surround the receipt of E9-1-1 calls and calls received on the 7-digit lines. Because cellular calls can be made from any location, the communication center has no real means of locating the caller. GPS technology is likely to be used to help locate cellular callers. AVL can assist by displaying the location of the caller as well as the location of the closest unit to the call, providing the cellular phone is capable of relaying this information.

Access to internal databases

CAD systems require access to information that reside on internal computer systems such as the department's enterprise information system, other police department workgroup applications, and city information systems. Specifically, from the CAD workstations, the operator will access alarm permit information, utility billing, license and permits, and other city databases as required. Dispatchers require quick access to these systems, absent of complicated log-on procedures. The advanced systems provide icons wherein the system immediately presents the functions for which they have security access when a dispatcher selects the icon.

Access to external databases

Both call takers and dispatchers require access to external systems. External systems are stand-alone computer systems, usually under the control of another governmental agency. The NCIC, the National Sex Offender Registry, and state criminal justice information systems are examples of external databases that communication centers require access. Often name and property inquiries occur by means of a single name search that queries multiple databases. External database capability varies from agency to agency. Generally speaking, most all agencies require access to state and NCIC systems. Occasionally, agencies require access to a regional system. As an example, agencies within Pinellas County Florida all share information with the county sheriff and use a software package known as Cop Link to share common information. Other similar regional systems exist throughout the country that requires a specific interface.

References

Ackroyd, S., Harper, R., Hughes, J. A., Shapiro, D., & Soothill, K. (1992). *New technology and practical police work*. Buckingham, PA: Open University Press.

Chu, J. (2001). *Law enforcement information technology: A managerial, operational, and practitioner guide*. Boca Raton, FL: CRC Press.

Gagne, A. (2015). CrimeStar Inc. (Version 10.6) [Computer Software]. San Jose, CA: CrimeStar Corporation.

Intelligent Transportation Systems, Joint Program Office, (n.d.). Success Stories: Next Generation 9-1-1. Retrieved http://www.its.dot.gov/ng911/index .htm.

chapter five

Police record management systems

Command and control of police resources are critical to service delivery in a timely and efficient manner. Computer-aided dispatch systems fulfill this role.

List of definitions

CAD—computer-aided dispatch
IJIS—integrated justice information system
MLI—master location index
MNI—master name index
MVI—master vehicle index
NYSIIS—New York State Identification and Intelligence System

Introduction

Police record management systems equate to what the author refers to as the enterprise information system (RMS) for the department they serve. The RMS is the main departmental database. It contains information germane to everyone in the department. Everyone in the organization needs to have access to the information contained in the enterprise database. The RMS is the main software system that the police department depends on for data storage and retrieval of critical information. Police departments commonly refer to this system as the record management system or the RMS. RMS is an older term, and although it is still a commonly used term, it does not affectively describe the functions performed by the RMS. RMS systems performed the functions required of the Records Bureau. Early RMS systems emulated manual record systems and provided little information to others within the department. The second-generation RMS system began providing access to information that many others in the organization began to recognize as vital if not crucial to performing individual jobs. Everyone in the department accesses today's enterprise information systems and uses the data to perform their jobs. The data stored on these systems are crucial to performing day-to-day operations, and today's police environment cannot function without a solid RMS.

Required access to the RMS information permeates the entire department and beyond. Since 9/11, police agencies throughout the United States understand the importance of being able to share data. The movement toward integrated justice information systems (IJISs) necessitates the ability to share data. Police agencies share data with other justice agencies and are making data available to the public using the Internet. Agencies provide interactive websites that allow citizens to obtain public information from the police RMS. The RMS allows citizens to contribute information by doing such things as allowing citizens to report minor crime over the Internet. These crime reports populate the RMS with these minor crime reports.

Although workgroup applications are discussed in Chapter 6, the following section describes their relationship to the RMS. Workgroups require access to the RMS. Workgroups often maintain a local database that contains information specific to that workgroup's functions. Property and evidence or personnel and training are prime examples of significant workgroup applications. The RMS in combination with individual workgroups forms complete computing environment within a police department.

Enterprise information system

The typical enterprise information system captures information through a series of modules. These modules encompass data capture through processes performed through the normal course of business in a police department.

The following is a list of modules that comprise a typical police enterprise information system:

a. Calls for service
b. Master name index
c. Master vehicle index
d. Master premise index
e. Incidents
f. Traffic accidents
g. Arrest
h. Juvenile arrest or other contact
i. Known offender
j. Field interview reports
k. Citations
l. Wants/warrants and protective orders

The following is a description of each of the previously mentioned functions and the internal linkages and external interface requirements typically found in an RMS.

The first three modules described (calls for service, master name index [MNI], and master vehicle index [MVI]) are systemwide modules that not only provide for data collection and retrieval but also function as indices and history files. The other modules discussed in this section capture information specific to an incident, arrest, booking, etc. Master name, vehicle, and premise indexes provide a historical perspective while tracking occurrences.

Calls for service

Police agencies require the ability to view computer-aided dispatch (CAD) data via the RMS system. As discussed in Chapter 4, CAD systems are real-time systems, and they do not permanently store data. Most CAD systems will keep data for thirty to ninety days before archiving the information. To save the information captured by the CAD system, the system writes data to the RMS. The CAD system will pass all data pertaining to a call to a call for service (CFS) module in the records system. This will include actions taken by the field officers as well as the dispatch center personnel. The system automatically populates the fields in the various reports with the basic call information. This shortens the report-writing time. In the event there is no formal report required, the system provides the officer with the ability to enter unlimited comments to the call record from his or her field computer. The CFS module can download the completed call at any time and accept a batch download of all the calls at the end of shift.

Linkages to other modules

The CFS module does not require any external interfaces. The system does require linkages to other modules within the RMS, which typically include the following:

- CAD system
- MNI
- MVI
- Arrests (adult and juvenile)
- Aliases, images
- Offense/supplemental reports
- Vehicle impound module
- Pawn module
- Associates files

- Field interviews
- Alerts and comments
- Crime analysis module
- Known offenders
- Probation/parole notices
- Alarms
- Misdemeanor citations
- Traffic Citations
- Traffic accidents
- Master premise index
- Property and evidence
- Personnel

In a quality system, the user easily moves among the previously mentioned modules. They can share information between all without any redundant data entry. As an example, an entry of a traffic accident report provides a link directly to the vehicle index. If the vehicle is already in the system, it should require updates to the vehicle module with the latest involvement information. This is also true for name and premise information.

Master name index

Police departments encounter people for many reasons such as arrestees, victims, and suspect. The MNI must maintain the names of persons and businesses police departments encounter and link them to their appropriate involvement with the department. Once the department enters a person into the MNI, the system links all future involvements to this record without creating a new record. The storage of all name information occurs in this one location with pointers to other modules where data pertaining to the individual reside. Persons, businesses of interest, organizations, or other name types can be defined by the user and entered into the MNI and thereafter linked to the events entered into the system. Figure 5.1 depicts an MNI.

Name entry can occur through other modules, such as the following:

- Traffic accidents
- Arrests
- Field interview reports
- Alerts and comments
- Vehicle impounds
- Pawn module
- Known offender
- Citations

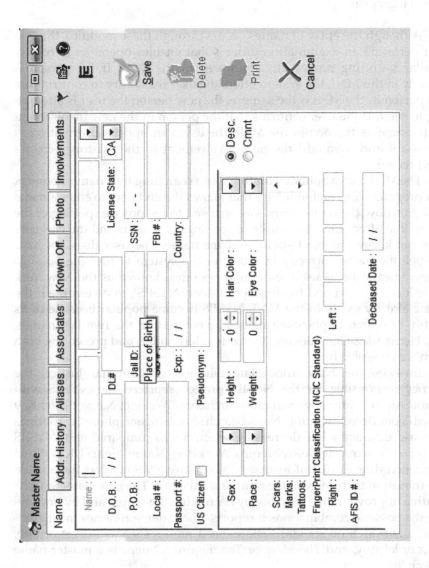

Figure 5.1 Master name index. (From Gagne, A., CrimeStar, Version 10.6, Computer software, San Jose, CA: CrimeStar Corporation, 2015.)

- Incidents
- MVI
- Master premise index
- Booking
- Fingerprint

Although the entry of names occurs through these modules, the system performs an examination process that enables operators to review similar sounding names already stored in the MNI. If the person is already in the MNI, the system offers the user the ability to confirm that the person in the MNI is the same as the new person the user is attempting to enter. If the user confirms that the person in the new involvement is the same as the one in the MNI, the user can update information as necessary and then add the new involvement to the existing person's MNI record.

The MNI uses a Soundex routine when searching for a name. Soundex is a programming methodology that allows the end user to enter a name based on how the name sounds as opposed to the precise spelling of the name. Too often, there are multiple spellings of a name and the end user may not know the exact spelling of the name. The user does not have to spell the name correctly in order for the system to find the possible name. Most systems use the popular Soundex, known as the New York State Identification and Intelligence System (NYSIIS), to determine if the name already exists in the MNI. NYSIIS became popular because of its ability to search hyphenated names by comparing the two last names, e.g., Hernandez-Gonzales and Gonzales-Hernandez, and presenting both names as possible hits.

In 1998, the New York State Division of Criminal Justice, the agency responsible for the NYSIIS project, replaced the NYSIIS with NameSearch® (http://www.name-search.com/Working/Name_SearchKey WordPhoneticcoding.htm). NameSearch's® intelligent phonetic routines increase accuracy while decreasing selectivity as compared with NYSIIS (http://www.name-search.com/Working/Name_SearchKeyWord Phoneticcoding.htm); unfortunately, not many RMS vendors have made the transition to the new name routine at this time. The new NameSearch® routine improves name searches by narrowing the search and by improving the possible combinations it reports. These name routines must automatically search on standard abbreviated names such as Robert or Bob, John or Johnny, and Theodore or Ted. Figure 5.2 depicts a master name search list.

A solid MNI will also include the ability to track information such as address changes, date of birth changes, aliases/monikers, known associates, physical descriptors about the person, and method of operation (MO) characteristics. A quality system must allow for name changes (such as

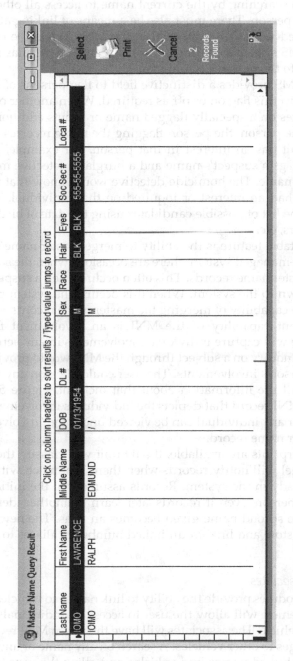

Figure 5.2 Master name search list. (From Gagne, A., CrimeStar, Version 10.6, Computer software, San Jose, CA: CrimeStar Corporation, 2015.)

women's maiden name or name through a previous marriage) and the capability when searching by the current name to access all other name records for that person. There must also be a means of linking all photographs associated with this individual in the MNI. When the end user requests the RMS system to perform a name search on an alias name, it provides a link to the person's actual name.

The ideal RMS provides a distinctive field to flag persons of interest. The user can turn this flag on or off as required. When another officer or detective inquires on a specially flagged name or inputs additional data pertaining to the person, the person flagging the name receives a notice that another unit has an interest in that person. For example, a homicide detective flags a suspect's name and a burglary detective makes an inquiry on that name. The homicide detective would know that the burglary detective had an interest or inquired on that individual. The end user can limit the list of possible candidates using the date of birth, social security numbers, etc.

Another notable feature is the ability to merge master name records. Even in the best-managed system, there are occasions when the same person has two master name records. This often occurs when a suspect gives an alias unknown to the system. When this occurs, the system provides the end user the capability of merging the master name records.

An important capability of the MNI is an involvement file. The involvement file will capture individual involvements in any activity. As an example, an inquiry on a subject through the MNI would provide a list of all of that person's involvements. The user could click on any involvement and see all the information about that incident. Figure 5.3 is an example of an MNI record that depicts the individual's involvements. The involvements for any individual can be viewed under the "involvements" tab of the master name record.

When fingerprints are available, the ID unit will classify the prints. The ID personnel will notify records when there is a match with someone who is already in the system. Records assume that the initial name entered is that person, even if records later learn of another identity for that person. The second name given becomes an alias. The new system must be able to store and link an unlimited number of aliases to a single MNI record.

Known associates

Modern MNI modules provide the ability to link names to vehicles so that a search on a vehicle will allow the user to access all individuals associated with that vehicle. The associates will have their own MNI record and may have linkages to other vehicles. A search on any name or any vehicle will display all linked names and vehicles and allow the user to access any name or vehicle associated with the original record. When accessing

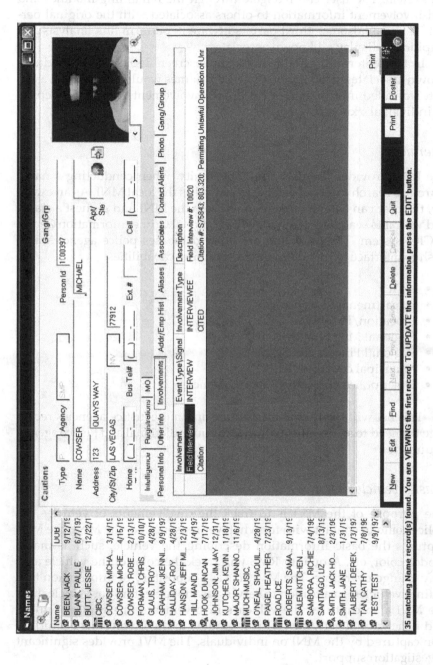

Figure 5.3 Involvements. (From Gagne, A., CrimeStar, Version 10.6, Computer software, San Jose, CA: CrimeStar Corporation, 2015.)

an associate, the user can look at that individual's involvements within the system. The user can navigate through the remaining modules and add involvement information to others associated with the original person. They can also use third party software to perform link analysis and graphically display all known associates.

In the center of the following sample screen depicts an individual's known associates. Clicking on one of the names would display that associate's detailed information or his or her involvements. Figure 5.4 depicts an individual's known associates.

Interfaces

The MNI provides the user the opportunity, when conducting a name search, to search external databases as well as the local MNI. As an example, the user can enter a person's name into the MNI and request a wants and warrants search through the FBI's National Crime Information Center (NCIC) system. The following are other databases police agencies may wish to interface to for added name searching capabilities:

- NCIC
- Department of Licensing
- Probation/Parole
- Regional Mug Shot System
- Regional Fingerprint System
- Municipal courts systems
- Other police and county sheriff agencies

This list will likely expand as more and more justice agencies recognize the need to share information across jurisdictional and justice agency boundaries.

Master vehicle index

The purpose of the MVI is to track the involvements of vehicles the police come in contact with for whatever reason. Like the MNI, the MVI captures the basic information describing the vehicle, such as make, model, color, etc. A quality RMS will track the color of the vehicle as it may change over time. The MVI acts as a repository of information that defines vehicles. In addition to serving as the repository for vehicle data, the MVI also captures the vehicle's involvements in various criminal and noncriminal activities. This is similar to the involvement information captured by the MNI on individuals. The MVI provides significant investigation support.

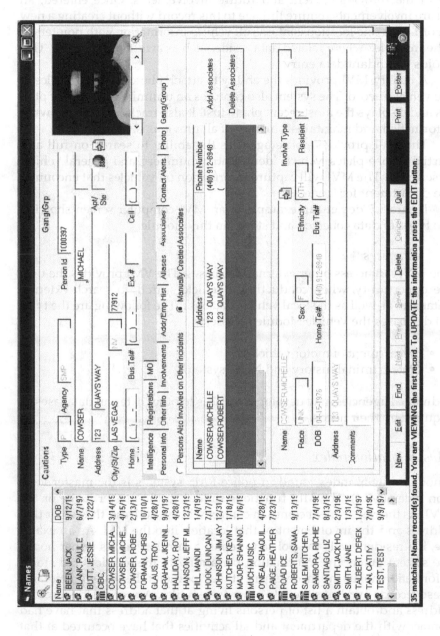

Figure 5.4 Known associates. (From Gagne, A., CrimeStar, Version 10.6, Computer software, San Jose, CA: CrimeStar Corporation, 2015.)

The MVI should function similarly to the MNI. The MVI should provide several data elements sufficient to describe the vehicle. It must track all of the vehicle's current and future involvements. Once entered, all future involvements require linkage to this record without creating a new record. This one location contains all vehicle information with pointers to other modules where related data reside, such as arrest and accident. This avoids redundant data entry.

A quality MVI provides the ability to attach photos of the vehicles to the vehicle record. The system also captures an unlimited number of photos and displays the most recent photo first. It also tracks registered owner information and maintains a history of all previous owners.

The MVI provides police agencies the ability to search on full and partial license plates, vehicle identification numbers, and general vehicle descriptors. The MVI will capture information on vehicles that encounter the department for any reason.

Figure 5.5 depicts an example of an MVI computer screen showing the types of data collected and stored in this module.

Interfaces

The MVI can access other external databases. The VMI provides the user the opportunity, when conducting a vehicle search, to search external databases as well as the local vehicle database. The following are the typical databases the Vehicle Module accesses:

- Department of motor vehicles
- State criminal history and NCIC system

Individual agencies may develop interfaces to other external databases as required by their needs.

Master location index

Another crucial index found in police RMS systems is the master location index (MLI). The MLI functions similar to the master name or the MVI. As the department comes in contact with an address, they enter that address and the involvement of that location into the MLI. As an example, if a resident calls the police to report a burglary at his or her home, the system enters the information pertaining to the location and stores information about the involvement at that location. The system maintains these records and links them to other system files. A user could search an address and obtain a list of persons living at that address that have had contact with the department and all activities that have occurred at that location. Figure 5.6 depicts a typical MLI.

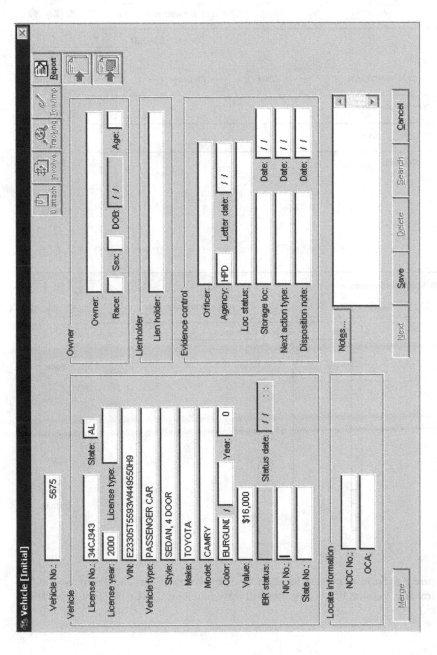

Figure 5.5 Master vehicle index. (From Gagne, A., CrimeStar, Version 10.6, Computer software, San Jose, CA: CrimeStar Corporation, 2015.)

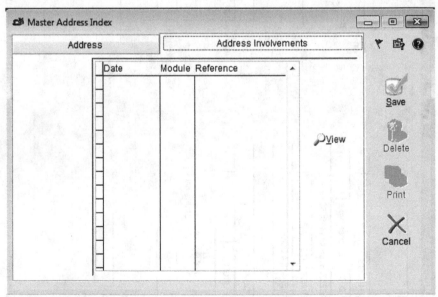

Figure 5.6 Sample master location and involvement screen. (From Gagne, A., CrimeStar, Version 10.6, Computer software, San Jose, CA: CrimeStar Corporation, 2015.)

If the MLI integrates with a geographic information system (GIS), the system will plot the location on the map. Clicking on the map location opens a window that displays the location information.

The capture of premise information can occur from several locations. The following is a list of the modules requiring linkage to the location index:

- Geofile
- Traffic accident
- Citation
- Arrest
- License and permits
- Field interview reports
- Master name
- Master vehicle
- Incidents
- CAD

Entry of information into this module occurs in one of two ways:

1. Automatically, when a user enters information in any of the previously mentioned modules
2. Manually, whenever a need arises to place information into the system pertaining to an address

The MLI becomes a critical file when an agency implements crime analysis mapping. The GIS relies on the MLI to plot activities at key locations.

Incidents

The incident module captures the basic information pertaining to reported crimes. The information contained in the incident module is the data typically found in a crime report that describes the basic information pertain to an incident. As an example, the incident module captures the date and time the incident occurred, the location of the incident, including the beat in which the incident occurred, and the reporting district as well as other information that defines the basics about the incident. Figure 5.7 depicts a sample incident screen.

In today's police agency, the records clerks enter the information from the incident report into the RMS. The implementation of an appropriate mobile computing system will eliminate redundant incident data entry. The field officer will enter the data and upload it to the enterprise database. This will transform the records personnel duties from data entry to quality control facilitators. With field computing, data entry occurs by the

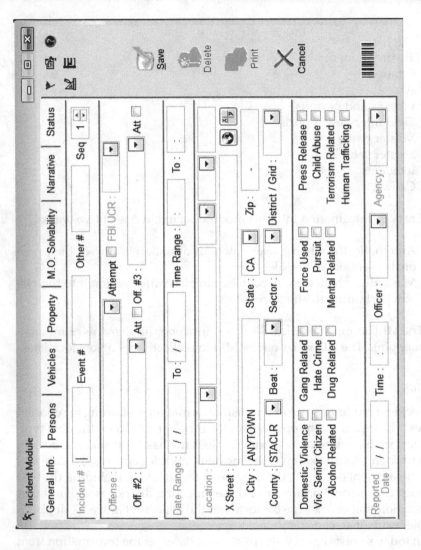

Figure 5.7 Sample incident screen. (From Gagne, A., CrimeStar, Version 10.6, Computer software, San Jose, CA: CrimeStar Corporation, 2015.)

field officer entering the report into the officer's mobile data computer. The officer enters the narrative of the report through the use of an industry-standard word processor, such as Microsoft Word or Word Perfect.

The use of personal digital assistants (PDAs) or tablet PCs is emerging as a means of officers capturing crime information. Ideally, the capture of the initial data occurs using a PDA with radio spectrum or Bluetooth capability back to the patrol vehicle or RMS for access from the MDC. This provides the field officer with the ability to access information while away from the vehicle. Once the officer is back to the car, the officer can upload the information into the in-car computer and complete the remainder of the incident report. Once the officer completes the report, he or she uploads it to a temporary file awaiting supervisory review and approval. When the supervisor approves the report, he or she forwards it to records for quality control. Once approved, the data automatically populates the incident record and other appropriate modules. The system automatically distributes the case to other appropriate units within the department. Employing the technology as described brings the incident module to as real time as feasible.

Modern RMS systems are making use of the Internet and web-based technologies. One way that this is occurring is by allowing citizens to enter minor incidents over the Internet. This requires the system to provide limited citizen access to the incident module. The recommended approach is to allow the citizen to enter a report on the Internet in a special file. The Internet incident module allows citizens to enter minor reports that the department deems appropriate for Internet reporting. These are typically minor crime reports such as petty thefts and minor malicious mischief. Once the citizen submits the report, the system assesses the report for completeness. If there are mistakes or incomplete information, the system prompts the citizen for the corrected or additional information. Once completed, the system enters the report into the incident module and the other associated modules such as property, MNI, MVI, MPI, accident, citation, and case management. A significant advantage to Internet incident reporting is that the data are immediately available to detectives.

Arrest

The arrest module is a critical component in any RMS. This module tracks all of the arrests and arrestee information captured by an agency. Every police department across the country captures information pertaining to the arrest of a subject. In the modern police department, the officer fills out the arrest form on his or her laptop or online in the actual arrest module. The arrest module captures information about the arrestee and the circumstances surrounding the arrest. Figure 5.8 depicts a typical arrest module.

Some agencies are moving toward the use of tablet PCs to capture the basic report information. The officer uploads the data from the tablet to the laptop or in-car computer. The officer can also conduct an MNI lookup to determine if the department has ever had contact with the individual before the current incident. From the tablet PC, the officer can also conduct wants and warrant searches of state, local, and national databases.

If the person has a previous arrest record, the data from the arrest module populate the appropriate fields in the new arrest record, eliminating the need for redundant data entry. The officer simply updates the record with any new information. Once the arrest report is complete, the data will be available in the RMS. The information must be sufficient to satisfy state and federal reporting requirements for the Federal Uniform Crime Report or the National Incident Based Reporting System.

Detectives and others use the arrest module as an investigation tool. It provides MO information pertaining to individuals. The system captures the physical descriptors of the suspect, such as hair color, eye color, scars, marks, and tattoos. Quality arrest modules also provide the entry of free-form text to describe the circumstances for the arrest.

Ideally, if the jail where the booking of an arrestee is to occur or if the system interfaces with the facility, the officer can enter the arrest information on his or her field computer and simultaneously upload the information to the jail facility's system and the RMS. The booking system populates with all of the arrest data. The jailer completes the booking form with the data required by the jail facility.

Linkages to other modules
The arrest module requires linkages to other modules for exchange of information and to look up information as required. As an example, the names entered into the arrest module must be verified through the MNI either to begin a new record or to add to an existing record.

The following is a list of those modules that the arrest module must be capable of interacting:

- Geofile
- Incident
- MNI
- MVI
- Master premise index
- Wants/warrants and protective orders
- Property and evidence

These systems also capture MO data on each suspect. Ideally, most modern systems provide user definable fields that describe the offender's MO. The following screen depicts MO data captured by an arrest module.

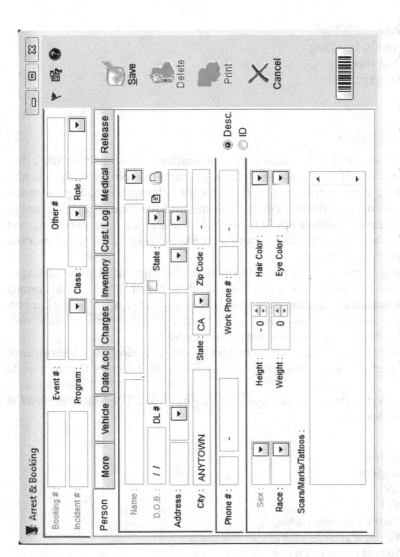

Figure 5.8 Sample arrest module. (From Gagne, A., CrimeStar, Version 10.6, Computer software, San Jose, CA: CrimeStar Corporation, 2015.)

Interfaces

The arrest module can access external systems to obtain information. The following is a list of the external database access typically required of this module:

- State/NCIC
- County booking
- Mug shots
- Fingerprints

Juvenile contact

The juvenile contact module captures similar information as the adult arrest module. It maintains these data separately to comply with state and federal regulations that require that juvenile information be kept separate from adult arrest information. All features and functionality discussed in the adult arrest module apply to juvenile contact (see Arrest section), and the juvenile contact module functions the same way as the arrest module with several exceptions.

The juvenile contact module requires the capture of parental information as well as details about the juvenile's school. The juvenile contact module is also an investigation tool. It must provide MO information pertaining to the individual. The higher-quality RMS systems provide user definable fields that describe the offender's MO.

Some systems use free-form text to capture clothing descriptions, whereas others allow the end user to define MO factors through code tables.

The system requires linkages to other modules. The following is a list of those modules:

- Geofile
- Incident
- MNI
- MVI
- Master premise index
- Wants/warrants and protective orders
- Property and evidence

The juvenile contact module must access external systems for information. The following is a list of the external database access required of this module:

- State/NCIC
- Mug shots
- Fingerprints

Known offender

Agencies throughout the country come in contact with individuals that consistently break the law. Police refer to these individuals as known offenders. To capture information about these individuals, the RMS incorporates a known offender module. The known offender module requires the ability to capture information pertaining to an individual who repeatedly commits crimes. This module is comprehensive and provides the ability to categorize the offender type such as a sex offender, burglar, and robber. The module must also interface to the crime analysis mapping system, particularly to allow the crime analysis system and investigators to plot the residence location of known offenders and the locations where known offenders tend to commit their crimes. This information is accessible to all officers. Investigators are able to enter known offender information, absent of an incident report. As an example, if a sex registrant moves into town, the system must accept the information pertaining to this person without an incident report.

Known offender modules also support the tracking of gang members. They capture data pertaining to the gang, affiliated members, gang signs, symbols, and other identifying information.

The known offender module is a significant investigation tool. It provides MO information pertaining to individuals. It contains the same data elements available in the arrest module but also tracks known associates of the frequent offender. From these affiliations, the system can develop link analysis charts showing the associates of known offenders.

Linkages to other modules

The known offender module requires linkages to other modules. The following is a list of those modules:

- Geofile/crime analysis system
- Incident
- MNI
- MVI
- Master premise index
- Wants/warrants and protective orders
- Property and evidence

The system captures MO data on each suspect.

Interfaces

The known offender module must access external systems for information. The following is a list of the external database access required of this module:

- TCIC/NCIC
- Mug shots
- Fingerprints

Field interview reports

For field interview reports (FIRs) to be of any value in a police organization, they must be available almost immediately to departmental personnel. With mobile computing, the officer can directly enter the FIR in the field at the time the officer captures the information. The RMS reports to the field officer if a field interview card is on file from a previous contact with this individual. This module provides the ability to capture physical descriptions, including clothing. The field officer requires the ability to research the individual further if necessary. The officer can initiate a wants and warrants check based on the information entered without having to reenter all of the key data. In addition, if there are mug shots available on a subject, the officer can view them on their laptop.

The storage of the name and address data occurs in the MNI and MLI. The system displays these data in the FIR module whenever displaying the FIR record.

Lastly, a quality FIR module supports record flags. Flags allow for special processing and are user definable. As an example, an investigator wants to know whenever field officers stop a certain individual. The investigator can set a flag so when this occurs, the investigator receives a notification from the system that an officer stopped this individual. The investigator can then view the field interview card and the reported actions taken by the field officer or contact the officer directly to learn more about the stop.

Citations

Every police department tracks citations, the number written, the type, moving, parking, etc. Some systems interface to the municipal court system to file and track the citation's progress. The RMS provides the ability to enter citations of many different types, for example, moving, nonmoving, municipal violations, etc. Ideally, officers write citations in the field, using mobile computers, similar to FI cards. It is conceivable that the FI module and the citation module could be one and the same, differentiated by a field that identifies the entry as either a citation or an FI. As part of the computing strategy, the officer will enter citations via the laptop or handheld PDA at the time he/she captures the information. If printers are added to the patrol vehicle, it allows citation printing in the vehicles. The system must also provide the ability to enter the information from a workstation. Through an electronic interface to the court system, the system will upload the necessary complaint data to the court system (if such capability is available in the court system). The intent is to eliminate any redundant data entry.

Like the FI module, the citation module shall support flags as described. It must also be able to assign and track issued citation books and voided citations.

Modern driver's licenses contain magnetic strips that store all of the pertinent information found on the face side of the license. As a result, FI modules incorporate the ability to integrate magnetic strip readers. As an example, police officers will swipe the subject's driver license through the magnetic strip reader. They also use a bar code wand to input information from the person's ID when completing a field interview. One way to accommodate the additional data entry requirement is to use PDAs to capture the necessary data and then upload the information to the mobile computer. The data from the PDA could be uploaded to the RMS at the same time.

Linkages to other modules

The module will require linkages to other modules within the system. The following is a list of those modules:

- MNI
- MVI
- Master premise index
- Field interview

Interfaces

The system must also be able to access other databases. The citation module provides the operator the opportunity to search external databases as well as the local database. The following are the typical databases the citation module accesses:

- TCIC/NCIC
- Municipal court system
- Mug shots

Wants, warrants, and protective orders

Enterprise information systems support, maintain, and fully automate a wants/warrants and protective orders module. These modules provide police departments the ability to enter persons wanted for questioning or with an outstanding warrant. In addition to the wants and warrants, the RMS tracks protective orders. The entry of a protective order updates the CAD system premise file to alert dispatchers to the protective orders. This module also includes the capability of displaying photographs of persons as part of the want, warrant, or protective record. Figure 5.9 is a sample of multiple wants and warrants module screens.

Interfaces

The wants/warrants/protective orders module provides the user the opportunity to search external and local databases. There is increasing pressure on law enforcement agencies to share data between jurisdictions. Wants/warrants/protective orders are a significant way of sharing critical data. This is a significant part of the IJIS movement.

The following are the typical databases the wants/warrants modules access:

- State/NCIC
- Municipal court systems
- Mug shots systems
- Fingerprint systems

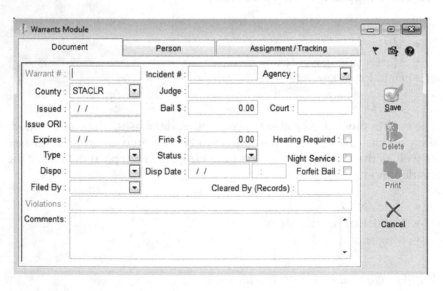

Figure 5.9 Sample wants and warrants module.   (*Continued*)

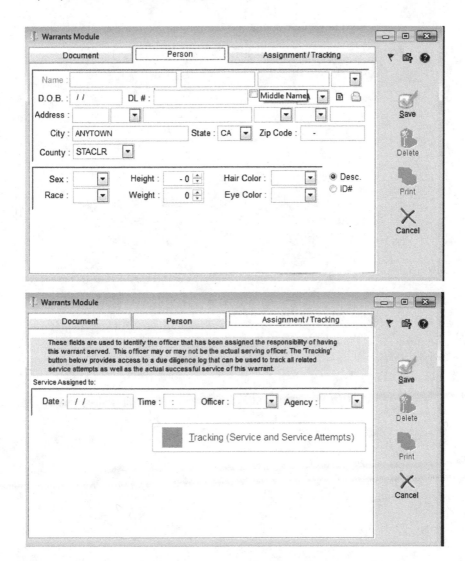

Figure 5.9 (Continued) Sample wants and warrants module. (From Gagne, A., Crime-Star, Version 10.6, Computer software, San Jose, CA: CrimeStar Corporation, 2015.)

Reference

Gagne, A. (2015). CrimeStar Inc. (Version 10.6) [Computer Software]. San Jose, CA: Crime Star Corporation.

chapter six

Police workgroup applications

Many units within police departments require specialized software to assist them in performing their day-to-day functions. These specialized software programs access the enterprise information system but stand alone as specialized software systems.

List of definitions

AFIS—Automated Fingerprint Identification System
Case management software
GIS—crime analysis and geographic information system
Mug shot and facial recognition systems
Property and evidence tracking systems

Workgroup applications

Workgroups are local networks that require data and functionality. Workgroups for the most part are beyond the scope of the enterprise database/RMS. They are unique to a work unit within the police department. Workgroups may consist of data that are specific to that workgroup. Functions not performed by other units or that preclude them from being a part of the enterprise database become workgroups. An example of a workgroup application would be property and evidence. The property and evidence functions require many features and functions that do not pertain to other work units within the department. For instance, this work unit requires the ability to manage property within the storage areas. Property and evidence need unique software to assist in this management process.

Workgroups come in a variety of applications. Some typical workgroup applications are as follows:

- Automated fingerprint identification systems
- Case management systems
- Crime analysis system
- Mug shot and facial recognitions systems

- Investigation, vice, intelligence, and narcotic tracking system
- Property and evidence systems
- Scheduling systems
- Pawnshop management
- Subpoena tracking systems
- False alarm management
- Others

Although the previously mentioned systems are prevalent in most agencies, there are other workgroup applications used in police agencies. New workgroups develop within organizations all the time, and although they are unique applications, they all require access to the enterprise database/RMS, and many of them also require access to external systems.

The following subsections of this chapter discuss the features and functions of these various workgroup applications.

Crime analysis and geographic information systems

In the 1970s, the Law Enforcement Assistance Administration (LEAA) began to promote crime analysis through a popular program known as the Integrated Criminal Apprehension Program. Initially, this program promoted the development of crime analysis throughout the United States. In the early days of crime analysis, promoters developed manual crime analysis processes. As computer technology advanced, the benefits of computerizing these processes became clear. In the late 1970s, LEAA recognized the need to aid in the development of software that would support crime analysts. LEAA funded the development of the nation's first crime analysis system known as Crime Analysis Support System (CASS). CASS was unique in that it allowed users to develop their own files, create unique searches, and develop unique reports.

As the discipline of crime analysis advanced, crime analysis systems advanced significantly over the years. Crime analysis units require timely access to data. A crime analysis system must have full access to the enterprise database/RMS and be able to download data to third-party analysis packages such as spreadsheets and mapping systems. Geographic information systems (GISs) typically encompass mapping systems. GIS is now a critical component of the crime analysis functions. In a comprehensive criminal justice information systems environment, the enterprise database/RMS interfaces with a GIS system and transfers data to the GIS for purposes of spatial analysis. One particularly popular crime analysis program is the Omega Group's CrimeView™ application. With this system, crime analysts download information from the department's record management system for analysis purposes. CrimeView™ provides a spatial view of crime by allowing crime analysts to plot the locations of crime, the residence of known offenders, and a variety of other data captured and stored in the enterprise database. Figure 6.1 presents a sample of a plot map depicting burglaries over the past six months.

Crime analysis supported by GIS can show crime trends and the movement of crime throughout the jurisdiction. Putting the map into motion using beginning and ending dates provides a graphical display of crime displacement and movement throughout the area under analysis.

Crime analysis systems work best when they have the ability to access current information in an almost real-time state. That is why a crime analysis/ GIS system requires integration with the department's enterprise database. When a real-time interface exists between a crime analysis/GIS system, the analyst has access to crime attributes such as crime type, time/date ranges, and location information. The analyst can query the enterprise database on ranges within these data elements and plot the information on a map providing a graphical display of the crime problem. The analyst can also combine other data, such as the last known residence of people who committed similar crimes. When plotting this information on the same map, a graphical display can be quite useful to an investigator seeking leads. These maps can display hot spots, statistical profiles, and spatial trends.

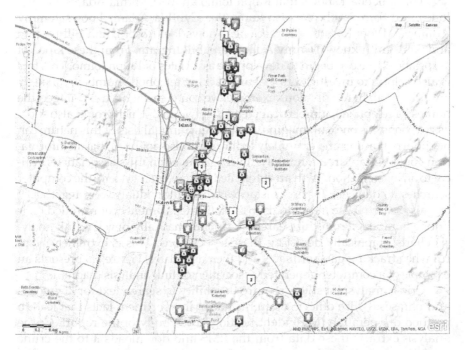

Figure 6.1 Sample plot map. (Courtesy of Zana, A. P., Intergraph Public Safety, ICAD, Computer software, Huntsville, AL: Intergraph Corporation, 2015.)

Dissemination is a significant crime analysis task. Using a good crime analysis system integrated with GIS facilitates the distribution of information throughout the department. It allows the crime analyst to share information with patrol, investigations, and other units within the department on a real-time basis. E-mail is a common methodology used to disseminate crime profiles, suspect information (such as wanted fugitives), mug shots, and other crime analysis bulletins.

Crime analysts use bulletins to disseminate information to various units within the department. One common bulletin is referred to as "be on the lookout" (BOLO). BOLOs often include mug shots as well as textual descriptions of the individual or individuals sought. Through the use of a good crime analysis system, crime analysts can develop a BOLO and disseminate it immediately to field officers' mobile computers and detectives' desktops and place the information on the department's website if so desired.

Another important component of a good crime analysis system is the ability to link associates to one another, which is called "link analysis." Investigators have performed link analysis for years before the development of information technology systems. Link analysis is the process of associating individuals who know or might know one another. Figure 6.2 presents a manually developed link analysis chart.

This link chart shows that Ralph Ioimo knows Cynthia Adams, George Jones, and Sam Smith. We also know that Cynthia Adams knows Tommy Adams and Joel Rosetti, George Jones knows Joel Rosetti, and Bill Ingram and Sam Smith know Tommy Adams and Bill Ingram. From these kinds of associations, we can begin to develop the associates of Ralph Ioimo. This tool is also helpful to investigators that are tracking telephone numbers called by an individual. In the previous example, we could easily have exchanged the names for telephone numbers called by Ralph Ioimo, which would also show associations. As one can imagine, maintaining annual lists of this nature can be time consuming and extremely tedious. It is also doubtful that all information could be captured manually. Investigators often miss associations critical to an investigation. With an automated link analysis system, the computer searches its database for any instances where individuals were together. It can also search these individuals to see if the department ever recorded their phone numbers. From this search, it can automatically develop link analysis charts graphically depicting these associations. This is extremely helpful when tracking gang affiliates and their associates. Figure 6.3 presents an example of a computer-generated association or link analysis diagram.

Crime analysis systems require the ability to search text for keywords and phrases. Police officers often include many pertinent facts that lead to method of operation (MO) identification in the body of the report. Crime analysis extracts these data from the RMS and downloads it to the crime analysis server. From these searches, the crime analyst extracts information and performs ad hoc searches and produces ad hoc reports as required.

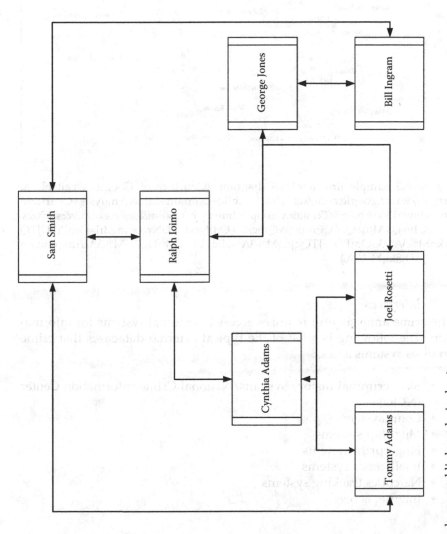

Figure 6.2 Sample manual link analysis chart.

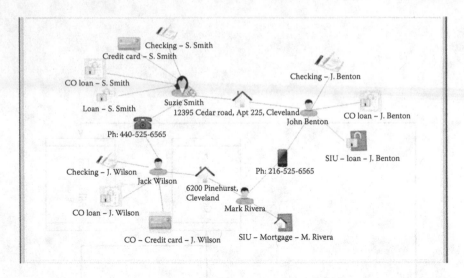

Figure 6.3 Sample link analysis diagram. (Courtesy of Google. Available at https://www.google.com/search?q=Public+Domain+Link+Analysis+Chart&hl =en&biw=1366&bih=667&site=webhp&tbm=isch&tbo=u&source=univ&sa=X&v ed=0CBwQsARqFQoTCPnn9qWQmckCFQdiJgod-wUNrA#imgdii=OmPfkUJTQ gjkqM%3A%3BOmPfkUJTQgjkqM%3A%3Bd_LFBb-4uHq0NM%3A&imgrc=Om PfkUJTQgjkqM%3A.)

Interfaces

The crime analysis unit requires access to external systems for information. The following is a list of the typical external databases that crime analysis systems access:

- State criminal history systems/National Crime Information Center (NCIC)
- Court systems
- Mug shot systems
- Fingerprint systems
- Intelligence systems
- Narcotics tracking systems
- Internet access

Automated fingerprint identification systems

Automated fingerprint identification systems (AFISs) are part of a group of biometric technologies that are growing within the criminal justice environment. Other biometric systems include but not limited to the following:

- Mug shot systems
- Facial recognition systems
- DNA systems
- Iris scan technology
- Retina scan technology
- Voice recognition systems

Of these technologies, fingerprint recognition is perhaps the oldest and the most widely used other than mug shots.

Most historians agree that the intentional use of fingerprints dates back many centuries. Pictographs exist that show primitive drawings of hands with crude attempts at displaying simple whirling ridges on three of the fingers (Moenssens, 1971). The science of fingerprint technology bolstered law enforcement's ability to solve a crime for many years. The classification of fingerprints and the analysis of latent prints occurred manually by the Federal Bureau of Investigation (FBI). The technical section of the FBI's Identification Division performed these tasks. In the early 1960s, the bureau employed a staff of approximately 1,300 fingerprint technicians that searched more than 1,000 fingerprint cards every day against a criminal file of cards representing nearly 15 million individuals (Lee & Gaensslen, 1991). As the fingerprint repository grew, it became more and more difficult to search the entire database. Contrary to the popular belief of the American public, the FBI would only search its database for serious felons. Because of the complexity associated with searching this large database, it was not possible to conduct a search for a typical residential burglary or routine robberies. It was not until the 1970s and the development of the nation's first AFIS did it become possible to conduct rapid fingerprint searches.

Early AFIS systems were expensive and affordable by only large agencies. In addition, AFIS systems increase in their investigative value when they encompass large databases. These two factors resulted in the development of regional AFIS systems, usually implemented at a county or multicounty level. These regional systems then link to state fingerprint databases and the FBI National Fingerprint Database.

Early AFIS systems consisted of large computer systems with significant data storage capability. On the front end of the system, there were terminals or workstations and sophisticated scanning devices used to capture fingerprint data. Before fingerprint data can be of use, it must first be captured and then stored in the system. Once in the system, there must be a way of matching the information and retrieving the data. These systems store two types of data: known subject fingerprints and unknown fingerprint data. Agencies implementing new AFIS systems enter known subject fingerprints into these earlier systems through the data captured off a standard fingerprint card. This included textual data pertaining to the subject as well as his or her fingerprints. These systems also store and categorize latent fingerprints often lifted at a crime scene where there is no known suspect. Latent fingerprints can be used to search the known subject files for a match. They can also be stored and matched at a later time upon the suspect capture.

Although modern AFIS systems still require paper scanners to read the fingerprint cards and latent prints lifted from a crime scene or an article of evidence, live fingerprint scanners capture fingerprints from individuals. This new technology is called *live scan*. There is a variety of live scan devices in use today. In jail booking facilities where the jailer would have to roll ink on a glass top and roll fingerprints manually by rolling the subject's fingerprint over the inked glass and then rolling the finger on a card, the jailer simply places the subject's hand on the glass of a scanner and digitally captures the fingerprints. These live scan devices capture the information temporarily stored in the workstation and then forwarded to the larger AFIS system. If the person arrested has fingerprints on file, the booking agency knows his or her true identity within minutes as opposed to days, weeks, or months as was the case in the older systems. These live scan devices make it possible for small agencies to link to a regional AFIS system. For this to occur, all the agency needs is a personal computer and a scanning device to check for fingerprint match. This technology makes fingerprints useful and affordable down to the field level. Figure 6.4 shows a sample fingerprint scanner and tablet.

Other means of capturing fingerprints occur through an optical reader or single fingerprint readers. These devices capture a single fingerprint and send the data to the AFIS system to verify identification. When

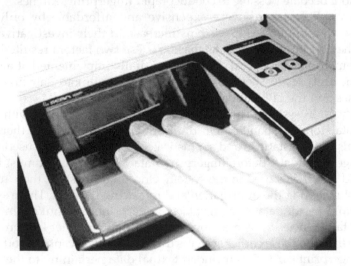

Figure 6.4 Sample fingerprint scanner and tablet.

the FBI rewrote NCIC in 2000, they incorporated single fingerprint identification into the new system, NCIC 2000. Single print optical or silicon
readers make it possible to incorporate them into mobile computing units
such as laptops in police vehicles. With the single fingerprint devices, the
officer can positively identify someone in the field. This technology will
only continue to grow over the next decade and become more sophisticated and useful in solving crimes.

Mug shot systems

Ever since the invention of the camera, the criminal justice system has
captured mug shots of arrestees or known offenders. Manual mug shot
systems consisted of a camera, usually mounted on a tripod or other
stationary device. The sophisticated systems had a photographer's background screen with appropriate lighting. The suspect would stand in
front of the screen with a placard hung over his or her neck with identifying information either handwritten on the placard or, in later years,
on plastic lettering to identify the subject and the associated case. One
might find a measuring stick in the picture to help identify the subject by
his or her height. They used a standard film camera to take the picture.
Usually, there were three poses used: front view, left-side view, and right-
side view. In addition to facial views, agencies commonly took pictures of
other identifying marks, scars, or tattoos found on the individual.

Once the booking officer took the pictures, they would remain in the
camera until the roll of the film was complete. The agency then would
send the film out for processing. For large and more affluent agencies, the
process took place in the department's photo lab. For all others, the photographs went to a commercial location for development. In either case,
the developed photos went to the records division for storage. Sometimes
the agencies obtained multiple copies of the photos for storage in different
locations. Records stored the photo with the subject's arrest file, whereas
the investigators stored the photos in the lineup or mug shot books so
that victims, witness, etc., could view these photos in hopes of identifying
known offenders. They categorized these books by year and usually by
race. They were cumbersome to use and often required significant time to
examine.

Law enforcement officers use mug shots to help identify suspects. If an
officer obtains the identity of a possible suspect during an investigation, to
make the case, the victim must identify the suspect as being the one responsible for the crime. In the past, investigators used manual photo lineups to
determine if the victim can identify the suspect. The officer would develop
what has commonly been known as a *six-pack*. A six-pack is an array of six
photographs with one of them being the suspect. These six-packs are a source
of controversy and often attacked by defense attorneys as bias by the officer.

Although the values of photographs are critical to the criminal justice process, it was not until the 1970s when the cost of information technology began to come down that mug shot systems began to appear. The early systems consisted of a camera, a workstation, a computer, a data storage device, and a printer. Mug shot systems normally included software that identified the person in the photograph. The new systems no longer require a placard in front of the subject's photograph to identify him or her, although some agencies still use the placard. Like AFIS systems, mug shot systems often functioned as standalone systems. This resulted in duplicate data entry of name information. A computer-to-computer interface is required to link with the record management system.

Digital photography has revolutionized mug shot technology. Many of the record management systems now integrate digital photographs into their systems, which allow mug shots to be included as part of the booking system. This eliminates the need for redundant data entry and computer-to-computer interfaces. With digital photography integrated into record management systems, agencies can store multiple photographs not just for mug shots but also for photos of scars, marks, tattoos, or anything else the agency wishes to photograph and store as part of an individual's record. The new systems also store photographs in reverse chronological order, which allows a historical perspective of the individual and the transformations of his or her looks, dress style, body art, and piercing that occur over time. Modern mug shot systems are capable of sophisticated searches that allow the user to develop automated six-pack lineups as previously discussed. When developing these six-packs, the user provides information about the suspect, and then the system selects the other photos that closely match the suspect. This automated generation of photo lineups helps to eliminate bias making the results of the lineup stronger court evidence. Figure 6.5 shows a sample of an automated photo lineup also known as a six-pack.

The traditional mug shot systems are evolving into facial recognition systems. Facial recognition systems provide the ability to search large databases of facial images for potential matches. Given still or video images of a scene, facial recognition systems can identify or verify one or more persons in the scene using a stored database of faces (Face Recognition Home Page, http://www.face-rec.org/general-info/). Facial imaging systems digitize facial images, which can be compared with other digitized facial images to obtain matches. Facial images and mug shot images are both part of the new emerging biometric technologies.

Property and evidence

Managing property and evidence within a police department is at best a complex task that demands the highest degree of accuracy. Before computers, property and evidence rooms maintained arduous manual files

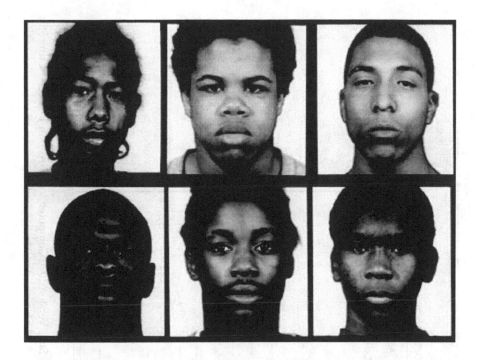

Figure 6.5 Sample computer-generated six-pack. (From Gagne, A., CrimeStar, Version 10.6, Computer software, San Jose, CA: CrimeStar Corporation, 2015.)

that tracked the location of property, where it has been and who has had access to it. In today's modern property and evidence room, computers track the precise location of the property and the person who has custody of it at the moment, as property and evidence often leave the property room for testing in laboratories and for trial presentations in courtrooms. Property and evidence systems are one of the complex workgroup applications found in police departments. They require interfaces to external systems such as state computers, NCIC, and other criminal justice systems to check the property for stolen or reported lost status. Figure 6.6 shows a sample property and evidence module screen.

Property and evidence rooms require a comprehensive system to manage the intake, storage, and disposition of all property that comes into the property and evidence room. When an officer enters the described property item, the entry should be made once and appended into the report so the description does not require reentry.

In an automated system, there needs to be a means of checking out property to an individual officer and to show that the court has the property. The system must have the ability to show that the court retained the property for the trial.

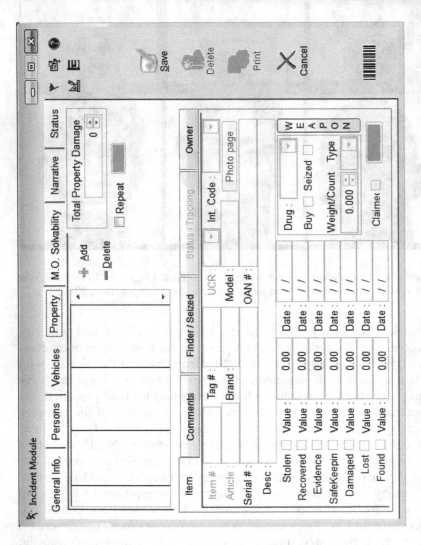

Figure 6.6 Sample property and evidence. (From Gagne, A., CrimeStar, Version 10.6, Computer software, San Jose, CA: CrimeStar Corporation, 2015.)

Property rooms can range from a single room, as often found in small agencies, to multiple storage rooms and facilities scattered throughout the jurisdiction. Agencies commonly use multiple rooms for property storage. The types of rooms found in a police agency are gun vaults, floor safes, refrigeration, and other distinctive storage locations. Property and evidence systems must be capable of storing room number, row number, section number, shelf number, and box number to track the precise location of the property. Property and evidence systems must have the capability of tracking an unlimited number of transactions.

Disposing of property is critical to property and evidence management. A quality property and evidence system provides the automatic disposition of a certain property. The system will notify the property and evidence supervisor when property is eligible for disposition. Disposition of property typically occurs through the case finally adjudicated. The basis of the case dispositions is the court disposition and time. Found property must be kept for a specified amount of time, and once that time expires, the property can be disposed. Property and evidence systems track and manage these critical times and notify the technicians that the property can be disposed. This efficiency is a critical capability required of all property and evidence systems.

The most modern of the property and evidence systems provides the officer the ability to enter all necessary information about the property that they book into evidence directly into the system. The property and evidence technicians provide the necessary quality control required to ensure that officers booked what they said they booked. If booked property has a serial number, the system automatically runs that serial number through the pawn system, the state criminal information system, and the NCIC to determine stolen property. Also, before the disposition of the property, the systems do an automatic check to ensure there are no holds or other cases pending for that property.

Property and evidence systems have the ability to track asset seizures. Asset seizures occur whenever a policing agency seizes the assets of a private person, often related to narcotic cases. As an example, law enforcement may seize an airplane that narcotic traffickers used to transport narcotics. As a result of the court trial, if the defendant(s) is found guilty under the asset seizure laws, the title of the airplane transfers to the law enforcement agency making the arrest. Property and evidence systems require the ability to identify an item of property confiscated or cash seized in relation to a case. The system tracks the results of the case and provides notification of the final court disposition. Upon receipt of the court disposition and forfeiture approval, the law enforcement agency responsible for the case receives custody of the property. Obviously, this is a significant requirement of all property and evidence systems.

Property and evidence require a photography capability that links to the property record. Digital photography makes it possible to link photos with textual records. This allows officers to photograph property and link it to the property and evidence record. Some systems provide property and evidence technicians the ability to attach photographs of the person to whom they release the property. Whenever entering property, it must be checked to ensure that the property links to a case or an incident number. The release of property should also be automated, capturing all necessary release information.

Several property and evidence systems provide the ability to link a single fingerprint to the record. Like photographs, the single fingerprint identification provides the ability to capture the fingerprint of the person receiving the property. This ensures the property's integrity in that it requires that the person removing the property from the property and evidence room is who they say they are. It also adds to the audit trail in that when checking out the property, the property and evidence technician can be assured of whom they released the property to, and there is no doubt of the chain of custody.

A property and evidence system requires full bar coding capability. All property entered into the property room will receive a barcode. Property and evidence rooms use bar code readers to check property in or out as well as when moving the property around in the property room. Property and evidence units constantly perform inventories of the various property rooms. In the old pencil and paper days, this was an arduous and time-consuming process. Today's modern property and evidence systems that use bar code wands make this process a much simpler task.

Property and evidence records need to be accessible in a "read only" mode that will allow anyone with the appropriate security to view the in custody property. Personnel who book property should also be able to provide property and evidence with disposition information. As an example, a detective should be able to view the property associated with one of his or her cases and let property and evidence know how and if the property can be released.

Linkages to other modules

A property and evidence system requires linkages to the executive information system and other workgroup applications for a variety of purposes. These systems share information with the following modules:

- Incident/offense
- Master name index
- Master premise index
- Master vehicle index
- Pawn slips
- Case management

Interfaces

Property and evidence systems require access to an external database. The property and evidence systems provide the user the opportunity to search external databases when conducting a search. Agencies require the ability to search external systems that affect property disposition. It is also necessary to know if another jurisdiction has a want on the custody property. The system checks external databases upon entering the property to see if there is a want by another department. The system will also check these external systems before allowing the property to be released. The following are the typical databases the property and evidence module must be capable of accessing:

- State criminal information systems
- NCIC
- Court systems

Case management

A prominent workgroup application found in most police departments is case management. Investigations require a system that will help them manage cases and information associated with those cases. The case management system tracks a case from its assignment to an investigator through final disposition. The investigation manager assigns cases to investigators based on a series of criteria established by the police department, known as solvability factors, which helps to determine the probability of solving a case. Solvability factors must be part of a case management system. The system captures these solvability factors and recommends follow-up based on the solvability score. The detective supervisor will maintain the ability to override any computer recommendation.

Once the investigation manager determines the case solvability is high enough to invest investigator time to try and solve, he or she assigns the case to an investigator through the case management subsystem. The data from the initial incident report entered into the enterprise information system populate the case management files. At this point, the case management system allows the investigation manager to assign the case to an investigator. When he or she assigns the case, they can establish the amount of time they wish to allot the investigator. This workgroup provides quality assessment capability to determine such things as detective case clearances, time consumed on an investigation, and other similar and relevant case management information. This application includes the accounting and analysis of investigator time/activity. It also provides the ability to track case dispositions, including case rejections and all other changes to the case.

The case management system provides the investigation manager the ability to establish key milestones for review purposes. Case aging is a fundamental capability within a case management system. Investigation managers review case aging reports to determine the progress of a case. After exhausting all leads, and there is no likelihood of solving the case, the investigation's manager can inactivate the case. As an example, if the manager determines that the case does not have a high solvability but that it is worth spending some investigatory time attempting to resolve, he or she can assign the case and establish a time limit for review. If, after a specified period, the investigator has not made any progress, the manager can inactivate the case and remove it from the investigator's workload. When the manager decides to inactivate the case, they assign a disposition for inactivating the case. The system then prints a letter to the victim(s) notifying the victim(s) of the case disposition.

Another feature of a case management system is the ability to balance workload among the unit's investigators. Good case management prevents one investigator from handling a disproportionate number of cases. A good case management system assesses investigator workload based on the amount of time spent on all of the cases as well as the number of cases assigned. Figures 6.7 and 6.8 present examples of case assignment and case aging modules.

A quality case management system includes several key reports and the ability to create ad hoc reports as required. The following is a list of the reports typically included with a case management system:

- Daily, weekly, monthly, and yearly investigator productivity reports
- Caseload reports
  - By officer
  - By unit
- Case disposition reports
- Cases cleared
- Pending investigations
- Suspended reports
- Active cases
- Inactive cases

The ad hoc reporting capabilities allow investigation managers to develop unique reports required to aid them in managing the investigation process.

Linkages

Case management systems link to several internal modules that are normally part of the enterprise information system. The case management system downloads information and also uploads data such as disposition

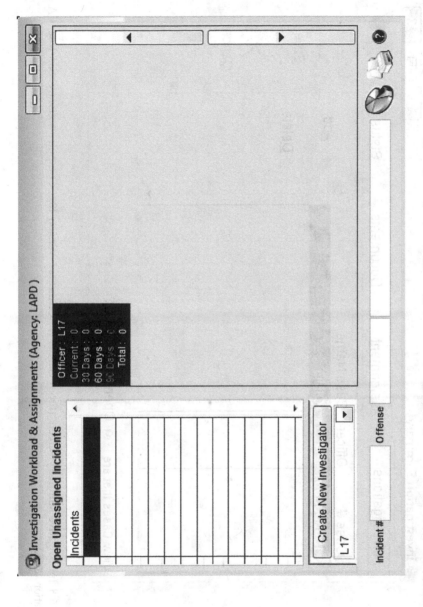

Figure 6.7 Sample case assignment and management screens. (From Gagne, A., CrimeStar, Version 10.6, Computer software, San Jose, CA: CrimeStar Corporation, 2015.)

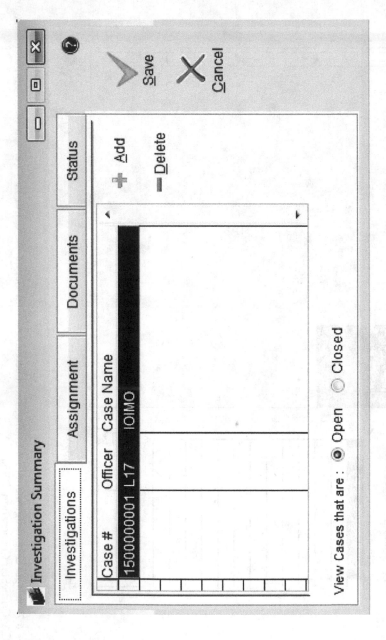

Figure 6.8 Investigative summary screen. (From Gagne, A., CrimeStar, Version 10.6, Computer software, San Jose, CA: CrimeStar Corporation, 2015.)

information to the enterprise information system. The responsibilities, however, lend themselves to linkages with other components of the RMS. Those critical components are as follows:

- Incident
- Arrest
- Wants, warrants, and protective orders
- Property and evidence

The case management system requires linkages to external systems to exchange information. Most of the external systems are terminal emulations that allow the system to access these external systems. The interface to the court system is a comprehensive exchange of information. This interface typically allows the investigators to file cases from the case management system directly with the courts. The court system also provides the final court disposition back to the case management system, which updates the enterprise information system with the final disposition.

Investigation, vice, intelligence, and narcotic systems

Investigation, vice, intelligence, and narcotic units performing different functions require similar software capabilities. These units require software to assist them in performing their jobs. These units often require the ability to track critical information on persons, locations, and vehicles that are often not part of the enterprise database/RMS. They require the ability to download information required to perform a variety of analytical and investigative processes. It should not be necessary for these units to maintain redundant databases to obtain the information investigators need. The enterprise database/RMS must treat an incident as a case and capture all information associated with that case. Supplemental reports should add to the data stored in the RMS with additional information added to the incident as required by these specialized investigations.

Each of these units requires a specialized module that provides the ability to profile suspects, track wiretaps, and provide informant management capabilities. These units maintain print media from external sources. As an example, the narcotic unit may send a substance to the laboratory to be analyzed. The laboratory will send a written report to the requesting detective notifying them of the analysis. These units require the ability to scan information into the system and attach the report to the case by the offense number. These units also write numerous supplemental reports that are narrative in nature and must be capable of assigning these reports to the initial crime report. The case number must remain the same, but each supplemental should be identified by a subnumbering system that will show the additional supplements, e.g., 01-1234567.01.

Each of these units requires the ability to track dial number recorder information, which includes wiretaps, PEN registers, and phone numbers associated with investigations. Link analysis and via charting are key tools for these units. Each detective unit needs to obtain statistics for management reporting. The investigator's module must also include a tickler system. The tickler must automatically remind the respective unit when a file requires purging other required transaction. If there is no activity on a file after a predefined period, the system notifies the supervisor. If appropriate, the supervisor can inactivate the case or reset the tickler date.

The following are the tasks the investigation system supports to satisfy the needs of these units:

1. Enter suspect information and get a list of case numbers involving suspects with similar characteristics together with the associated suspect names and/or descriptions.
2. Enter vehicle information and get a list of case numbers involving vehicles with similar characteristics together with the associated license numbers and/or vehicle descriptions.
3. Enter MO information and get a list of cases having similar MOs, including target and point of entry information.
4. Search for cases by property descriptions.
5. Search for all subjects arrested for offenses within a given time frame.
6. Create uniform crime reports or national incident-based reporting system reports for public release.
7. Search for associates of a suspect.
8. Search report narratives for text strings.
9. Search pawnshop records for property and suspects.

The following are features and functions required by various investigation units that must be part of a new system.

1. Retrieve data from anywhere in the database using a SQL command line.
2. Provide complete documentation of the system table composition, including all field names and the linkages between tables.
3. Enter MO information and get a list of suspect names and/or descriptions and/or vehicle descriptions associated with that MO in past cases, in addition to the case numbers.
4. Enter vehicle information and get a list of suspect names and/or descriptions from involved cases.
5. Create reports listing offenses that include suspect information, including names, personal descriptions, vehicle descriptions, and whether arrests occurred.

6. Create a report that displays alias names in place of or along the side of street addresses.
7. Create summary reports, displaying total offenses broken down by type, location, data, and time without restriction. This must include locations, as well as by beat, and Reporting District (RD).
8. Create reports by connecting to any table in the Automated Information System (AIS) database, including fields from different tables when linking the tables by a common field.
9. Produce crime maps displaying offense locations and areas of intense activity.
10. Create reports listing all of the suspect's associates and their criminal histories, including dates, offense, and location of the offense.
11. Search for suspects or arrested persons living within a defined radius of a location previously involved in offenses.
12. Create reports of parolees living within defined geographic areas.
13. Create reports listing arrested subjects, the location of the offense they committed, and their MOs.
14. Search arrest and traffic citations for vehicle information.
15. Search gang affiliations and gang member associates.
16. Search field interview data for suspects and vehicles.

Interfaces

Investigators require access to external systems to obtain investigatory information. The investigative support systems require access to external databases to obtain information and to contribute data to these databases. The following are the typical systems the investigative support system integrates with:

- Department of Corrections
- Utility billing
- Tax records
- Census data
- State/NCIC
- Mug shot systems
- Fingerprint systems
- Internet access

Pawnshop

A critical component in most police departments is the management of pawnshops and pawned property. Pawnshops are a prime source for individuals to fence stolen property. Most jurisdictions require pawnshops to report every piece of property pawned in their shop. In many jurisdictions, pawnshops manually report pawned property. These pawnshops fill out information about the person pawning the property as well as a comprehensive description of the property pawned. In a totally manual system, the pawnshop submits these slips to the police department. In manual environments, someone might review the slips and forward them to an investigator. In some environments, the agency files them by property type and in alphabetical order. If there is an automated system in place, they enter the slip into the computer system. A manual system becomes cumbersome to use and rarely provides any usable information when entry of the slips does not occur in a timely manner.

Modern systems use an automated pawnshop reporting process. This module captures the appropriate information for all pawned data. The ideal system provides Internet capability that allows pawnshop owners to enter pawn data into the pawnshop management module. This occurs at the time a person pawns the property. If appropriately setup, at the time the pawnshop operator enters the property, the system performs a check to see if there are any similar stolen or lost pieces of property. If recorded stolen or lost pieces of property exist, then the pawnshop and the police department receive notification. This improves the chances of trying to capture the person trying to pawn the stolen property and enhances the ability to recover stolen property. Pawnshop dealers are supportive of these automated systems because it cuts their losses associated with purchasing stolen property.

Regardless of the method used to enter the data, a quality pawnshop system must be capable of searching the lost and stolen property contained within the executive information system, as well as property and evidence module. If there is a match, the system notifies the person in charge of the pawnshop or another identified person about the pawn entry received that matches lost or stolen property reported. When entering lost and stolen property, a similar search occurs to ensure that a piece of property already pawned does not turn up as a stolen piece of property.

Linkages to other modules

The pawnshop module requires linkages to the executive information system and other workgroup applications for a variety of purposes, usually to look up information. These systems share information with the following modules:

- Master name index
- Vehicle module
- Incidents
- Arrests
- Property and evidence

False alarms

False alarms are a significant problem for police departments throughout the United States. Every year, Chicago police respond to more than 300,000 burglar alarms, 98% of them false, which translates to the equivalent of 195 full-time police officers (Sampson, 2003). Most agencies report somewhere between 96% and 98% of all alarms being false (Sampson, 2003). Obviously, this is extremely costly to the nation's police departments. Most cities respond to this problem by implementing false alarm ordinances.

A typical false alarm ordinance requires the alarm owner to register their alarm with the department and pay a user fee. If the establishment experiences two or more false alarms, the department begins to take punitive actions. The agency usually begins by sending the alarm registrant a warning letter. If another false alarm occurs within a specified period, the alarm registrant receives a citation. Most alarm ordinances provide for increasing higher fines if the false alarm continues to be a problem. Some will go as far as refusing to respond to anymore false alarms at that location.

False alarm modules must interface with the computer-aided dispatch (CAD) system. The CAD needs to check the alarm module to ensure that there is a valid permit on file. It must also determine the response, responsible party, and other necessary information. The CAD system must also pass the closed call information, particularly the call disposition to the alarm module. If the alarm is legitimate, there is no action required on the part of the alarm module. If the alarm is false, the alarm module requires the information pertaining to the alarm. It will generate the appropriate after action response.

The false alarm module also serves as a financial system in that it requires the ability to post payments, track delinquencies, and generate all necessary correspondence. They also need to issue permit numbers; recognize renewals; generate letters, invoices, and notices of revocation; and generate no permit notice if an alarm response occurs and there is no alarm permit on file.

The false alarm module obtains the violation information from the CAD system. The system tracks the alarm activity as part of premise history. If there is a status change on the alarm, such as the loss of the alarm permit, an update to the CAD system occurs immediately. The alarm information must be available through the premise history file. The alarm module must contain the following minimum fields:

- Permit by site
- Occupant information
- Permit number
- Dates of validity
- Emergency contact
- Alarm company information

The system must also capture information specific to the false alarm. The minimum data elements required are as follows:

- Cause of alarm
- Date of alarm
- Method of contact
- Number of alarms
- Action taken
- Mechanism to assess fees
- Mechanism to wave fees
- Notices
- Violations
- Fees unpaid

Linkages to other modules

False alarm modules require linkages to other modules within the system. The following are examples of some of the modules that the false alarm module must link to:

- Master name index
- Master premise index
- CAD
- Call for service
- Citations
- Incidents

In a quality system, the user should be able to move between the previously mentioned modules with information shared between all and absent of any redundant data entry.

Subpoena tracking module

A significant workgroup application is the subpoena tracking module found in most quality systems. Subpoenas are a fact of life in police agencies. Patrol officers, detectives, and civilian employees regularly receive subpoenas to testify in court on both criminal and civil cases. Managing subpoenas is a significant task in most departments. Before the implementation of information technology systems, agencies logged subpoenas in a book. The person's supervisor would give the recipient the subpoena. The recipient would sign to signify that he or she received the subpoena. The supervisor would sign, indicating he or she was the one who served the recipient.

Most criminal justice system providers offer automated subpoena tracking systems. These systems have the ability to accept electronic subpoenas or the ability to enter the subpoena into the system. Many police agencies establish an interface between the courts and themselves, which facilitates this process by sending the subpoena electronically to the appropriate individuals. The system records the date and time the officer read the subpoena. Once the person served reads the electronic message, the system sends a return message to the serving agency that indicates the details of the subpoena service. This eliminates any manual intervention and improves the efficiency of subpoena processing.

Police agencies require the ability to track these subpoenas and the costs associated with court attendance by department personnel. Some agencies receive reimbursement for employee time spent testifying in court, particularly on civil cases. The system should track the status of the subpoena and record if the officer attended court and if so the amount of time spent in court. The system will calculate the allotted reimbursement amount for each employee.

Linkages to other modules

The subpoena tracking system requires linkages to other modules, including personnel and scheduling. When an officer goes out on extended sick leave, or vacation, the department enters this information into the system, and the system sends this information to the court liaison to ensure the officer will not appear delinquent. Police personnel often receive multiple subpoenas, and commonly the appearance time conflicts with other cases. This module requires the ability to schedule court appearances to prevent overlapping court appearance requests. When the system receives the subpoena, it must check the officer's court appearance and report any conflicts back to the issuing agency for their resolution.

Summary

Workgroup applications vary from agency to agency. All information technology systems support workgroup applications of one kind or another. Those discussed in this chapter are only some of the workgroup applications found. They are the most common of all workgroup applications, but there are others such as the following:

- Personnel and training
- Laboratory information management systems
- Narcotic tracking systems
- Special operations management systems
- Others

As time progresses and information technology advances, the list of workgroup applications will grow.

References

Boba, R. (2005). *Crime analysis and crime mapping*. Boca Raton, FL: CRC Press.

Chu, J. (2001). *Law enforcement information technology: A managerial, operational, and practitioner guide*. Boca Raton, FL: CRC Press.

Gagne, A. (2015). CrimeStar Inc. (Version 10.6) [Computer Software]. San Jose, CA: Crimestar Corporation.

Lee, H. C., & Gaensslen, R. E. (1991). *Advances in fingerprint technology*. New York: Elsevier.

Menzel, R. E. (1999). *Fingerprint detection with lasers* (2nd ed.). New York: Marcel Dekker, Inc.

Moenssense, A. A. (1971). *Fingerprint techniques*. Chilton Book Company.

Sampson, R. (2003). *False burglar alarms*. Problem-Oriented Guides for Police Series Guide No. 5. Washington, D.C.: U.S. Department of Justice.

Zana, A. P. (2015). Intergraph Public Safety. ICAD [Computer Software]. Huntsville, AL: Intergraph Corporation.

chapter seven

Mobile computing

Mobile computing is the future of information technology in law enforcement. It represents the officer's mobile office and requires all the capabilities found at the desktop.

List of definitions

Automated license plate recognition
Bandwidth
CDMA—code division multiple access
CDPD—cellular digitized packet data
FCC—Federal Communications Commission
MDT—mobile data terminal
PDA—personal data assistant
UHF—ultra high-frequency
VHF—very high-frequency

Introduction

Mobile computing is advancing at a galloping pace. Estimates are that 80% of all police agencies use some form of mobile computing, and that number is likely to increase well into the 95% range by 2015 (Roberts, 2011). Mobile computing encompasses additional technologies not possible 10 years ago. Technologies, such as single fingerprint identification, digital photography, and other similar technologies are now at field officer's fingertips.

The following sections describe the history of mobile computing, mobile computing and dispatch operations, field report writing, mobile officer data mining, and radio data transport versus cellular communications.

History of mobile computing

Police departments throughout the United States are implementing mobile computing systems rapidly. This technology has evolved significantly since the early 1960s from basic message status terminals (MSTs) to advanced laptop computer systems and complete office automation. The early MST systems served as communication devices between the dispatch and the field units (Nunn, 1993). Their original intent was to reduce radio traffic. The devices introduced in the late 1960s to early 1970s simply provided field units with the ability to press a status key that would reflect a status change, such as arrived at the scene, available, etc. (Ioimo & Aronson, 2003). These terminals were only one-way communications devices. Field officers could update their status, but dispatchers could not send information to these devices (Ioimo & Aronson, 2003). The MST evolved over the years to include a digital display of four lines by 40 characters. They also have the ability to function over conventional and trunked radio as well as cellular. Some industries still use these devices, but they are no longer used in public safety. Figure 7.1 is a sample of a modern MST.

In the late 1970s and early 1980s, the mobile data terminal (MDT) was developed. These devices provided two-way communications between the dispatch and the field units. They consisted of a screen for display of data, a microprocessor, and a keyboard. The use of these devices provided the dispatchers the ability to capture call data and send dispatch information to the MDT, without voice radio transmission. Officers were able to view these data on their terminals. The use of the MDT in the vehicle allowed officers to enter their status as a call progressed without radio transmission. The field officers were also able to perform standard want and warrant checks on persons and vehicles (Ioimo, 2003). They received the information directly on their MDT screen. This eliminated the need for dispatchers to perform the inquiry and report its results over the radio. They also provided car-to-car communication without the use of voice radios (Ioimo, 2003). Figure 7.2 is a sample of a typical MDT.

Although these devices improved conditions for dispatchers, they did little to enhance the tasks field officers perform. Early research indicates

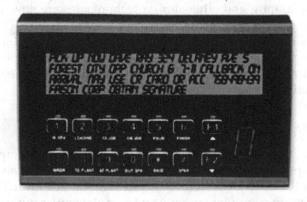

Figure 7.1 Message status terminal.

Figure 7.2 Mobile data terminal (Motorola 9100).

that field computing benefits areas within the department other than patrol (Kraemer & Danziger, 1985; Northrop, Kraemer, & King, 1993). There is evidence to suggest that when officers receive information that they can act upon, the technology then becomes useful and results in field officer task improvements (Nunn, 1993). In an evaluation research project of five north central Texas police agencies, Nunn (1994) was unable to show any efficiency gains at the field officer level except recoveries of stolen vehicles. With the new MDT system, officers gained the capability of inquiring on vehicle license plates without having to request the dispatcher to perform the search for them. This resulted in many more vehicle license plate inquiries and thus increased hits on stolen vehicles (Nunn, 1994).

Other research shows that detectives' efficiencies improve from the use of field computing (Kraemer & Danziger, 1985; Kraemer, Danziger, Dunkle, & King, 1993; Northrop et al., 1993). In their study of detectives, Kraemer et al. (1993) found that detectives' productivity improved with information technology that provided ad hoc inquiry capabilities. This access to information allowed detectives to search vast amounts of information by formulating searches that pertained to cases on which they were working (Kraemer et al., 1993; Northrop et al., 1993). Detectives also improved their investigative capabilities. They obtained information about crimes within hours as opposed to days, which was the typical lag time for detectives to obtain crime reports.

As police departments began to transition from the MDT to laptop computers in their vehicles, a trend to use the laptop for field report writing developed. The Houston Police Department was one of the first police departments to use laptops for field report writing and MDTs for communications with dispatch and access to TCIC/NCIC (Ioimo, 2003). Officers would take reports on their laptops and transport the completed report to the main system via a floppy disk. The laptops were removable and not linked to any fixed system. The software Houston used was in-house developed. As technology improved, Houston began to upload reports to their in-house developed record management system.

The popular COPS-MORE program of the 1990s fueled the development and proliferation of mobile computing systems. The laptops replaced the MDT and offered greater flexibility and capability. Although there are no official statistics available, current estimates are that 80% of the nation's police departments have implemented laptop computers (Ioimo & Aronson, 2004). By 2015, it is estimated that more than 90% of police departments will use mobile computing systems. Figures 7.3 and 7.4 are samples of both a permanently mounted laptop and a portable laptop.

With the proliferation of field computing, we have seen many articles claiming success of laptop technology appear in the trade journals. Many received national attention as being model programs. Empirical research does not support these claims, particularly at the end-user level. In a study conducted of several police agencies, Rocheleau (1993) discovered that there is a significant difference between the perception of how field computing has affected efficiency and reality. In this study, Rocheleau discovered that when surveying individuals in the departments that implemented this newer technology, the upper management believed that field reporting significantly improved task efficiency. This research showed a significant gap between management's perspectives of how computerized field computing benefits the department and how the field officers perceived its benefit. The data showed that field officers did not perceive field computing to be a benefit in performing their jobs. The

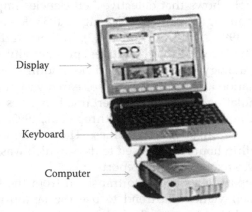

Display ⟶

Keyboard ⟶

Computer ⟶

Figure 7.3 Motorola MW 800.

Figure 7.4 Panasonic tough book laptop.

research results confirmed the officer's opinions of this technology's usefulness (Rocheleau, 1993). Later research supported this, which indicated that officers saw the benefit potential of mobile computing, but as used, field computing was not doing much for police officers (Ioimo, 2000).

The reason the initial implementation of laptop computers did not seem to benefit police officers was because the new technology did not offer anything that would help them improve their job tasks. Initial laptop implementations simply computerized the reports that police officers manually took on a form. If an officer takes a report on a form or enters the data into a laptop, there is little if any job enhancement from the new technology. Others within the organization benefited from field computing. Detectives received cases as soon as the officer completed the report and the supervisor approved it. This was a matter of hours versus days in the manual system. Records personnel benefited in that it eliminated the need for data entry from the forms into the enterprise database. Finally, administrators benefited in that they received information almost immediately, which allowed them to prepare for inquiries on cases receiving intense media coverage.

Mobile computing has improved significantly over the past 10 years. As this technology advanced, mobile computing expanded to encompass many field investigative tools that helped to improve the field officer's ability to perform his or her job. Today's patrol vehicle is the patrol officer's mobile office. The typical field mobile computer not only performs the functions of the early MDTs but also provides field officers with all of the technology that they would have at their desktop. Geographic information systems provide critical crime analysis information directly on the field officer's laptop. Field officers can request plot maps of the crimes occurring in their beat. They can also request an overlay of the suspects that live in their beat and that commit a certain crime. Laptop technology and digital photography are prevalent in most modern police vehicles. Digital photography allows officers to integrate photographs with their reports. It also allows the officer to take a photo of a suspect and immediately include the suspect in a field photo lineup. Single fingerprint identification technology is also part of the mobile office. All of these technologies have come together to improve and enhance the field officer's mobile computing capabilities.

Data radio and wireless technology as transport mediums

To understand how mobile computing operates requires a basic understanding of radio technology. The Federal Communications Commission (FCC) assigns frequency bands to various groups. Early public safety radios functioned on the very high-frequency (VHF) range (30–300 MHz). Public safety used the 150-MHz band, and this is where many field computing systems began. Later the FCC assigned the 400- to 500-MHz band to public safety, moving to the ultra high-frequency (UHF) range (300–3000 MHz). The need for more bandwidth and technology advances soon saw public safety operating on the 800-MHz band. Most recently, the FCC assigned the 700-MHz frequency band to public safety. The importance of the frequency range to mobile computing is its data transmission speed. The lower frequency bands were slow with maximum transmission speeds of 2400 baud. Moving up to the 400-MHz band provided data transmission speeds of 4800 baud, and 800 bands doubled that data throughput capability to 19.2 baud. The recent 700-MHz frequency assignment provides a whole new dimension as it moves data radio into the broadband spectrum with speeds of 763–800 MHz. Table 7.1 depicts the data speed for each of the spectra.

The early implementation of mobile computing used radio for the transport of data. Frequency spectrum has been a premium for many years. In large metropolitan areas, many agencies are in competition for a limited number of frequencies. In some instances, this limited the advancement of mobile computing. When law enforcement function was primarily in the VHF range, with data transmission speeds in the 2400- to 9600-baud range, it was not practical to use these devices to take reports and transmit them to the department's record management system. This frequency range did open the way to two-way communications between the dispatch center and allowed field units to inquire into the local, state,

Table 7.1 Radio frequency ranges

Radio frequency range	Data throughput
75–150 MHz	2400 kilobytes per second
400–500 MHz	4800–9600 kilobytes per second
800–900 MHz	19.2 kilobytes per second
700–800 MHz	3.2–4.8 gigabytes per second

and national databases. This spectrum also provided the ability for field units to communicate with one another.

The move into the 800-MHz frequency range increased the data throughput capability to 19.2 Kbps, which made it possible for small agencies to write reports using field computers and transmit those reports to the record management system. Many agencies began to dedicate frequencies strictly as data frequencies, thus avoiding contention with voice transmissions. Clearly, the busier police agencies faced greater challenges when it came to system performance. Larger agencies still experienced system degradation when it came to transmitting data. These system performance issues kept these systems from becoming more robust and capable of transmitting large volumes of data. The inclusion of functionality such as crime analysis mapping, mug shots, and other capabilities was not possible primarily because of data throughput restrictions.

In 2005, the FCC assigned the 700-MHz frequency band to public safety. This occurred after a long debate with the cellular providers seeking the 800-MHz band for its use. Nextel uses the 800-MHz band for part of its service, which interferes with law enforcement agencies operating on this same band. After a lengthy debate, the FCC agreed to assign the 800-MHz frequency band to Nextel and the 700-MHz frequency band to public safety. There are significant advantages to the 700-MHz frequency range because it operates in the UHF band and is part of the broadband technology. The 700-MHz band provides data throughput of up to 4.8 gigahertz per second. This opens up significant capabilities for the expansion of mobile computing. With this throughput, field officers have the same capabilities in the field that they have at their desktops. The transition to the 700-MHz frequency range will take some time to complete. There is a cost associated with moving to this technology because agencies will have to convert their existing systems to the new spectrum. This usually entails new antennas, base equipment, and mobile radios. Depending on the size of the agency, this could be extremely costly. Many agencies just upgraded their systems to the 800-MHz band and are not likely to reinvest in this new infrastructure for quite some time.

There are other transport mediums used for mobile computing. Cellular technology provided faster data throughput. The use of cellular digitized packet data (CDPD) became popular in the late 1990s as an alternative to radio. Through the use of CDPD, it became possible for officers to function in their vehicle as they do at their desktop. The technology used was transmission controlled protocol/Internet protocol (TCP/IP). This provided access to the department's enterprise database by field officers. It did not require additional software to inquire the enterprise database. Police departments throughout the country began using this technology, often in conjunction with traditional radio systems. The traditional radio provided voice communications and integration with the department's computer-aided dispatch (CAD) system as well as state and national databases. CDPD provided the data radio capability to access the department's record management system.

Cellular technology made further advances with an enhanced version of CDPD known as code division multiple access (CDMA). CDMA provided greater capacity to the cellular network. CDMA does not assign a frequency to each user. Instead, every channel uses the full available spectrum (Beal, n.d.-a, b). As a result of this technology, police agencies obtained better performance and greater capacity.

The development of evolution data optimized (EVDO) enhanced CDMA technology significantly. EVDO is a wireless radio broadband data standard adopted by many CDMA mobile phone service providers. It significantly enhanced CDMA data throughput, which is critical to law enforcement's ability to transmit large files and to access data on the enterprise database.

The industry generically uses the term Wi-Fi when referring to 802.11 broadband, whether 802.11b, 802.11a, or dual band. Wi-Fi stands for wireless fidelity. The 802.11b frequency range has a 2.4-GHz data throughput, and 802.11a operates a 5.0-GHz data throughput. This technology offers the ability to share data across any brand of equipment, which promotes interoperability. Wi-Fi technology requires a series of transmitting devices be installed throughout the community, referred to as a Wi-Fi net. The drawback with Wi-Fi as a transport medium is its costs. To put a net over the entire jurisdiction is costly. Often cities will assume the cost of implementing a Wi-Fi net and share the technology with other agencies such as transportation, public works, fire, and police. This helps to defray the cost. Some cities make this a service that they provide to citizens and visitors to the community. The airport is a common place for Wi-Fi. Cities usually charge for this service, but it allows visitors, particularly business people, the opportunity to access the Internet from wherever they are at within the city. This provides law enforcement high-speed access to the department's record management system.

Agencies using Wi-Fi net often set up "hot spots" throughout the city. When a police vehicle comes in close to a "hot spot," data stored on the mobile computer such as reports upload to the enterprise database. Often these hot spots are fire stations or schools.

In 2005, Motorola released a competitive broadband product to compete with the 802.11 technology. It is a dedicated 4.9-GHz broadband system. The Motorola 4.9 system functions similar to the 802.11 technology. Throughout the jurisdiction are radio antennas, and as police units come within range of these locations, data transfer between the base station and the vehicle.

In summary, today there are three systems used for high-speed data transfer: the 700-MHz radio spectrum, the Wi-Fi 802.11, and Motorola's 4.9-GHz system. Each of these systems provides high-speed data through-put. This makes mobile computing a powerful in-vehicle computer system. It allows field officers the same access and capabilities as if they were using a desktop. These technologies will continue to advance, enhancing mobile computing.

Mobile computing security

As with all information systems, security is critically essential. Security is especially pertinent in a mobile computing environment. The most secure mobile environment is one that operates over a private radio system. Other transport mediums require different types of security. For those systems using the public networks, such as CDMA and EVDO and other Internet transport, an effective means of security is through a virtual private network.

Mobile computing and dispatch operations

Mobile computing started as a means of providing relief to overcrowded radio frequencies and to reduce the workload on dispatchers. The integration of MDTs and laptop computers with CAD systems provided a means for two-way communications between dispatchers and field officers. Since the development of MDTs, officers have been able to query state and national criminal history systems to check for wants and warrants. This off-loaded a significant burden from the dispatchers and also provided flexibility to field officers. Officers could perform their own license plate checks, run suspicious subjects for wants and warrants, arrive themselves on the scene of a call for service, and clear the call once completed. All of this can now be accomplished without dispatcher involvement.

With mobile computers, dispatchers could send the initial call record to the field unit so the field officer would have location information, the reporting party's name, and other pertinent information about the call. Some of the busier agencies would send multiple calls at a time to the field unit for them to handle accordingly. Some agencies provide the pending call list to the officers so they can see the calls awaiting dispatch. Some agencies found this was not the best practice. Some officers would abuse the system by keeping themselves unavailable so another unit would handle a call that they did not want to handle.

This interaction between the CAD system and the mobile computing system increased as computing power increased. In today's dispatch environment, CAD systems are capable of accessing information from multiple sources that in the past was impossible. CAD systems integrate with other information systems and field support systems, such as mapping. With the power of today's mobile computing units, dispatchers can send the X, Y coordinates to the field mobile computers, and the officer can pull up a map in the car and see the exact location of the call and obtain premise and hazard information pertaining to surrounding locations.

Officers also have the ability to send dispatchers information that they previously spoke over the radio and the dispatchers had to enter into the CAD system. As an example, when an officer completes a call, he or she enters the final disposition directly through the mobile computer. This includes comments the officer finds germane about the call and its outcome. These comments become part of the dispatch record for others to review at a later time. In the past, officers would verbally provide this information over the radio, and dispatchers would enter it into the call for service record. These and other enhancements significantly improved dispatcher performance and lessened the dispatcher's work burden.

Like any new technology, procedural issues arose in many departments that had to be addressed. Mobile computing changed the way many agencies conducted business. Because of the ability for dispatchers to dispatch units to a call without radio contact, other units in the area were often not aware of another unit's activities. Many considered this to be a safety issue. Officer train themselves to listen to the radio, so they know what is going on in the immediate and surrounding areas of their beat. With silent dispatching, as dispatching through mobile computers came to be known, officers were not aware of the other officer's activities. This proved dangerous when suddenly another officer requested assistance or an incident another officer was working got out of control and required other units to assist. This led to many agencies abandoning silent dispatching and adopting a combination of voice and CAD to mobile computer dispatching. All serious or potentially serious calls were dispatched using both voice and mobile computer so that other officers could hear what was going on.

Another supervisory problem that came to the public's attention through the Rodney King case is the officer's use of text messaging. Text messaging is a strong capability of mobile computing. It allows officers and supervisors to communicate with one another without the use of the radio, thus freeing valuable airtime. Unfortunately, many officers misused this capability. In many agencies, there was little supervisory control over the car-to-car text messaging, which led to many abuses. What most officers did not realize is that the department saved these text messages and could be recalled at a later date and time. In the Rodney King incident, by going back to the saved messages from the night of the incident, investigators found that the officers used the text messaging capability to make racial slurs that were later used in court against both the officers and the civil lawsuit against the city. Instances of sexual harassment of female officers and off-color jokes and comments are all problems experienced with abuses of the mobile computing system. Providing Internet access to officers in the field also opens up potential abuses of these systems.

Departments that keep a strict watch over the system minimize these abuses and how officers are using this capability. Letting it be known to the officers that periodic spot checks of their activities on these mobile devices will occur usually eliminates the problem. Following through with discipline for such abuses usually ensures appropriate behavior. Agencies that implement mobile computing systems must ensure they develop appropriate policies to address the use of these devices. Agencies should also ensure they articulate these policies to those using field mobile computers.

Field report writing

Field report writing was one of the first enhancements to mobile computing brought about primarily by laptop computers. One of the first police departments to begin using laptop computers for field report writing was Houston, Texas. Houston issued laptops to all of its officers. Houston minimally configured these laptops and used 3.5-inch floppy disks as their storage medium. Officers would enter incidents, arrests, and other reports through a commercially available word processor and save the information in the floppy disk. At the end of their shift, officers would upload the report to the department's record management system.

As mobile computing became more widely spread, the main focus of this new technology was on field report writing. Many agencies soon began implementing laptops in the patrol cars with some form of field report–writing system included. The COPS/MORE program of the 1990s significantly enhanced mobile computing. Most of the COPS/MORE grants included mobile computing, which in turn included field report writing.

In the early implementations of field report writing, there were problems. These problems related primarily to the data transport infrastructure. Most radio systems could not adequately handle the volume of data, particularly in the 2400- and 4800-baud rate for data transfer. Even at high transmission speeds, this was problematic. Large agencies quickly bog down the system by transmitting reports. Consequently, the mobile computing as a means of transmitting reports was slow and difficult to use.

Other issues, such as report review processing, needed to be addressed. One of the methods of addressing the report review process was to send the call from the mobile computer to a report review-pending file. From this file, the supervisor could review the report and send it back to the officer in the field for required changes. Others in the department could review the unfinished report, but knowing that it was an unapproved report. If the supervisor required corrections, he or she could e-mail the report back to the officer. Once the officer made the corrections, he or she would send the report back to the supervisor with the corrections highlighted. Once satisfied with the report, the supervisor could enter his or her approval code, which would then send the report to the record management system for permanent storage. Figure 7.5 depicts the field report–writing processing.

The benefits of this new technology for the field officer were somewhat dubious at first. If an officer took a report on a piece of paper or a laptop computer, there were not many differences. Others in the department did benefit from this new technology because they would have quicker access to the report data than they would have with the manual system (Kraemer & Danziger, 1985). Officers recognized that this technology could benefit them by providing more information related to their job (Ioimo, 2000). Field mobile reporting also improved the quality of preliminary investigations. It forced police officers to complete a comprehensive preliminary investigation by prompting the officer taking the report with investigatory questions that might otherwise go unexplored.

The mobile office

Mobile computing has moved forward through the addition of other technologies. These technologies provide the officer with significant access to data. Having access to data helps police officers to perform their jobs more efficiently. The concept of a mobile office has emerged as the standard for mobile computing in law enforcement. Unlike their detective counterparts, field officers do not have a standard office with a desk, file cabinets, and a desktop computer system. Today's police cruisers are the field officers' mobile office. Police officers work from their vehicles and require access to critical information that will help them to perform their jobs efficiently. The mobile office is not a concept unique to law enforcement. Businesses have embraced the mobile office concepts and have significantly grown mobile office capabilities that go beyond laptop computers.

The typical mobile office consists minimally of a laptop computer. Advanced mobile office implementations include printers, magnetic strip readers, digital photography, cellular telephones, and other office tools. The mobile office should include print capability so the field officer can

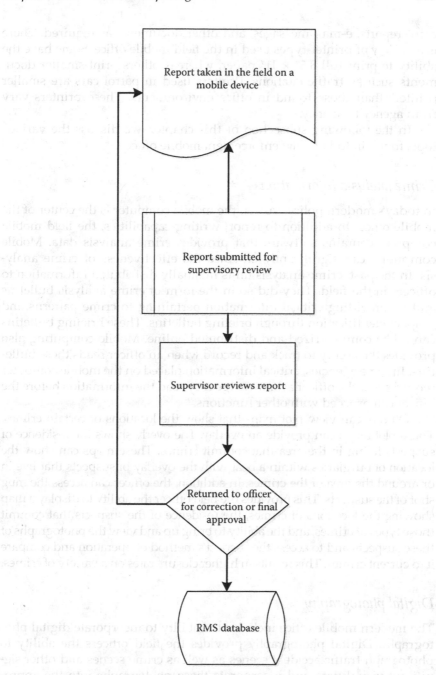

Figure 7.5 Field report–writing processing.

print reports, e-mail messages, and other documents as required. There is a variety of printer types used in the field mobile office. Some have the ability to print full 8.5" × 11" paper, whereas others print smaller documents such as traffic citations. Printers used in patrol cars are smaller printers than those found in office environments. These printers vary from agency to agency.

In the following subsection of this chapter, we discuss the various tools found in today's law enforcement mobile office.

Crime analysis information

In today's modern police cruiser, the mobile computer is the center of the mobile office. In addition to report-writing capabilities, the field mobile computer contains software that provides crime analysis data. Mobile computing can significantly enhance the effectiveness of crime analysis. In the past, crime analysis units manually distributed information to officers in the field. They did so in the form of crime analysis bulletins and by providing critical information pertaining to crime patterns and suspect identification through briefing bulletins. These briefing bulletins can all be computerized and distributed online. Mobile computing also provides the ability to track and record when an officer reads these bulletins. In some agencies, critical information placed on the mobile computer requires that the officer acknowledge they read the information before the officer can proceed with other functions.

Officers can view plot maps that show the locations of certain crimes. These plot maps can provide an overlay. The overly shows the residence of suspects living in the area that commit crimes. These maps can show the location of burglaries within a beat with the overlay of suspects that live in or around the area of the crimes. In addition, the officer can access the mug shot of the suspects. This provides the field officer the ability to display a map showing the locations of crimes, the residence of the suspects that commit those types of crimes, and the ability to bring up and view the photographs of these suspects and to access the suspect's method of operation and compare it to current crimes. This results in higher closure rates on a variety of crimes.

Digital photography

The modern mobile office includes the ability to incorporate digital photography. Digital photography provides the field officers the ability to photograph traffic accident scenes as well as crime scenes and other significant visual data and incorporate these photographs into the appropriate report. This digital photography capability enhances the quality of a report and often provides detailed information that is not otherwise a possibility. Digital photography also provides the ability to incorporate mug shots and to generate a photo lineup in the field that includes the suspect's photograph. Driver's licenses include magnetic strips that electronically contain all of the licensee information, including the licensee's photograph. This capability allows officers to create a photo lineup close to the time that the incident occurred while victim and witness memories are fresh. Using the digitized photograph from the driver's license, the field officer can create a photo lineup by drawing upon photo databases for similar photographs to include in the photo lineup. This instantaneous capability results in the quick resolution of crimes and increases in crime clearances.

Wireless mobile video

In addition to digital photography, wireless mobile video cameras are also part of the mobile office environment. Typically, police permanently mount cameras in the vehicle to video officers during traffic stops or other similar activities. Early mobile video provided officers the ability to video tape vehicle stops and refer to the tape as necessary after the event. Today with wireless networking, we can download video clips remotely, watch events as they happen, transmit data, monitor multiple patrol cars at the same time, automate notification of certain events from the car to the dispatcher—even turn things around, and give a department remote control of some of the vehicle's functions. For instance, a dispatcher can connect to a patrol car and see what an officer is dealing with as it is happening and even remotely do things such as turn on a car's siren or lights or disable the ignition on a stolen cruiser.

One of the newest wireless video technologies is the automated license plate recognition systems. These systems provide the ability to scan license plates as a patrol car is patrolling through the city streets using optical character recognition. These systems constantly scan license plates comparing them automatically against multiple local, regional, state, and federal databases of interest to law enforcement. The system alerts the officers both audibly and visually when a positive match occurs so that the officer can take appropriate action (Digital Video Systems, 2006). Every license plate scanned by the system is also date, time, and GPS encoded. The officer can wirelessly download the data captured, consolidated on a single server and analyzed using crime information management tools for postincident investigation or other requirements. In the past, officers had to run license plates by entering them manually to access these databases. With license plate checks occurring automatically, officers will undoubtedly recover more stolen vehicles, capture more wanted suspects, and increase their productivity.

Biometric tools

The positive identification of people that field officers come in contact with is always a challenge. Biometric tools are a means of positive identification that until recently were not possible at the field or patrol officer level. Biometric technology is rapidly advancing in several areas, which can be pushed out to the field level. One prevalent biometric technology now used in the field is single fingerprint identification. With the implementation of NCIC 2000, field officers have the ability to use single fingerprint biometric technology to help confirm the identity of subjects they come in contact with in the field. A fingerprint cradle attached to the mobile computer captures the fingerprint data and transmits the information to local, state, and national AFIS systems to confirm the identity of the subject. If the subject's fingerprints are on file, the system will report back to the officer in the field the true identity of the subject. When integrated with other biometric systems, additional information can be forwarded to the officer in the field. As an example, upon submitting a subject's fingerprint and if a mug shot is available, that mug shot along with the positive identification of a subject can be sent to the officer's mobile computer for his or her review.

Reference information

Reference information is also vital in the field mobile office. In the past, field officers often carried reference materials with them, such as penal codes, vehicle codes, drug identification reference manuals, and other similar reference documents that field officers rely on to do their jobs. Today this information is computerized and available online through the officer's mobile computer. This information provides the ability for field officers to look up and display information such as weapons. Officers can look up a weapon type and see a photograph of that weapon. More importantly, they can show these photographs to victims and witnesses to obtain positive identification. Like weapons, officers often require the ability to obtain photographs of vehicles. This allows officers the ability to display several vehicles to show to victims and witnesses for the identification of suspect vehicles. Another useful function is for police officers to store information about community leaders that they can access as needed. When problems occur in a neighborhood, the officer can access information pertaining to the leaders of that community and engage him or her in helping to solve the problem. These are several examples that show the use of mobile computing that further the field officer's capabilities.

Briefing information

Before a patrol officer's shift, police officers attend a briefing. Patrol briefing is a long-standing tradition within police departments that dates back to the days of Sir Robert Peel. In modern police departments, briefings usually occur before each shift coming on duty. The public learned about police briefings during the popular television series *Hill Street Blues* (Bochco & Kozoll, 1981–1987), when all of the officers gathered and the police sergeant stands before the gathering of officers and provides information pertinent to wanted suspects, vehicles, and other information officers need to know. During the briefing, the officers often engaged in both professional and social interactions and of course at the end of the briefing, the sergeant always concluded with, "Be careful out there." The show did an excellent job of depicting the "police briefing."

As the television series depicted, police briefings involve the transfer of information both formally and informally. Mobile computing assists in providing the formal distribution of information. Mobile computing systems provide briefing information to officers in the field. This does not replace the traditional briefing format but augments it. The officers can access the information presented at the briefing whenever necessary. Officers that come on duty in the middle of a shift, and do not have the ability to attend the formal briefing, can still obtain all of the necessary information from the online briefing. The agency can place photos or composite drawings of wanted suspects or vehicles in the online briefing information.

Some agencies use the online briefing as a means of ensuring officers obtain the appropriate briefing information. At the time an officer gets in his or her car and turns on the computer for the first time that day, the system forces the officer to read the briefing information and acknowledge that he or she read the information. This not only ensures that the officer receives the necessary information but also provides an audit trail confirming he obtained the information.

Cellular telephones

Police departments have adopted the use of cellular telephones as part of the mobile office environment. Cellular phones provide the officer with the ability to contact victims, witnesses, and others necessary in the course of performing their tasks. Cellular telephones that provide walkie-talkie-type capabilities also provide added benefits. Officers working a case can talk to one another without having to use the tactical frequencies or the department's main frequency. Cellular phones reduce officer dependency on radio communications, which improves radio channel usage.

Cellular phones also have the ability to combine telephony, text messaging, and Internet access. Microsoft wants to put "trustworthy computing" into next versions of software for cell phones. For this purpose, the cell phone transmissions need specific control and other information channels such as Bluetooth, infrared, card slots, and in-phone memory encryption.

The future of mobile computing

Mobile computing continues to advance on all fronts. This technology provides significantly robust capabilities to the officers in the field. As these advances occur, there is more integration of a wide variety of technologies. The ability to access the department's enterprise database from any officer's location provides enormous capabilities. In the future, mobile computing will provide several new capabilities that will likely affect law enforcement, such as the following:

Convertible laptops

Many police departments are beginning to use the new convertible laptop computers. These computers convert from a standard laptop to a pen-based system, allowing the officers to display a report in the standard crime report format that they would have used on a manual form. These convertibles allow the user to turn the screen around, close the device, and use a stylus to enter data. These devices provide the capability for the agency to take all of their existing forms and place them on the laptop. Officers can use the pen technology to enter information on the report the same way they would use a pen on a paper form. In addition, these forms can use drop-down menus for the selection of data required of a field. The stylus can also capture signatures required on forms, such as traffic citations. The officer can remove the convertible laptop from the vehicle and, through wireless technology, maintain communications with the agency's computer systems both internal and external. Several vendors are building these convertible laptops in ruggedized versions so they can withstand the stresses placed on them through field use. Figure 7.6 is a sample of the Panasonic Toughbook convertible computer, which is one of the most popular in use today.

Agencies that elect to use these devices are not likely to mount them in the vehicle as currently done with a standard laptop computer. If mounted, they are likely to be removed, so when the officer leaves the vehicle, he or she can easily remove the convertible and take it with him or her. The cost of maintaining a permanently mounted laptop and providing officers with convertibles is currently cost prohibitive. As the price of this technology begins to drop, police agencies will assign police officers a convertible laptop. Agencies will also have permanently mounted devices in their vehicles.

Tablet personal computers (PC)

A variation of the convertible laptop is the tablet PC. The tablet PC differs from the convertible in that it does not support a keyboard the same way

Figure 7.6 Panasonic Toughbook convertible computer.

a convertible does. The tablet PC uses a stylus to enter data the same way that the convertible does but without the keyboard capability. Rugged versions of the tablet PC are available, and they are mountable in vehicles where a detached keyboard can be used to key in data. Figure 7.7 depicts a ruggedized tablet PC.

Police agencies are beginning to provide a tablet PC, in addition to a permanently mounted PC. Like the convertible PC solution, the cost of providing both devices can be prohibitive.

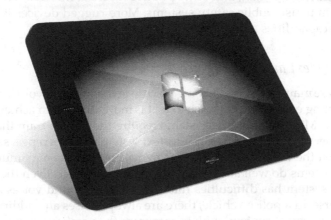

Figure 7.7 Rugged tablet PC.

Personal digital assistance

Personal digital assistants (PDAs) are gaining popularity as a mobile digital device that field officers can carry and use to collect information for reports and access local, state, and national criminal information databases. Another significant use of this technology is to collect the basic information required for crime reports, traffic accident reports, field interview cards, and other report information. The PDA is convenient to the way officers currently do business. Many officers carry small spiral notebooks that fit in their shirt pockets. They use these notebooks to capture information about crime as well as notes pertaining to their investigation of that crime. They later take this information and develop the formal crime report. By using a PDA, they can capture the face sheet information pertaining to a crime, traffic, or an arrest report. They can also jot down notes about the incident. Some PDAs offer graphic software that allows officers to do crime scene and traffic accident diagrams. Significant advantages of a PDA are that it is lightweight, and they are low cost, which makes them ideal for foot, bicycle, and motorcycle patrol officers (Chu, 2001). The PDA provides full access to the local, state, and national databases. This makes them an ideal tool for traffic citations because they can immediately collect data, check state and national databases for wants and warrants, and print the citation to give to the citizen. This eliminates the need for clerks to enter citation data.

These devices are capable of incorporating GPS chips, which provides the ability to track officers outside the vehicle. Figure 7.8 depicts a typical PDA.

Through the use of Bluetooth technology, the PDA can be used to upload crime report data to laptops, desktops, and other IT devices. Further integration occurs through intelligent gateway servers, HTML-based software, and TCP/IP transmission protocols. This permits access to the Internet, e-mail, and other public sources of information in addition to the in-house public safety systems. More rugged devices with cellular phone capabilities are appearing every day (Chu, 2001).

Voice to text and text to voice

There are many attempts at using voice to text and text to voice in the mobile computing environment. Voice to text is more difficult to achieve than text to voice. Most voice-to-text systems require the user to train the system to his or her voice. Training a voice-to-text system requires repeat sessions that build on the last session. Once the system reaches its maximum capacity, most systems do well at recognizing the trained voice. Even the best voice-to-text system has difficulties filtering out background voices and noises. Of course, in a police vehicle, there are always noises and additional voices the system must contend with to recognize the user's voice. As an example, a good use of voice to text is for the officer to notify dispatch when they are

Figure 7.8 Personal digital assistant. (Courtesy of Google. Available at https://www
.google.com/search?q=Public+Domain+Personal+Digital+Assistant&espv=2&biw
=1366&bih=667&tbm=isch&tbo=u&source=univ&sa=X&ved=0CFIQsARqFQoTC
Niwt8SVmckCFUozJgod6_4NkQ#imgdii=Wdg4uU-wZjhJ6M%3A%3BWdg4uU-wZj
hJ6M%3A%3Bki4Jjqc9NjcLqM%3A&imgrc=Wdg4uU-wZjhJ6M%3A.)

in pursuit and to call out the unit's constantly changing position during
the pursuit. Unfortunately, during a pursuit, there are lots of background
noises that interfere with voice recognition; the most notable of course is the
vehicle siren. With this activity, voice to text could help the most, but in all
probability, it is the most useless. For these reasons, we do not see a great
deal of use for voice-to-text systems in police vehicles.

What has proven more useful for mobile computing is text to voice.
Most systems that use text to voice use prerecorded messages, statements,
and commands. For example, a prerecorded message allows the officer
to press a function key and a message broadcasted that states the unit
identification and notifies dispatch and all other units that the unit is clear
and available, such as "1A12 is clear." Other uses of text to voice are when
a dispatcher dispatches a call to an officer. The dispatcher can dispatch

the call to the mobile computer via the text capability, and the system announces the call when the officer acknowledges the call on his or her laptop. There are many other uses of text to voice. Broadcast messages across districts can be formulated and sent to all field units and repeated as many times as necessary. One of the main concerns often raised by field officers is that because of mobile computers, they do not know when a fellow officer has run a suspect for wants or warrants and a hit comes back. Using text-to-voice technology, dispatch verbally broadcasts the want or warrant information to all units. This would let the other officers know if an officer has stopped a wanted suspect. These are only a few of the uses for text to voice. Through the integration of other technologies into the mobile computing environment, the development of other uses continues.

Technology integration

The future in mobile computing is in the integration of a variety of technologies found in the patrol car. This integration must allow officers in the field not only to access data but also to use that data in meaningful ways. In the future, the decentralization of information systems will be required to enhance field mobile computing. Decentralization means deploying applications directly to remote servers, desktops, and mobile devices so that remote workers can have the same quality of service as workers seated at their desks. Mobile applications should not be viewed as a distinctive stand-alone category, requiring a noteworthy development effort, special support, and unique platforms, but rather they should be viewed as an extension of existing applications, in which the adjustment of architecture occurs to enable distributed, rather than centralized, deployment (Margolis, 2006). The real benefit of mobile computing is the ability to provide field units with the same information and capabilities that their office counter parts have at their desktops. As mobile computing technology advances, this will become a reality.

References

Beal, V. (n.d.-a). CDMA—Code division multiple access. Retrieved from http://www.webopedia.com/TERM/C/CDMA.html.

Beal, V. (n.d.-b). Wi-Fi. Retrieved from http://www.webopedia.com/TERM/C/CDMA.html.

Bochco, S. & Kozoll, M. (1981–1987). *Hill Street Blues* [Television Series]. Los Angeles: NBC.

Chu, J. (2001). *Law enforcement information technology: A managerial, operational, and practitioner guide*. Boca Raton, FL: CRC Press.

Digital Video Systems (2006). *License Plate Recognition*. Retrieved from http://news.thomasnet.com/fullstory/486994/1782, 2006.

Ioimo, R. & Aronson, J. (2003, September). *The Benefits of Police Field Mobile Computing Realized by Non-Patrol Sections of a Police Department.* International Journal of Police Science & Management, 5(3) 195–206.

Ioimo, R. & Aronson, J. (2004, December). Police Field Mobile Computing: Applying the Theory of Task-Technology Fit. Police Quarterly, 7(4) 403–428.

Ioimo, R. E. (2000). *Applying the Theory of Task Technology Fit in Assessing Police Use of Field Mobile Computing.* Dissertation Abstracts International, Nova Southeastern University 2000, 292 pages; 9988001.

Kraemer, J. N., & Danziger, K. L. (1985, January/February). Computerized data-based systems and productivity among professional workers: The case of detectives. *Public Administration Review*, 196–209.

Kraemer, K. L., Danziger, J. N., Dunkle, D. E., & King, J. L. (1993, June). The usefulness of computer-based information to public manager. *MIS Quarterly, 17*(2), 129–151.

Margolis, H. (2006). PeerDirect: Enabling enterprise applications to run disconnected. from http://www.mobileimperative.com/documents.asp?grID=305&d_ID=1800#.

Northrop, E., Kraemer, K., & King, M. (1993). Police use of computers. *Journal of Criminal Justice*, 259–274.

Nunn, S. (1993, April). Computers in the cop car: Impact of the mobile digital terminal technology on motor vehicle theft clearance and recovery rates in a Texas city. *Evaluation Review, 17*(2), 182–203.

Nunn, S. (1994). How capital technologies affect municipal service outcomes: The case of police mobile digital terminals and stolen vehicles. *Journal of Policy Analysis and Management, 13*(3), 539–559.

Roberts, D. J. (2011, January). Technology is playing an expanding role in policing. *Police Chief*, 72–74.

Rocheleau, B. (1993). Evaluating public sector information systems: Satisfaction versus impact. *Evaluation and Program Planning, 16*, 119–129.

chapter eight

Crime analysis and crime mapping

At the core of today's intelligence-led policing is crime analysis, which has been enhanced through the integration of crime mapping.

List of definitions

CASS—Crime Analysis Support System
CopLink—links, persons, vehicles
GIS—geographic information system
ICAP—Integrated Criminal Apprehension Program
LEAA—Law Enforcement Assistance Administration

Introduction

Crime analysis provides an intelligent way of providing police service. For years, police departments across the country functioned on "gut-level intuitions" about where crime was occurring, the profile of the subject perpetrating crime, and other assessments about crime. Police departments have always tried to understand the crime problems within their communities. Pin mapping, which has been around since the early 1900s, was an attempt on the police department's part to try to understand crime patterns. Wanted posters, which have been around since the beginning of policing in the United States, are another means of disseminating useful information designed to help police capture wanted criminals.

Today, crime analysis has evolved into a focused discipline that utilizes several technologies associated with the collection, analysis, and dissemination of crime information. Current trends are to abandon the older methodologies of policing and adopt new approaches that focus on information and analysis of that data. The popular term today is "intelligence-led policing" (ILP). ILP cannot occur without strong crime analysis capability. Mapping is also an essential element of ILP. Crime analysis uses mapping to highlight crime problems and other factors that impact these problems.

The history of crime analysis

Crime analysis is not a new concept in law enforcement. The analysis of crime and crime patterns has occurred ever since organized policing began. Crime analysis provides a scientific means of analyzing crime. As the reader progresses through this chapter, the reader will see that crime analysis occurs in a variety of ways and for a variety of purposes. As technology has advanced, so has crime analysis.

Perhaps one of the most significant people in promoting technology in policing was August Vollmer, who was the police chief in Berkeley, California, from 1905 to 1932. Vollmer introduced many new technologies into law enforcement, including pin mapping. Vollmer used colored pins, which represented different types of crimes. The analyst placed these pins on the map at the location where one of these crimes occurred. This provided a pictorial view of crime patterns and the location of crimes.

Crime analysis, as we know it today, evolved over time. In Vollmer's days, tactical crime analysis took the form of pin maps. Analysis of crime data in these early days focused on providing statistical information tracking the numbers of robberies, burglaries, rapes, homicides, etc. The advanced police agencies compared this information from year to year, month to month, and season to season. Today, we consider this to be a part of administrative crime analysis, which we will discuss in greater detail later in this chapter.

The recognition of crime analysis as a formalized process began with the advent of the Integrated Criminal Apprehension Program (ICAP) in the 1970s (Austin et al., 1973). The Law Enforcement Assistance Administration (LEAA), as a major component of the ICAP project, promoted crime analysis. At the core of all ICAP grants was the establishment of a crime analysis unit. From that time forward, crime analysis has been an established discipline within the criminal justice community and has significantly advanced, becoming a core component of police operations. Crime analysis, during these early days, was primarily a manual process. Crime analysis was a tedious task. The crime analyst would receive a copy of all crime reports. In some police departments, the crime analyst was a single individual. In large agencies, there would be multiple analysts, usually with a supervisor. These agencies divide analysis activities into personal and property crimes. Analysts create pin maps from the data they collected from the reports. They would also read each report and create manual forms to tally the data and compare the data, looking for patterns and similar method of operation (MO) data. These crime analysts would provide written reports that they distributed throughout the police department. They often posted maps in the patrol briefing rooms. They would present weekly reports that they would distribute to the officers on a beat-by-beat basis, informing the officers as to the criminal activities in their beats. These early crime analysis units were task tedious, and acceptance of the information by police officers was a challenge. Most of the crime analysts were nonsworn, and acceptance of the information they provided was skeptical to these officers. Early crime analysts had to earn their credibility. They did so when information they provided led to solving a crime(s). The following case study demonstrates this office to crime analyst relationship of the 1970s:

In 1978, in a southern California city, a suburb of Los Angeles, the police department was dealing with a suspect that was going to elementary schools all over town, exposing himself to little girls as they walked home from school. The department put a small task force together trying to catch this sex offender. One of the children identified the suspect as having blonde hair and driving a green Camaro. After the Crime Analyst searched the sex offender file, he reported to the task force that there was a known sex offender that matched the description of the suspect. This person recently registered with the police department about a month before the incidents started to occur. He had blonde hair, but the car he was driving was a Mercury Cougar, unknown color. The task force refused to follow up on the crime analysts lead because they said the little girl said it was a green Camaro. Two weeks later and four indecent exposures later, the task force caught the suspect. He was driving a green Mercury Cougar. It was the suspect the crime analyst had identified two weeks earlier.

This scenario was quite common in the early days of crime analysis, and to a large extent, they still exist today. Officers would not accept the information provided by the crime analyst because he was not a sworn police officer. Police culture often serves as a real barrier to the implementation of new programs as well as new technology (Greene et al., 1994). Police officers tend to cling to their traditions of random patrol, rapid response to calls for service, and arrests without regard for data that might suggest alternatives (Phillips, 2012). After the previously mentioned incident, however, the officers began going to the crime analysts with cases they were working, asking for his assistance. The previously mentioned success story established credibility and respect that still exists to this day.

Later in the ICAP era (circa 1977), LEAA funded the International Association of Chiefs of Police for the development of the first computerized crime analysis software system known as the crime analysis support system (CASS). CASS was a standalone system that provided crime analysts the ability to develop their own files. It was a prelude to today's database software, like Microsoft Access. Crime analysts were able to develop their own files to capture information that was pertinent to them and to develop specialized files as necessary. CASS consisted of seven main capabilities:

1. *Crime pattern detection*—the identification of related or similar crimes based on geography, trends, and common suspect and methods of operation.
2. *Crime suspect correlation*—addressed the methods used to develop crime files that assisted identifying perpetrators by several means, after the identification of a pattern or a known MO.
3. *Target profiles*—discussed demographic data that have a direct effect on a community and focuses on a "community services" approach to crime prevention, placing the emphasis on increasing the analysis of the human environment so that programs may be developed to prevent and reduce crime.
4. *Forecast crime potentials*—dealt with predicting time and location of future events. This was an inferential step that proceeded from pattern analysis.
5. *Exception reports*—based on crime threshold establishing limits for crimes and how those limits could be utilized for triggering operational planning on exceeding those limits.
6. *Forecast crime trends*—primarily dealt with the prediction of crime volume in the time domain based on various statistical techniques.
7. *Resource allocation*—a cost-effective method of distributing police manpower and equipment. Managing resources, money, time, and materials was the central underlying theme of this module (Chang et al., 1979).

These seven principles became the basis of crime analysis throughout the United States. The automated software developed included these seven principles.

CASS was a freeware to any police or law enforcement organization that wanted to install it. It was a Cobol program, a popular programming language from the 1960s. It ran on several different minicomputers and early business microcomputers. Companies could obtain CASS at no charge if they wanted to provide implementation and training services to agencies wanting to use CASS. Several companies obtained the software and enhanced it and offered it for sale as an enhanced product.

Since these early days of CASS, information technology has progressed significantly. CASS is no longer an available system. Most companies that provide criminal justice software systems have incorporated the basic crime analysis features and functions into their record management system (RMS). They enhance crime analysis capabilities by incorporating electronic mapping. New geographic information system (GIS) software replaced the old pin maps that integrated with the RMS.

Crime analysis has progressed significantly since these early days, and so has the technology used in crime analysis. Modern crime analysis environments include several different types of analyses that make up the broader caption of crime analysis:

1. Intelligence analysis focuses on criminal activities of individuals or groups of offenders. It is typically related to organized crime, gangs, drug traffickers, prostitution rings, financial fraud rings, or combinations of these criminal enterprises (Santos-Boba, 2013).
2. Criminal investigative analysis describes criminal profiling. Criminal profiling entails the process of constructing "profiles" of offenders who have committed serious crimes (Santos-Boba, 2013). This profiling should not be confused with racial profiling.
3. Tactical crime analysis is the study of recent criminal incidents and potential criminal activity through the examination of characteristics such as how, when, and where the activity has occurred to assist in pattern development and for lead investigation, suspect identification, and case clearance (Santos-Boba, 2013). According to Boba, tactical crime analysis has three goals: (a) to link crimes and thus identify patterns, (b) to identify potential suspects of crimes or crime patterns, and (c) to link solved crime to open cases and thus help to clear or close cases.
4. Strategic crime analysis is the study of crime problems and other police-related issues to determine long-term patterns of activity, as well as to evaluate police responses and organizational procedures (Santos-Boba, 2013).
5. Administrative crime analysis is the presentation of compelling findings of crime research and analysis based on legal, political, and practical concerns to inform audiences within police administrations, city government/councils, and citizens (Santos-Boba, 2013).

Intelligence analysis

Intelligence analysis is a process of collecting information or data pertaining to individuals and criminal activity. It differs from pure crime analysis in that it tends to focus on individuals whereas crime analysis focuses on types of crimes. Certainly, the two overlap and have the same goals of capturing perpetrators and reducing crime. Intelligence analysis can mean different things to different police organizations. Unfortunately, it is often conceived as a highly secretive and sometimes subversive activity that is morally ambiguous or takes police close to legal and ethical boundaries (Ratcliff, 2007). The author believes that Swanson, Territo, and Taylor (2008) provide the most accurate definition of intelligence analysis, which is as follows:

> Intelligence analysis is the identification of networks
> of offenders and criminal activity, often associated
> with organized crime, gangs, drug traffickers, pros-
> titution rings, and terrorist organizations.

Dr. Jerry Ratcliff (2007) further defines criminal intelligence analysis as the creation of an intelligence knowledge product that supports decision making in the areas of law enforcement, crime reduction, and crime prevention. All of this is ILP. At the heart of ILP is crime analysis.

Since 9/11, a renewed emphasis on intelligence analysis arose. Immediately following 9/11, there were many questions as to what prior knowledge each of the federal police organizations held regarding the terrorists. Concerns, as to the sharing of information among the various federal agencies, as well as the local law enforcement agencies (police and sheriffs), received significant public attention. As a result, there was a reorganization of many of the federal agencies as well as the birth of Homeland Security. More importantly, there was recognition that local, state, and federal agencies collected an enormous amount of information and that there was a need to analyze that information and distribute the findings in a timely manner to those with the need to know. From this recognition, fusion centers occurred.

Unfortunately, there is no clear definition as to the purpose and function of the fusion centers. The general concept of a fusion center is that they should serve as a clearinghouse for all potentially relevant information that can be used to assess local crime and terror threats and aid in the apprehension of more traditional criminal suspects (Swanson et al., 2008). What many of them across the United States are doing is collecting data about subjects and groups. They provide a place where all law enforcement agencies can contribute information about criminals and potential terrorists. Fusion center intelligence analysts analyze this information and distribute their findings to all law enforcement agencies. Their tasks and functions clearly support ILP.

Intelligence-led policing

Intelligence analysis provides the necessary data for police executives, managers, supervisors, and planners to base their approach in dealing with crime from an enlightened position. It intimately understands the problems at hand and uses solid information to develop responses to those threats. ILD provides police managers a means of responding to the community's crime problems based on the analysis of intelligence information from which the agency developed a response.

The National Criminal Intelligence Sharing Plan (NCISP), released in 2003, contained 28 recommendations for substantial changes in local policing (NCISP, 2003; Swanson et al., 2008). The focus of the recommended changes was to address crime problems through the analysis of intelligence information, with emphasis on predictive analysis derived from the discovery of hard facts, information, patterns, intelligence, and good crime analysis (Swanson et al., 2008).

In ILD, agencies capture data pertaining to suspected and known criminals. Typically, crime analysts store these data on computer systems through sophisticated software systems that provide analysis capability. Software typically associated with intelligence analysis is systems that capture personal information that is also capable of linking individuals to other individuals or gangs. These link analysis systems, capture information pertaining to the person, their vehicles, known associates, criminal activity in which they engage, and locations that they frequent, such as bars or nightclubs. One extremely popular link analysis software package used in ILD is a package known as CopLink. CopLink provides a graphic interface showing associations between persons, locations of property, and other intelligence information (Miller, 2008). Figure 8.1 depicts a typical CopLink association graphic display.

Intelligence analysis incorporates the use of GISs to map information pertaining to individuals as well as groups of individuals or gangs. Crime analysis utilizes these same techniques to map crimes, known suspects, hot spots, and other crime-related activities.

GISs and crime mapping

GISs and crime mapping are a critical tool used by crime analysts. It is necessary to understand this technology and how it is used as all types of crime analysis use GIS and crime mapping. Although mapping is a critical crime analysis tool, the intent of this section is to expose the reader to the various types of maps and their use in crime analysis. Although mapping has always been a part of crime analysis, older pin maps were difficult to manage, and they were not easily maintained. It was difficult to create different types of maps, and although many early crime analysis units used different types of maps, automated mapping systems eliminated this problem.

Today, most communities have a GIS system supported and maintained by a GIS department. The GIS department maintains the base

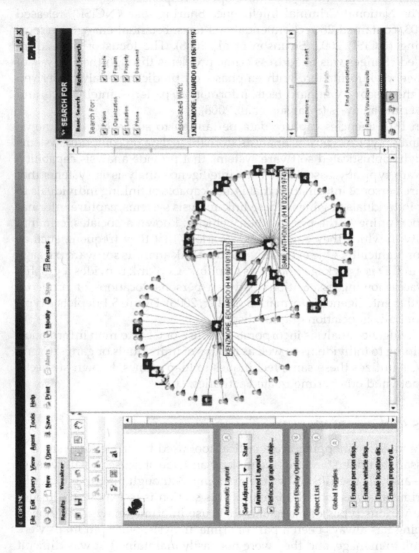

Figure 8.1 CopLink association graphic display. (From Coplink, Retrieved November 5, 2015 from https://www.google.com/search?q=coplink+public+domain, 2015.)

map that all departments within the community use. The base map contains all the roadways within a political jurisdiction. Most of these maps include an area outside of the community boundaries. From the base map, there are layers built to display information about several things or combinations of things. In crime and intelligence analysis, maps display data about crime. There are many different maps used to describe crime problems. Maps are a tool that can best describe crime problems. There are many different types of maps used to accomplish analysis mapping. The software used to develop these maps is from companies that specialize in mapping software. Such companies like Intergraph, Environmental Science Research Institute (ESRI), MapQuest, MapInfo, and other similar companies provide mapping software from which the crime analysis maps can be built.

Crime mapping types

There are several different map types used to display crime and other critical crime analysis data. In the next section, we discuss some of the different uses of maps. The maps presented are just some uses. There are many types of maps, which crime analysts use. The types of maps used are dependent on what the crime analyst is trying to present. As an example, the crime analyst may want to depict the location of burglaries and layer that map with the "known burglars" that live in that area. Multiple crimes could also be displayed with a known offender plotted with these crimes. To use an adage "a picture is worth a thousand words" and much more can be done to make a point by using maps in this way.

Mapping can be integrated with other digital technologies. As an example, digital photographs can be linked to an address. A user can click on that address and bring up a photograph of that location. Multiple photos can be linked to that address. This can be an extremely useful tool to the end user. A dispatcher could click on the address of a call and obtain a photo of the location. Other types of data can also be linked to an address, such as floor plans and other similar data.

The following is a mapping layer that depicts homicides in Washington, DC. This is a plot map. This map is a pin map, referencing homicides with colored pins on a map on a wall. This map is a thematic map because it presents a theme. In crime and intelligence analysis, these are the most common types of maps. Figure 8.2 depicts a homicide plot map.

The same data used to produce the previously mentioned map of homicide locations calculates densities of the crime within census tracts in Washington, DC. The gray areas are census tracts in the city where no homicides occurred in 1994 and 1995. The solid red tracts ranked highest in density of homicides, ranging from 55 to 157 homicides per square mile (National Institute of Justice, n.d.a). (Census tracts are smaller than a square mile, so the

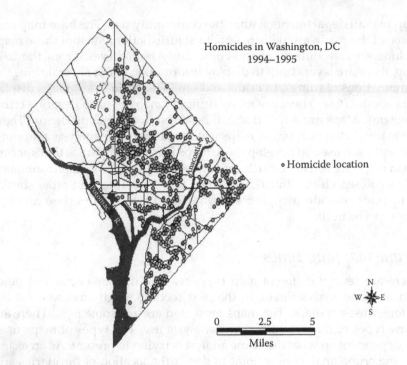

Homicides in Washington, DC
1994–1995

• Homicide location

Figure 8.2 Homicide plot map. (From Sadler, D., *Images for Public Domain Crime Maps,* Available at https://www.google.com/search?q=public+domain+crime+maps &rlz=1T4VRHB_enUS619US625&tbm=isch&tbo=u&source=univ&sa=X&ved=0CC 0QsARqFQoTCNP6uLSS-sgCFYJAJgodt2ADCw&biw=1680&bih=808, 1995.)

actual numbers of homicides occurring in each are often considerably less than its density value in the map legend.) The choropleth map shows discrete distributions for particular areas such as beats, precincts, districts, counties, or census blocks. Figure 8.3 depicts a homicide density map.

Figure 8.4 is a combination of choropleth and thematic mapping. This map compares homicides with poverty in 1994. It displays the percentage of persons in each tract that fall 50% or more below the poverty level and the homicides. More homicide incidents seem to have occurred in the poorer tracts.

Patrols in many departments hold briefings regularly with the aid of maps on recent crime trends. These types of maps are "pattern" maps. The following map shows not only the locations of three crime types over a 12-day period but also the recent incidents in larger red icons over that same time frame. Crime analysts will use this map to track the direction of crime and to provide predictive information to patrol. The map shows the direction of the serial robberies and tells they are following the freeways. The pattern is an especially useful concept in crime analysis, as

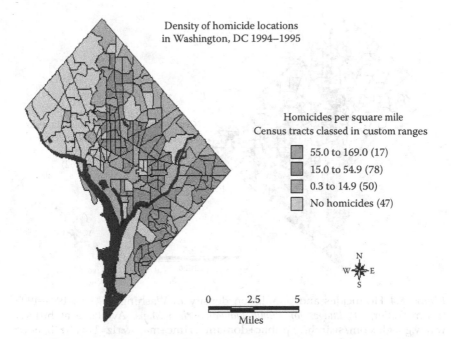

Figure 8.3 Homicide density. (From Sadler, D., *Images for Public Domain Crime Maps*, Available at https://www.google.com/search?q=public+domain+crime+maps &rlz=1T4VRHB_enUS619US625&tbm=isch&tbo=u&source=univ&sa=X&ved =0CC0QsARqFQoTCNP6uLSS-sgCFYJAJgodt2ADCw&biw=1680&bih=808, 1995.)

so much of what crime analysts do involves describing or analyzing the pattern of crime occurrences (National Institute of Justice, n.d.b). The classification of patterns consists of random, uniform, clustered, or dispersed. Figure 8.5 shows a sample trend map.

The identification of "hot spots" is a core crime analysis function. Mapping helps to identify these hot spots by highlighting them with different colors that depict frequency. The following is an example of a "hot spot" map showing vehicle theft "hot spots." The bright red colors show a high number of incidents in those areas. Figure 8.6 shows a sample hot spot vehicle theft map model.

Many crime analysts consider the recovery locations of stolen vehicles to be more relevant in solving crimes than the location from which the vehicle is stolen. Unless a thief has an alternate mode of transportation, he or she will likely leave a stolen automobile close to some desired destination, quite possibly a chop shop where stolen cars are stripped down for parts. The density map presented in Figure 8.7 shows the number of automobiles recovered per square mile that had originally been stolen in Baltimore County (see Figure 8.6) (National Institute of Justice, n.d.a). Figure 8.7 depicts stolen vehicle recovery locations.

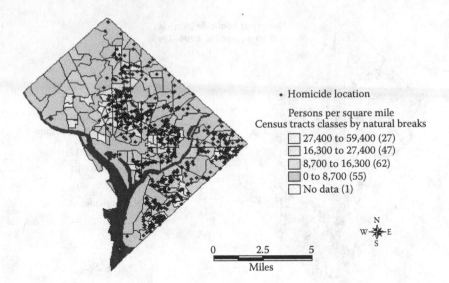

Figure 8.4 Homicides and population density in Washington, DC, 1994–1995. (From Sadler, D., *Images for Public Domain Crime Maps*, Available at https://www.google.com/search?q=public+domain+crime+maps&rlz=1T4VRHB_enUS619US625&tbm=isch&tbo=u&source=univ&sa=X&ved=0CC0QsARqFQoTCNP6uLSS-sgCFYJAJgodt2ADCw&biw=1680&bih=808, 1995.)

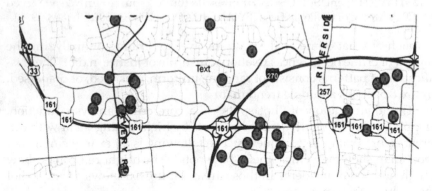

Figure 8.5 Trend mapping.

In combining the use of these maps, we can see the location of stolen cars and overlay that map with the location of recovered cars. The analyst can then make assessments about the crime. They can determine patterns and help direct patrol so that they will understand the stolen vehicle problem and how patrol might be able to combat the problem. Other types of crimes can also be analyzed in the same way.

HotSpot—Past 5 years

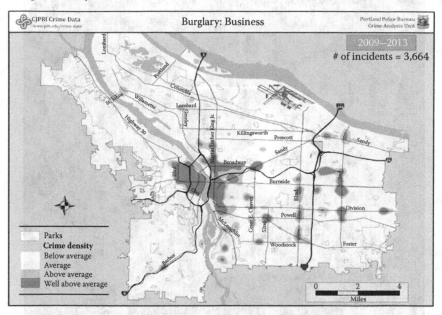

Figure 8.6 Hot spot vehicle theft map model. (From Sadler, D., *Images for Public Domain Crime Maps*, Available at https://www.google.com/search?q=public+domain+crime+maps&rlz=1T4VRHB_enUS619US625&tbm=isch&tbo=u&source=univ&sa=X&ved=0CC0QsARqFQoTCNP6uLSS-sgCFYJAJgodt2ADCw&biw=1680&bih=808, 1995.)

Crime analysis and information technology

As discussed previously, crime analysis has not always had the advantages provided by information technology. Mapping is one critical component, but there are many other automated tools that crime analysis uses today that are vital to understand. Some of these tools are components of the RMS, but others are external tools. The crime analysis process consists of the following steps:

1. *Collection of data*—There are many different ways of collecting data that crime analysts use. Typically, this information comes from the crime and arrest reports and calls for service data created by the department and entered into the RMS. Other sources of information are available from within the department and through external sources that aid in the crime analysis function. What should be recognized about data is that the more accurate and complete the data from the crime and arrest reports, the better the output. The old

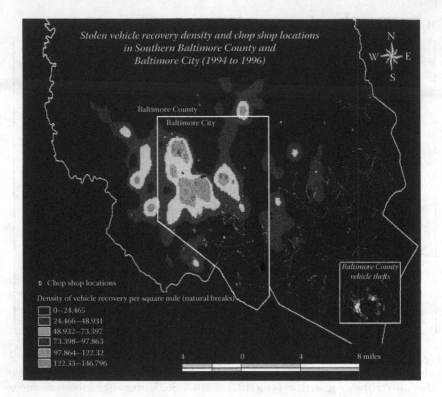

Figure 8.7 Stolen vehicle recovery locations. (From Korandzic, E., Stolen Vehicle Recovery Locations, *Images for Public Domain Crime Maps*, Available at https://www .google.com/search?q=public+domain+crime+maps&rlz=1T4VRHB_enUS619US625 &tbm=isch&tbo=u&source=univ&sa=X&ved=0CC0QsARqFQoTCNP6uLSS-sgCF YJAJgodt2ADCw&biw=1680&bih=808, n.d.)

cliché "garbage in, garbage out" holds true in the collection of crime analysis data.

2. *Collation of data*—In the early manual days of crime analysis, this was a tedious process. In today's environment, information technology makes it easier to collate data. Volumes of data can be sorted into categories pertinent to specialized files. These data can be further broken down into specialized variables as might be required.

3. *Analysis of data*—This is a key function of the crime analyst. The analyst uses several information technology tools to analyze the collected and collated data. Many of the RMS systems on the market today include crime analysis tools within the RMS. There are also several stand-alone systems that capture information from the RMS and then

provide the crime analyst with the ability to analyze the data in more detailed formats. The following are examples of some external tools:
  a. GISs (such as ESRI, Intergraph, MapInfo, etc.)
  b. Spreadsheets (such as Microsoft Excel)
  c. Desktop databases (such as Microsoft Access)
  d. Link analysis software (such as CopLink)
  e. Investigative software (such as Xanalys)
  f. Crime prediction software (such as PrePol)
These are a few of the external tools used to analyze crime data and to present that data in a format understandable to the end users.
4. *Dissemination*—In the early days of crime analysis, dissemination came in the form of written documents describing crime problems in an area or by providing beat reports describing the crime problem in a particular beat or district. Pin mapping visually depicts crime problems. With information technology, the dissemination of information has become much more sophisticated. Crime analysts have the ability of putting together automated beat reports. These reports can be disseminated to the beat officers through their e-mail or directly through the mobile computer. GIS information can also be sent directly to the mobile computer. As an example, through this technology, beat maps can be available to officers in the field that support ILP by allowing officers to see where crimes are occurring in his or her beat. Officers can use these maps to see where known offenders live in their beats. Photographs can also be linked so officers can click on a known offender dot on the map and his or her photo will be displayed. Many other information dissemination tools are available to the crime analyst.

Information technology and crime analysis

There are several different forms of crime analysis that require different types of information technology. This number can vary, but the following is the traditional types of crime analysis (Santos-Boba, 2013):

- Tactical crime analysis
- Strategic crime analysis
- Operations analysis
- Administrative crime analysis
- Intelligence analysis

In each of these different types of crime analysis, the technology used differs to some degree. It is essential to understand the purpose and function of each of these different forms of crime analysis. The following subsections describe these functions and the technology used.

Tactical crime analysis

Tactical crime analysis deals with immediate criminal offenses to promote quick responses to a crime problem. It provides information to assist operational personnel in the identification of crime trends and the arrest of criminal offenders. The primary goal is to identify crime trends and patterns/series. The goal of tactical crime analysis is to connect offender and modus operandi information from several offenses in an attempt to provide ILP leads to patrol, to investigative leads, to help solve crimes, and to clear cases after apprehension and arrests. Tactical crime analysis seeks to identify patterns of crimes that are not easily linked together. Tactical crime analysis focuses on crimes in which the offender and the victim do not know one another and on crimes that are predatory in nature. The following is a listing of the types of crimes tactical crime analysis focuses on:

- Theft from vehicle
- Auto theft
- Vandalism
- Commercial burglary
- Residential burglary
- Indecent exposure
- Public sexual indecency
- Rape
- Robbery

Crime analysts use a variety of information technology tools in processing the data for tactical analysis. The pertinent data used for tactical crime analysis are the following:

- Crime type
- Modus operandi
- Person data
- Vehicle data

This information typically comes from the crime or arrest reports and the data entered into the RMS. From the RMS, the crime analyst typically uses the ad hoc reporting tools to develop specialized reports. The crime analyst also uses ad hoc tools to conduct analysis pertaining to the crime problem. Crime analysis will use mapping tools available through the RMS or an external GIS system to identify movement pertaining to the tactical issues at hand.

In addition to the RMS tools, a crime analyst will use spreadsheets and desktop database systems as necessary to analyze and track activities. Spreadsheets allow the crime analyst to capture unique variables that can be further analyzed. Information from spreadsheets can also be accessed by other tools like the GIS systems which can further assist in the tactical analysis.

Strategic crime analysis

Strategic crime analysis focuses on long-term strategies as opposed to current crime activity that tactical crime analysis faces. Strategic crime analysis focuses on criminal activity over a period of time. It is looking at things like identifiable trends, crime growth, or reduction of crime. External factors are also crucial in strategic crime analysis. Things like a new factory that will employ many new employees and bring other factories into town will have an impact on policing activity as well as criminal activity. Strategic crime analysis focuses on these types of activities as they can, and likely will, have an impact on things like calls for service, criminal behavior, beat distribution, and configuration. This form of crime analysis focuses on the effectiveness of policies and procedures. The main concern of strategic crime analysis is with long-term criminal problems. As an example, the community has a significant residential burglary problem that has been worsening for the past 3 years. This would be a problem that strategic crime analysis seeks to analyze and propose solutions to address the problem.

Many of the automated tools that the strategic crime analyst uses are the same as those the tactical crime analyst uses; it is the way that they use these tools that are different. Many of the RMS systems provide reports that show month-to-month and year-to-date statistics. Strategic crime analysts will use spreadsheets to analyze much of this information. This form of analysis is called temporal analysis—the analysis of data in relationship to time. These data are typically comparative data. Figure 8.8 shows a strategic crime analyst's use of a graphical display of information pertaining to commercial burglary and commercial thefts over a time:

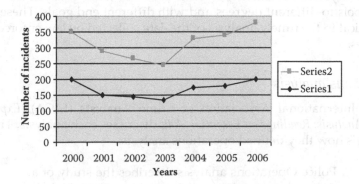

Figure 8.8 Commercial burglary and commercial thefts.

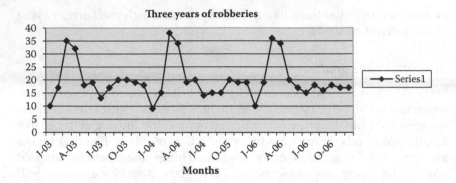

Figure 8.9 Seasonal robbery trends.

These data can also depict certain patterns by the time of year. As an example, if a community is a winter resort, there may be trends that the police and the community need to be aware of to address the identifiable problem. Figure 8.9 shows robberies are at their highest during the winter months of January through April. Figure 8.9 depicts seasonal robbery trends.

There are different external systems that the strategic crime analyst also requires access. Typically, they concern themselves with future building plans that might be on the drawing board that the building department is dealing with and will likely be implemented in the future.

Figure 8.10 shows a typical spreadsheet analysis that depicts the number of robberies by the time of the day and day of the week. From this spreadsheet, further analysis occurs that can determine tactical approaches to dealing with this robbery problem.

These are the types of information technology tools used in strategic crime analysis work functions. Other forms of crime analysis use these same tools to different degrees and with different end goals. These tools are critical to the timely analysis of the data collected by law enforcement agencies.

Operations analysis

In the International Association of Crime Analysts (IACA), *Exploring Crime Analysis: Readings on Essential Skills* discusses each analysis. The following is how they defined operations analysis:

> Police Operations analysis describes the study of a police department's policies and practices, including its allocation of personnel, money, equipment,

	Sunday	Monday	Tuesday	Wednesday	Thursday	Friday	Saturday	Total
00:00–00:59	10	2	4	3	7	9	15	50
01:00–01:59	13	1	0	0	3	9	18	44
02:00–02:59	8	0	0	0	0	2	12	22
03:00–03:59	3	0	0	0	0	0	5	8
04:00–04:59	0	0	0	0	0	0	0	0
05:00–05:59	0	0	0	0	0	0	0	0
06:00–06:59	0	0	0	0	0	0	2	2
07:00–07:59	0	2	0	1	1	0	3	7
08:00–08:59	0	0	0	0	0	0	0	0
09:00–09:59	0	0	3	5	0	0	4	12
10:00–10:59	0	2	1	0	0	3	0	6
11:00–11:59	0	0	0	0	0	0	0	0
12:00–12:59	2	2	0	0	4	5	0	13
13:00–13:59	0	0	0	0	0	0	0	0
14:00–14:59	5	0	0	0	3	4	3	15
15:00–15:59	0	0	4	0	2	5	2	13
16:00–16:59	1	0	2	0	1	3	3	10
17:00–17:59	0	0	0	0	0	0	0	0
18:00–18:59	0	0	0	0	0	0	0	0
19:00–19:59	2	3	6	4	4	5	5	29
20:00–20:59	2	4	3	3	5	5	7	29
21:00–21:59	2	3	4	6	12	19	21	67
22:00–22:59	4	6	7	7	9	11	12	56
23:00–23:59	8	2	2	2	8	9	9	40
Total	**60**	**27**	**36**	**31**	**59**	**89**	**121**	**423**

Figure 8.10 Crosstab of data of robberies.

and other resources, geographically, organization-
ally, and temporally, and whether these operations
and policies have the most effective influence on
crime and disorder in the jurisdiction. (Bruce et al.,
2008)

Operations analysis pertains to the operation of the police department and not with the resolution of crime patterns or prevention of crime
and disorder problems (Santos-Boba, 2013). The technology that is necessary to meet operations analysis surrounds the operations of the police
department. It encompasses patrol workload used to assign officers to
shifts and to configure beat structures. Operations analysis and strategic
crime analysis are similar as they base many operations decision on long-
term trends (Bruce et al., 2008).

The data used in operations analysis come from a computer-aided
dispatch (CAD) system and an RMS. Some of these systems have analysis tools that assist in this analysis. CAD systems provide data that show
the locations of calls for service, the number of calls for service, and the

amount of time consumed handling these calls. Utilizing subgeographic reporting districts that comprise beats, it is possible to determine beat structures that equalize workload among all beats. This same data can be used when cities incorporate additional areas into the city limits. Some operations analysts use external tools to assist in their analysis such as spreadsheets. There are some software packages that are specific to operations analysis, particularly when dealing with patrol workload analysis.

Not all crime analysis units support operations analysis as a separate unit. The functions this unit typically employ overlap strategic crime analysis. Usually, the functions and tasks of the operations analysis merge into strategic crime analysis. Large agencies are more likely to establish operations analysis as a separate analytical unit.

Administrative crime analysis

Administrative crime analysis differs from the other types of crime analysis in that the information gathered and analyzed tends to be for public information. The focus is on nonoperational personnel. This is also perhaps the oldest form of crime analysis. Administrative crime analysis focuses on things like comparing crime statistics from one year to another, addressing crime trends, and addressing problems that might be of interest to a group. The presentation of administrative crime analysis depends on the following:

- The audience
- The purpose of sharing the information
- The contexts of individual situations

Audiences for administrative crime analysis information include people in the following areas:

- Police and city management
- Citizens
- Other groups with various interests (such as business owners, neighborhood organizations, news media)

The context of the presentation of the information can affect the presentation of administrative crime analysis information

- Social/political climate
- Legal concerns
- Practical concerns

As specified by the IACA, examples of administrative crime analysis would include the following (Bruce et al., 2008):

- A report on demographic changes in the jurisdiction
- A historical research project on crime during the prohibition period
- Miscellaneous crime statistics to support grant applications
- Preparation of uniform crime report (UCR) or incident-based reporting system (IBRS) reports
- Creation of charts and graphs to support the chief's presentation to the city council
- Creation of patrol deployment maps for a special event
- Provision of a list of individuals with warrants by police beat and seriousness of offense

The data used for this analysis come from RMS, CAD systems, and other standard tools that are in place. One significant tool used by administrative crime analysts is the Internet. Administrative crime analysts often manage the police department's website. On this website, they provide crime statistics that show the types of crimes, usually the UCR eight major criminal offenses that have occurred in the community and how they compare to previous years. The use of the Internet to list wanted suspects, including mug shots, expanded over the years. In particular, the Internet can assist as follows:

- Reduce the workload for crime analysts
- Avoid answering crime-related judgment questions
- Increase awareness of community problems and encourage citizens to get involved with solving them
- Inform the public
- Share information with crime analysis scholars
- Share information with other police agencies
- Ensure that audiences maintain a source of accurate information about crime and disorder

There are disadvantages of police agencies' use of the Internet to publish crime analysis findings, which include the following:

- Commercial entities might use the information for profit
- Current and potential criminals might use the information to commit crimes
- Information about crime in the area
- Neighborhood might negatively affect those areas
- Audiences might misinterpret the information provided

Other information technology tools used for these efforts are typically off-the-shelf office automation tools, primarily spreadsheets, and word processors.

Predictive policing

Throughout history, policing has been reactive to actual crime activity. Over the years, we have seen improvements to the way policing is performed. Through the use of crime analysis, police departments have been able to implement proactive policing strategies. Law enforcement has used crime analysis data to describe crime patterns and to better deploy resources to address crime problems. Throughout the years, we have seen police agencies adopt problem-oriented policing, community-oriented policing, ILP, hot spot policing, and other techniques to better address crime problems.

Predictive policing harnesses information that each of these other techniques uses and takes the information to a much more sophisticated level. Predictive policing harnesses this information in a way that attempts to predict where and when crimes are going to occur. The National Institute of Justice describes predictive policing as follows: "Predictive policing tries to harness the power of information, geospatial technologies and evidence-based intervention models to reduce crime and improve public safety" (National Institute of Justice, n.d.c).

Predictive policing is a means of forecasting and predicting crime using sophisticated techniques that require computer analysis. It includes computer-assisted queries, statistical modeling (e.g., regression analysis), spatiotemporal analysis, and advanced hot spot identification models to perform crime linking; geospatial tools and other information technology support (Perry et al., 2013) are needed. These software tools are found in combination with current criminal justice software and business modeling software.

In the Rand study, they pointed out four myths about predictive policing that surround information technology used in this model.

> *Myth 1: The computer actually knows the future.* Some descriptions of predictive policing make it sound as if the computer can foretell the future. Although much news coverage promotes the meme that predictive policing is a crystal ball, these algorithms predict the risk of future events, not the events themselves. The computer, as a tool, can dramatically simplify the search for patterns, but all these techniques are extrapolations from the past in one way or another. In addition, predictions are only as good as the underlying data used to make them.

Myth 2: The computer will do everything for you. Although it is common to promote software packages as end-to-end solutions for predictive policing, humans remain—by far—the most important element in the predictive policing process. Even with the most complete software suites, humans must find and collect relevant data, preprocess the data so they are suitable for analysis, design and conduct analyses in response to ever-changing crime conditions, review and interpret the results of these analyses and exclude erroneous findings, analyze the integrated findings and make recommendations about how to act on them, and take action to exploit the findings and assess the impact of those actions.

Myth 3: You need a high-powered (and expensive) model. Most police departments do not need the most expensive software packages or computers to launch a predictive policing program. Functionalities built into standard workplace software (e.g., Microsoft Office) and GISs (e.g., ArcGIS) can support many predictive methods. Although there is usually a correlation between the complexity of a model and its predictive power, increases in predictive power have tended to show diminishing returns. Simple heuristics have been found to be nearly as good as analytic software in performing some tasks. This finding is especially important for small departments, which often have insufficient data to support large, sophisticated models.

Myth 4: Accurate predictions automatically lead to major crime reductions. Predictive policing analysis is frequently marketed as the path to the end of crime. The focus on the analyses and software can obscure the fact that predictions, on their own, are just that—predictions. Actual decreases in crime require taking action based on those predictions. Thus, we emphasize again that predictive policing is not about making predictions but about the end-to-end process. (Perry et al., 2013)

Predictive policing is going to grow in the years to come, especially as computer technology advances. It is important to understand the concepts as described in this section.

Intelligence analysis

Until recently, crime and intelligence analysis were two separate units within law enforcement organizations. Although many of the functions each unit performed were similar, intelligence analysis focused on individuals and groups where crime analysis focused less on individuals and more on crime patterns, crime types, and other crime-related factors. Rarely did the two units work together. Crime analysis units tended to be staffed by civilians, whereas intelligence units staffed by sworn personnel. There are still many departments across the country that still function this way; however, we are seeing more and more of these units combined.

Much of the data captured by intelligence units comes from operations functions. The data come through surveillance of criminal locations, wiretapping, undercover investigations, and other similar functions. This obviously differs from the functions and tasks we have been discussing thus far as it pertains to crime analysis. This is not the actual analysis function. This information becomes criminal intelligence when used to form a broader picture of criminality used by decision makers to direct enforcement, prevention, or further intelligence resources. Intelligence can be broken down into groups similar to crime analysis:

- Tactical intelligence
- Operational intelligence
- Strategic intelligence

Tactical intelligence is the most common level of criminal intelligence. It supports frontline enforcement officers and investigators in taking case-specific action to achieve enforcement objectives.

Operational intelligence is the creation of an intelligence product that supports area commanders and regional operational managers in planning crime reduction activity and deploying resources to achieve operational objectives. It supports decision makers who are responsible for geographic areas or who command enforcement teams. Operational intelligence helps decision makers decide which organized crime groups are most vulnerable to enforcement and which areas of a city require the most resources. Operational intelligence often sits above tactical intelligence because only after a decision maker determines priorities will tactical intelligence be used to support any enforcement objectives.

Strategic intelligence provides insight and understanding into patterns of criminal behavior and the functioning of the criminal environment and aims to be future-oriented and proactive. Strategic intelligence seeks to influence long-term organizational objectives and to contribute to discussions of policy, resource allocation, and strategy (White, n.d.).

The events of 9/11 and the demonstrated need to share information have inspired the concept of integrating crime and intelligence analysis (Carter, 2004). In summary, criminal intelligence analysis provides information on prolific offenders and organized criminal groups, and crime analysis provides the crime context of the environment in which they offend. Both are essential to a full understanding of crime problems and recidivist criminality and are prerequisites of good decision making and effective crime reductions (National Institute of Justice, n.d.c).

The technology required to meet the needs of this combined effort is not any different. The information technology that integrates both crime and intelligence analysis tends to deal with linking people together and linking people to criminal activity (NIJ, n.d.). Link analysis software helps to achieve this goal.

Today, crime analysis and crime mapping have become critical components within law enforcement. Current emphasis on intelligent-led policing promotes crime analysis as the key component in providing the data to make intelligent decisions. The previously mentioned tools and approaches are critical to the implementation of crime analysis departments.

References

Austin, R., Buck, G. A., Cooper, G., Gagnon, D., Hodges, J., Martensen, K., & O'Neal, M. (1973). *Police crime analysis unit handbook*. Washington, DC: LEAA.

Bruce, C., Gwinn, S. L., Cooper, J. P., & Hicks, S. (2008). *Exploring crime analysis*. (2nd ed.). Overland Park, KS: International Association of Crime Analysts.

Carter, D. L. (2004, November). *Law enforcement intelligence: A guide for state, local and tribal law enforcement*. Retrieved from http://www.cops.usdoj.gov/pdf/e09042536.pdf.

Chang, S., Simms, W., Makres, K., & Bodner, A. (1979, May). *Crime analysis support system: Descriptive report of manual and automated crime analysis*. Washington, DC: Law Enforcement Assistance Administration.

CopLink White Paper Knowledge Computing Corporation (2008, November). COPLINK (White Paper). Tucson, AZ.

Greene, J. R., Bergman, W. T., & McLaughlin, D. J. (1994). Implementing community policing: Cultural and structural change in police organizations. In D. P. Rosenbaum (Ed.), *The challenge of community policing: Testing the promises* (pp. 92–109). Thousand Oaks, CA: Sage.

Korandzic, E. (n.d.). *Stolen Vehicle Recovery Locations*. Images for Public Domain Crime Maps. Available at https://www.google.com/search?q=public+domain+crime+maps&rlz=1T4VRHB_enUS619US625&tbm=isch&tbo=u&source=univ&sa=X&ved=0CC0QsARqFQoTCNP6uLSS-sgCFYJAJgodt2ADCw&biw=1680&bih=808.

Miller, C. (2008, October). *CopLink CompStat analyzer automates crime data analysis*. Law Enforcement Technology.

National Institute of Justice (n.d.a). *Why Map Crime?* Retrieved from http://www.cops.usdoj.gov/html/cd_rom/tech_docs/pubs/WastIsCrimeMappingBriefingB.

National Institute of Justice (n.d.b). *Mapping Crime: Principle and Practice.* Retrieved from http://www.scrilbd.com/doc/1212253/Criminal-Justice-Reference-178919.

National Institute of Justice (n.d.c). *Predictive Policing.* Retrieved from http://www.nij .gov/topics/law-enforcement/strategies/predictive-policing/Pages/welcom .aspx.

NIJ Quick Click: I. Why Map Crime? Quick Links. (n.d.). Retrieved from http://www .cops.usdoj.gov/html/cd_rom/tech_docs/pubs/WhatIsCrimeMapping BriefingB.

Perry, W. L., MchInnis, B., Price, C. C., Sminth, S. C., & Hollywood, J. S. (2013). *Predictive policing: The role of crime forecasting in law enforcement operations.* Rand Corporation.

Phillips, S. W. (2012, September). The attitudes of police manager toward intelligence-led policing. *FBI Law Enforcement Bulletin*, 81, 9.

Ratcliff, J. H. (2007, August). *Integrated intelligence and crime analysis: Enhanced information management for law enforcement.* Washington, DC: Police Foundation.

Sadler, D. (1995). *Images for Public Domain Crime Maps.* Available at https:// www.google.com/search?q=public+domain+crime+maps&rlz=1T4VRHB _enUS619US625&tbm=isch&tbo=u&source=univ&sa=X&ved=0CC0QsARq FQoTCNP6uLSS-sgCFYJAJgodt2ADCw&biw=1680&bih=808.

Santos-Boba, R. (2013). *Crime Analysis with Crime Mapping.* Thousand Oaks, CA: Sage Publications, Inc.

Swanson, C. R., Territo, L., & Robert, T. W. (2008). *Police Administration Structures, Processes, and Behavior.* Upper Saddle River, NJ: Pearson-Prentice Hall.

United States Department of Justice (n.d.). Retrieved from http://www.cops .usdoj.gov/Default.asp?Item=2790.

United States Department of Justice. (2003). *The National Crime Intelligence Sharing Plan.* (Award No. 2000-LD-BX-0003). Washington, DC.

White, M. B. (n.d.). Enhancing the Problem solving capacity of Crime Analysis Units. Retrieved from http://www.cops.usdoj.gov/Publications.

chapter nine

Corrections information technology

Corrections management systems encompass a wide variety of software systems necessary to manage institutional systems as well as community corrections.

List of definitions

CC—Community corrections
CMS—corrections management system
JMS—jail management system
PDA—personal digital assistant
Property and evidence tracking systems

Introduction

There are two major components to the correctional system in the United States: institutional incarceration and community corrections. There are three levels of (local) institutional incarceration, that is, county or city jails, state prisons, and federal penitentiaries. For the most part, the severity of the crime determines where an individual is placed in the correctional system. The type of law violated will determine if an individual is sentenced to a state penitentiary or a federal prison. If a person violates a federal law, they are tried in federal court and sentenced to either a federal penitentiary or federal probation.

Community corrections differ significantly from jails or penitentiaries. Community corrections encompass the management of individuals who committed a crime and either served time for that crime and was released early from prison or was never incarcerated and was sentenced to community corrections for supervision. This chapter discusses the various correctional information systems used in community corrections as well as in jails and prisons.

History of correction information technology

Corrections management systems (CMSs) had similar beginnings as that of law enforcement computer-aided dispatch systems and record management systems (RMSs). Most of the early systems were developed through funding provided by the Law Enforcement Assistance Administration (LEAA); however, there were early systems custom built by prison authorities. In either case, these early systems were mainframe based and migrated over time to microcomputer and client server technology. Most of the systems were written in COBOL and, like the hardware, migrated over time to today's modern software languages. As with other criminal justice systems discussed in this text, correctional systems evolved over time and have become sophisticated systems that correctional agencies rely upon to accomplish their required tasks.

Jail booking/intake systems

Regardless of the size of the correctional facility, all jails and prisons require the ability to capture basic information about a subject entering the facility. In the old manual systems, a police officer would complete a booking form that went with the prisoner to the long-term facility. Quite commonly, when an officer got to the jail with his or her prisoner, they would wait in line to bring the person before the booking officer. When the officer and the suspect were finally before the booking officer, the booking officer would ask the questions and complete a booking form. This could be a manual form, but as jail facilities began to be computerized, the booking officer would enter the information directly into the computer and print out the completed booking form to give to the arresting officer for his report.

Today, police agencies commonly use a jail booking system to capture information pertaining to an arrestee or detainee. Many police agencies across the country no longer support their own jail facilities. They rely upon the sheriff's jail facility to house their prisoners. In some instances, there is a regional facility that multiple police agencies use to house prisoners and detainees that they arrest. Agencies that use a regional facility to house their prisoners will often maintain their own booking/intake system, which is a module of their RMS. This booking/intake system usually interfaces to the sheriff's or regional jail facilities, booking, and jail management systems (JMSs). This interface will pass data to the long-term facility to help eliminate redundant data entry. In some instances, the officer completes the booking form from his or her laptop and uploads it to the regional facility, thus eliminating the need for the booking officer to enter the information. The booking officer then adds the information pertinent to the incarceration itself, e.g., medical screening, and other required profiles discussed in the following sections.

Jail booking/intake components

The jail booking/intake module typically requires the ability to capture information pertaining to the subject. This is usually basic information such as the following:

- Subject name
- Subject's alias
- Booking date and time
- Personal information and descriptors
- Address
- Next of kin
- Arrest information
- Inmate classification
- Gang affiliation
- Medical history
- Personal property
- Suicide attempts
- Employment
- Other information that a booking facility might require

There are several critical functions that the system must perform when data are entered into these fields. Figure 9.1 shows samples of the jail booking screens.

Some of the data elements are obvious and require only a simple entry. Other data elements trigger other actions by the jail booking module. The following sections describe the tasks performed when the jailer enters these key data elements.

Subject name

This is a fairly straightforward data element. This is where the jailer enters the name of the subject being booked. Names are typically broken down by first, middle, last, and suffix, the suffix being titles like junior, the II or III, etc. When the jailer enters the name, several tasks occur. The first is usually a search of the database to determine if this subject has ever been booked at this facility in the past. This name search is similar to that of a master name search in a RMS. It is Soundex based and provides a list of potential candidates, based on the name entered.

If the subject was previously booked, the personal data from his or her previous booking populate the new record. The jailer will update the information as appropriate and enter the information pertaining to the new booking.

The second task that occurs when the name is entered is a want and warrant check. This can be both a local check to determine if the person

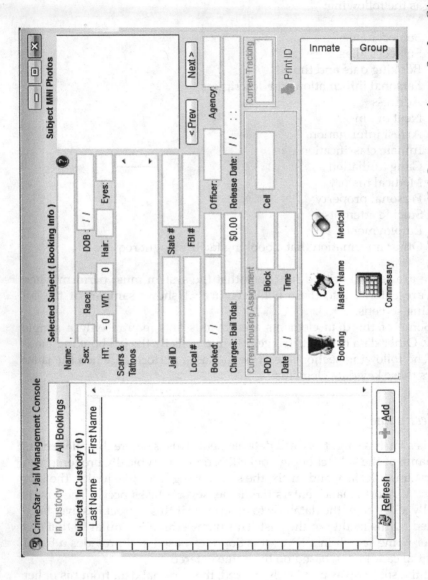

Figure 9.1 Sample jail intake/booking screen. (From Gagne, A., CrimeStar, Version 10.6, Computer software, San Jose, CA: CrimeStar Corporation, 2015.)

has any local wants and warrants as well as an external check, which checks both the state and the NCIC systems. The importance of this check is to ensure there are no other holds for this person in other areas of the criminal justice system.

Subject's alias

The booking system also captures the subject's aliases. This is a critical capability that is a must for all JMSs. Subjects commonly try to deceive jailers by providing an incorrect name at the time they are booked. They often repeatedly use the same alias, but there are many subjects that will use multiple aliases. The jail booking system has the capability of searching the database by an individual's alias and linking that alias to the person's real name. When there is an automated fingerprint identification system (AFIS) integrated with the jail booking system, the AFIS system assists in the positive identification of the subject. We discuss AFIS systems later in this chapter.

Personal information

When the jailer enters the personal information pertaining to the subject being booked, if the person was previously booked in that jail, the JMS compares the new information with that information already on file. Many JMSs will track this history. One data field in particular is date of birth. Subjects being booked often provide different dates of birth in an attempt to deceive the booking officer. Booking systems commonly provide a drop-down box that shows the previous dates of birth used by this individual.

Other fields provide historic information. As an example, people often change their hair both in styles as well as in color. People also gain and lose weight, grow and shave off facial hair, and obtain new tattoos. A good JMS will capture this information and store it as easily retrievable history.

As part of the personal information, the systems typically have the ability to produce an identification bracelet that includes a photograph of the subject as well as a bar code with all of the person's identifying information. These bracelets affix in a similar manner as those used in hospitals to identify patients, except they are made of hard plastic and not easily removed. With the bar code affixed to the bracelet, the inmate can use the bracelet in the commissary (discussed in the next section), the infirmary, the cafeteria, and for anything else the jail or prison deems appropriate.

Inmate classification

Before housing a subject, the jailer must classify the type of subject about to enter the corrections facility to determine if the inmate has any special needs. This classification looks at a variety of critical elements. Some of the classification questions typically found are as follows:

1. Does the subject have special medical needs?
2. Is the subject suicidal?
3. Is the subject affiliated with any gangs?
4. Is the subject violent?
5. Is the subject a repeat offender?
6. Is the subject an escape risk?
7. Is the subject notorious and require special confinement outside the general prison population?
8. Does the subject have known enemies?
9. Is the subject here long term or short term?
10. Other important information

Each of these questions when answered in the affirmative will spawn other functions from the system. Classification is most critical to housing of prisoners. A quality CMS will guide the end user through a series of questions and will also make recommendations based on the responses to these questions. The following two sections are examples.

Suicide attempts

Suicide-prone individuals require special attention in a jail facility. The JMS must capture information about any suicide attempted by the individual being booked. Any threats of suicide must be documented and taken seriously. If the person were previously booked into the jail, the system must notify the jailer of these attempts. This must be linked to the master name search. When the jailer enters the individual's name, it should provide an immediate suicide alert and store that information as a part of the booking record.

Gang affiliation

Gang affiliation is a critical function in a CMS. Gang members have a very different view of prison than most of us. Gang activities do not stop because the gang member was arrested. They continue their activities while in jail. In addition to identifying the individual as a gang member, it is important that gang members be separated from other rival gang members. As an example, the jailer would not want to house a member of the Bloods with a member of the Crypts. The JMS must be capable of identifying gang members by tattoos, clothing, and other identifying features, and when booking an individual, as information is added to the booking module, the system should alert the jailer that the individual being booked is or might be a member of one of the known gangs. Gang members will often openly admit to being a member of a gang. The gang component of the booking module must have the ability to capture the information about the gang to which the individual belongs. The booking system will often make a cell assignment recommendation. Before making that recommendation, the system must check to ensure that there are no gang conflicts.

Medical history

At the time of prisoner intake, the system must capture the subject's medical history. This includes all known medical and mental conditions. As part of the medical history, the system captures all medications the subject currently takes. Both the subject's medical history and the medications he or she is taking are important to ensure appropriate care is given while the subject is in custody. These systems also capture medical incidents that occur while the subject is incarcerated and they become part of the individual's permanent record. In the event he or she returns to the jail, that history is available to the jailer. The jailer can then update that information as required.

A quality CMS provides a series of user-definable medical questions as well as standardized questions pertaining to an inmate's medical condition. Certain responses to a particular question might spawn a series of additional questions. During intake, the response to certain questions might stop the booking process and require a medical doctor's approval before the inmate is taken into the facility. The JMS must record this information.

Personal property

As part of the booking or intake process, all of the person's personal property is confiscated. This requires that all property taken from the subject be inventoried and stored. The system captures the type of property, the quantity, and its storage location. Money and jewelry are typically important because inmates will often complain upon release from jail that they had a certain amount of money when they were booked into jail and that money was either missing or not the same amount when they were released. Modern jail/booking systems will not only capture the amount of money but also require the person's signature verifying the amount. This is also true of jewelry removed from the subject. Many systems provide the ability to photograph the property and attach the photo to the inmate's intake record. The personal property module also uses bar code systems to place a bar code label on the property to track it through the system. The system will capture where the property is stored and if moved where it was moved to and who moved the property.

When the person is released from jail, their property is returned at the time of release. The system requires the signature of the subject to verify that they received the property. If there is a dispute, the system allows the jailer to record the discrepancy for further follow-up. Like the intake process, many systems provide the ability to photograph the property and attach the photo to the inmate's release record. A common practice is to photograph the inmate receiving his or her property and attach the photograph to his or her record.

Corrections management information systems

Once the person is booked into jail, they move into the general population. The management of prisoners within a complex facility comes with many tasks that require the correctional officer to perform. Automating these tasks saves critical time and enhances the correction facilities capabilities to effectively manage large inmate populations that jails and prisons face in today's environment. CMSs are both decision support systems as well as record management keeping systems or data warehouses. CMSs typically include the following:

1. Inmate tracking
   a. Cell
   b. Movement
   c. Identification
   d. Disciplinary
   e. Visitor
   f. Phone
2. Medical tracking
   a. Doctors, dentists, and nurses
   b. Prescriptions/medication tracking
   c. Inmate billing
3. Accounting
   a. Inmate funds and agency billings
4. Commissary
   a. Inventory tracking
5. Scheduling
   a. Court
   b. Medical
   c. Work release
6. External interfaces
   a. State/NCIC
   b. Fingerprint
   c. Mug shot
   d. VINE
   e. Others

Although commercial corrections management software packages vary in their features and functionality, the previously mentioned modules are typical of most CMSs. Each of these modules is discussed in the following sections.

Inmate tracking

Inmate tracking requires the ability to manage an inmate and all that is associated with that individual. Tracking an inmate is complicated and requires several modules to ensure the appropriate management of the inmate. The following sections discuss the various modules typically found in a CMS used to track and management inmates.

Cell tracking

To begin the inmate tracking process, the cell to which the inmate is assigned must be captured. In addition to the cell block and the specific cell assigned, the system must track the cellmate and ensure that there are no reasons that the cellmates need to be separated. Previously, we discussed ensuring that natural enemies are kept separate, but there may be other reasons to ensure the separation of inmates. The cell tracking component of inmate tracking provides that capability. It is important to track all cells, past and current, that an inmate has occupied. Inmates move from cell to cell for a variety of reasons, e.g., solitary confinement and segregation (medical, high profile offender, etc.), and the system must track these movements and assist the housing management with these movements.

Movement tracking

Inmate tracking encompasses the ability to track inmates as they move about the institution. Biometrics and smart card technology are being used in CMSs today. This technology is playing an increasingly important role in correctional institutions as a means to address critical health, safety, and security issues (Seymour, Baker, and Besco, 2001). This technology is being used to track inmate movement 24 hours per day. With this technology, the inmate can be given a path they are to take when going from one location in the institute to another. The path is preloaded into the computer, and through the radio device attached to the inmate, the control officer or bridge, as it is sometimes referred to, can follow the inmate from departure to destination. GPS technology is also being used to accomplish the type of inmate tracking. The following depicts a typical facility map used to track inmates (InterAct Public Safety, n.d.).

Alerts are triggered and displayed to staff at the originated destination points when scheduled movements are not initiated or transit times are exceeded (Seymour et al., 2001).

Inmate identification

Another significant aspect of inmate tracking pertains to inmate identification. We have all read stories or have seen television reports where inmates were mistakenly released from jail or prison. These incidents are not only a major embarrassment to the involved agency but also dangerous, particularly if the inmate released is a violent offender. Many of the CMSs on the market today accommodate the ability to track and record the movements of an inmate. The most common, and perhaps simplest, are bar-coded wrist bands that include the inmate's photograph. The bar code contains important information about the inmate. The correction official can scan the bar code and display at his or her workstation all of the important information pertaining to the inmate, including the inmate's photograph.

Biometrics is becoming increasingly popular in identifying inmates. This technology is more precise and reduces the risk of misidentification. Biometrics provides a means of ensuring the person being released is whom the institution intends to release. In addition to prisoner release, there are other uses of biometrics within a correctional facility, such as movement from one location to another within the facility, ensuring visitors are who they say they are, training classes, and other similar personal identification requirements. The biometrics used in corrections is fingerprint readers or live scan devices that process fingerprint images. Hand geometry can be used to capture characteristics about an individual's hand that can be stored and later used to compare an image to the stored image.

Facial recognition is used frequently as a means of identifying individuals. Facial recognition uses a digital camera to capture a facial image. The digital image is analyzed and compared with the digital image on the smart card. Comparison points include the distance between the eyes and the nose and the location and shape of cheekbones. The digital image can be compared with other digital photographs for positive identification.

Iris recognition is another biometric CMSs are beginning to use. This technology uses a video camera to produce a digital image that is converted to a code. The code is encrypted and compared with a stored image.

Lastly, voice recognition measures the cadence, pitch, and tone of a specific phrase spoken by the subject and compares the results to encrypted data stored on the computer (Miles & Cohn, 2006). When one or more of these measures are used, the risk of releasing the wrong individual is substantially reduced.

Disciplinary tracking

Managing discipline is a critical task in a jail or prison environment. Inmates can reduce their sentence time with good behavior; likewise, they can increase their time or lose the good time they earn when they violate jail or prison rules. The system must track this information and keep accurate records in calculating good and bad time. In the past, correctional officers would issue citations for violation of jail or prison rules and regulations. These hand citations were tracked manually. The accurate tracking of this information created many problems. With the current CMSs, correctional officers use a personal digital assistant (PDA) to issue citations electronically. The electronic citation is uploaded through a Wi-Fi environment directly to the CMS. It eliminates delays and data entry and ensures accuracy. All disciplinary information is stored in the CMS. PDAs provide a great deal more information to the correctional officer. With the PDA, the correctional officer can obtain all of the information pertaining to an inmate, not just disciplinary information.

Visitor tracking

Tracking visitors is another important feature of a CMS. Visitors present challenges to the correctional facility. Visitors are the major source of introduction of drugs and weapons into the prison environment. Correctional facilities must screen visitors. Most facilities require that a potential visitor fills out an application. In a manual system, this is done manually, and the application goes into a file where someone reviews the application and then runs the subject for wants and warrants. It is not uncommon for visitors to have a want or a warrant and find themselves arrested when they come to visit an inmate. Likewise, the correctional facilities have been embarrassed to learn someone who was wanted was allowed to visit an inmate and not be detected. The automated system seeks to minimize this type of risk.

The inmate also has a right to reject visitors. When the inmate rejects the visitor, they are taken off of the approved visitor list or never added. A modern CMS has the ability to require the potential visitor to enter the information, either through accessing the system through the Internet or through a workstation provided at the jail or prison facility. Once the application is completed, the system automatically runs the potential visitor for wants or warrants or other criminal history information. The system must also link the visitor to the prisoner being visited. The supervisor has the ability to review the application and reject the individual.

Some facilities require visitors to submit to being fingerprinted. Obviously, this is controversial, and not all correctional facilities require fingerprint identification. At a minimum, the visitor will be run for wants and warrants. After the visitor is cleared, an identification badge or bar-coded wrist band is created by the system that includes the visitor's photograph, and in some systems, it includes the name of the inmate being visited. This prevents an unwanted visitor from using an approved visitor's identification. Each time the visitor comes to visit, the bar code is scanned, and another want and warrant check is performed to ensure the person is not wanted for a crime at the time they enter the facility to visit an inmate.

Searching visitors is a significant issue in today's prisons. Too often, weapons and drugs are smuggled into jails and prisons by visitors. Correctional facilities must ensure the safety of inmates and prison staff and to ensure persons entering prisons are not introducing these items. Prison and JMSs must track all incidents associated with visitors attempting to pass contraband to prisoners. Quality CMSs will track each incident and link it to the visitor, which can be used to prevent the visitor from returning to the prison.

The system must also capture information pertaining to the number of times the visitor visits a particular inmate. The system must capture the date of the visit, the time the visit began and ended, and the time the visitor left the facility. This information is stored in the inmate's file.

Prisoner phone logs

Another feature of modern CMSs is phone logs. Prisoners are often afforded time to make phone calls. This time is limited and has to be scheduled. The use of the phone is also a privilege; inmates often earn phone privileges based on good behavior. Modern CMSs track phone logs to determine whom prisoners are calling. They track the number called, the owner of the phone, the date called, the time called, and the length of the telephone conversation. This information is stored as part of the inmate record. Many of the correctional facilities today have digital phone systems specifically designed for prisons. These phones are interfaced to the CMS and pass this data to the CMS but are not typically a part of the main system. The numbers called can be used to develop contact trees showing the numbers called by the inmate and are often used in other investigations.

Medical tracking

Medical tracking is an important feature of a quality CMS. Medical tracking includes the management of all medical, dental, and psychiatric services provided to a prisoner. Most major jails and prisons throughout the country support sophisticated medical tracking. These facilities often contract with outside medical organizations for the more important services such as surgeries, but routine medical services and specialty services such as dialysis, HIV, orthopedic, and OB prenatal care for all pregnant inmates are usually available on site. Some locations have infirmaries that function as on-site hospitals. Figure 9.2a and b are examples of a dental and a medical facility, respectively, at the San Diego Jail facility.

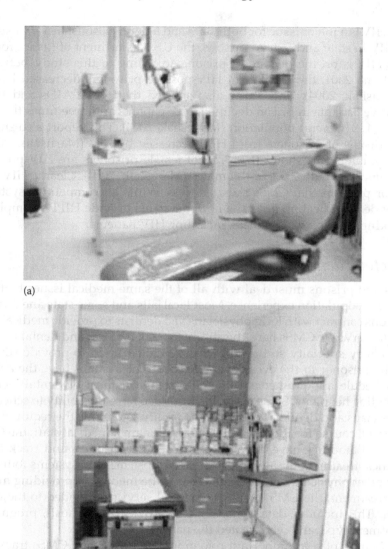

Figure 9.2 San Diego Jail (a) dental exam room and (b) medical exam room.

Medical management at a jail or prison facility is similar to that of any other medical office. CMSs provide complete medical history on all inmate patients. These systems track all diagnoses and treatments administered.

Many jail and prison systems contract with outside medical professionals as opposed to their being full-time employees. These systems track these persons, their qualifications, licensing, etc.

HIV is a major issue for both state and federal prisons. In a 2001 study of HIV in state and federal prisons, the U.S. Department of Justice found that HIV is on the decline in prison. According to this study, between 2000 and 2001, the number of HIV-positive prisoners decreased by 5% (Marushak, 2004). This study also showed that while AIDs and HIV-positive patients in prison declined, HIV patients are three times the rate of the U.S. general population (Marushak, 2004). This report also shows that deaths of prisoners from HIV decreased by 75% (Marushak, 2004). Lastly, the report shows that 3.2% of female prisoners are HIV positive as compared with 2.0% of the males (Marushak, 2004). Clearly, HIV is a major problem that CMSs must address. While all competitive systems provide a medical module, the newer systems provide HIPPA compliant tracking of all patient medical, including HIV patients.

Doctors, dentists, and nurses

Jails and prisons must deal with all of the same medical issues that the regular population experience. Most local jails and some state and federal prisons contract with local physicians and dentists to provide medical and dental services. CMSs have the ability to track medical and dental professionals by specialty so that they can be called upon to provide service to the prisoner in the event one is needed. The systems have the ability to schedule appointments with the external medical or dental facility, including hospitals. Some of the facilities also have the ability to schedule physicians and dentists to come to the facility to provide the required services. Of course for those facilities that maintain a medical staff, the CMS medical modules have the ability to schedule prisoners and track their medical treatment in the same fashion as those medical systems found in any other physician's office. Regardless of the method of providing medical treatment, the CMS tracks the medical services provided to the prisoner. This includes date, time, services provided, diagnosis, prognosis, treatment type, and who treated the patient.

Nurses play an important role in inmate healthcare. CMSs track the nurses in the same way that they do physicians and dentists. In most prisons, there are multiple nurses on staff, and they carry out many of the health services ordered by physicians. The CMSs track all treatments provided by the nurses.

Inmate medical billing

Not all prisoners are indigent; many do have health and dental insurance. Some prisons charge the inmate for medical and dental care. Modern CMSs have the ability to bill prisoners for their care. They also bill the prisoner's insurance carrier in the same way physician and dentist offices do. These systems have the ability to electronically bill the insurance carrier. They capture the diagnosis codes, procedure codes, and other pertinent medical billing data required by insurance companies in the same fashion that non-prison medical offices do.

Most prisons track the costs associated with prisoner medical care regardless of whether the prisoner has health insurance or not. Prison management software systems provide this capability. If prisoners are working, such as trustees, the prison may attempt to collect for the prisoner's medical treatment through earnings they receive from their outside employment.

Inmate accounting

When someone enters a corrections facility, a fund account is established, which allows inmates, relatives, or even friends to place funds in that account. The inmate may use that money for things like commissary purchases. These funds may also be used to pay bills outside the corrections system. Inmates commonly pay such obligations as restitution, support payments, and other similar obligations. Inmates may also work outside the prison through work furlough and work release programs. CMSs must be capable of tracking this information. Many jails and prisons charge inmates a percentage of these wages to offset the cost of their incarceration. All financial transactions must be tracked by the CMS.

Inmate accounting systems differ little from that of business accounting systems. They require general ledgers, accounts receivables, accounts payable, and payroll to track all of these transactions. The system tracks prisoner's income as well as expenses. Prisoners must also file income tax returns just the same as the rest of us, and these systems must be capable of generating and autofiling these returns on behalf of the prisoner. Inmates may also have outside obligations that they must address, e.g., restitution, child support payments, etc. The inmate accounting module tracks all of these obligations and provides accurate accounting of income and expenses associated with each inmate.

Commissary and food service management

All prisons have commissaries and, of course, food service, but not all commissaries and food service are managed by the prison. Prisons began to outsource commissary and food service functions to private sector firms several years ago. CMSs required either a module that manages these components or an interface to a third-party system that is providing these services. In this section, we focus on the requirements of the commissary and food service management module. Interfaces are handled separately.

As with food service, commissaries are being outsourced to private corporations for management. Often, the company managing food services also manage the commissary. There are still corrections facilities that operate and manage their commissary. CMSs provide commissary management modules. In the following section, we discuss the commissary management modules typically found in CMSs.

Commissary

All correctional facilities have commissaries where inmates can purchase a variety of products. Typically, these are toiletry items, books, stationary, food snack items, and other similar products. The commissary module provides several functions: a tracking system for commissary stock items, a privilege log to establish prisoner accounts, and a transaction log to maintain commissary stock and prisoner accounts as items are purchased (Cisco, n.d.), which are all part of the commissary module of the CMS.

Commissary inventory tracking subsystem

The commissary in any correctional facility functions as a store, with inventory items that require tracking. The commissary module functions similar to a point-of-sale system that would be used in any store. The system tracks purchases and subtracts each purchase from the in-stock total. A warning is posted in the transaction log when an item reaches an assigned reorder point. A warning will also post when an item is out of stock. A special feature is the restriction code—a code can be attached to each commissary item that, when matched by a restriction code in a prisoner privilege record, will post a warning in the transaction log when a prisoner tries to purchase the item (Cisco, n.d.).

Commissary privileges

In terms of the inmate, the use of the commissary is a privilege. The inmate often earns commissary privileges but can also lose those privileges. Prison officials must be able to manage commissary privileges as necessary. This requires the CMS commissary module to track prisoners by ID, name, and provide the ability to restrict inmate privileges.

Commissary transactions

The commissary module must track all purchases and adjust inventories and track commissary purchases by inmate. Inmates do not purchase items with cash but rather through their account. Funds are placed in their account that the inmate can use to make purchases. Most correctional facilities limit the amount that the inmate can spend as well as the number of any one item that the inmate may purchase. The commissary module must be able to address these transactions based on the conditions discussed previously. The system must track each purchase by prisoner ID, date of purchase, and starting and ending balances on the prisoner's account. Correctional facilities always limit the amount that an inmate may spend as well as the number of any one item that they can spend it on, e.g., cigarettes. The commissary module must be able to accommodate these requirements.

Sentence management

Sentence management modules are part of comprehensive CMSs. Sentence management encompasses a broad range of tasks. There are several components and subcomponents to a sentence management module. The following are the major components that we will discuss in the succeeding sections:

1. Sentence compliance
2. Inmate rehabilitation
3. Inmate reintegration

Quality prison management systems provide the ability to manage these three critical elements associated with sentence management. The following sections discuss these three elements of sentence management and how criminal justice information systems address each component.

Sentence compliance

When someone is sentenced to jail or prison, specific sentencing criteria are established either by the judge invoking the sentence or, in many instances, the law specifies sentencing conditions. As an example, a judge may sentence a subject to a set number of years in prison but may also stipulate a minimum amount of time the person must spend in prison before he or she is eligible for parole. In addition, an inmate may earn time off of his or her sentence for good behavior, specialized programs, or other reasons. An inmate may also earn additional time on his or her sentence for events that occur in the prison, or for other crimes. A CMS must capture this information and diligently track compliance with each requirement.

Systems that provide user flexibility are preferred. User flexible systems allow correctional facilities to tailor the sentence compliance fields based on code tables. Sentence compliance issues change over time. If those changes impact a specific data field, the agency can make the necessary adjustment through the code table without requiring changes to the software code itself.

Although an inmate is confined, they can often obtain sentence time reduction through several different ways. Of course, there is the proverbial time off for good behavior, whereby an inmate that complies with everything required of him can earn a reduction in required confinement time. Sentences can be reduced by the courts through appeals or they can be commuted. Sentences are often reduced as a result of prison overcrowding that is quite prevalent in today's corrections environment. The CMS must be capable of tracking the amount of time an inmate earns toward release and the various types of time as just described. Likewise, an inmate can also receive additional time for a variety of reasons, including violation of prison rules or regulations. Prisoners can also earn more time as a result of additional sentences the might receive related to other charges. The CMS must be capable of tracking this time as well.

Quality corrections management software is capable of tracking sentence compliance. It tracks these various conditions that can either add or subtract time from an inmate's required time. Another key component to sentence compliance is to track the various holds that might be placed on an inmate. There is nothing more embarrassing to a corrections facility than to release an inmate who is wanted in another jurisdiction. It is not uncommon for an inmate to be required to serve one or more sentences in one jurisdiction and then be transferred to another facility in another jurisdiction where he or she will be required to serve another sentence. Today's CMSs track these holds to ensure the inmate is not inappropriately released.

Inmate rehabilitation training

Many prisons throughout the country provide rehabilitation training to inmates in an effort to help the inmate develop the necessary skills to find gainful employment once they leave prison. On June 30, 2006, 2,245,189 prisoners were held in federal or state prisons or in local jails (Office of Justice Programs, 2007). These prisoners will be released after serving less than 50% of their sentences according to the U.S. Department of Justice (Office of Justice Programs, 2007). Providing these inmates with the necessary skills for them to make a living is important if we are going to reduce recidivism.

To manage rehabilitation, training requires software that is capable of tracking the courses, the faculty, or trainers that are capable of providing this training as well as tracking the necessary information pertaining to the inmate. CMSs provide the ability to capture the information pertaining to each specific course, the prerequisites required of the inmate to take the course, and the courses required to provide the inmate with certain certificates of completion for the training that they received. As an example, many corrections facilities provide the inmates with the ability to earn their general education degree (GED). To prepare the inmate for this test, there are a series of courses that are taught. The CMS must capture all pertinent information pertaining to these courses, including the instructor who taught the course. It must capture the inmate's information, including any test scores associated with the course. This information needs to be stored and recallable as necessary.

The rehabilitation training module needs to capture all pertinent information pertaining to the instructors. For certain courses, the instructors must maintain specific qualifications. As an example, instructors that teach first aid and CPR must maintain instructor qualifications, which fall due on a periodic basis. A quality rehabilitation training module will notify the training manager when instructors require renewal of these qualifications.

Inmate release and reintegration

The CMS must be able to track the release of an inmate. Releasing an inmate requires the capture of critical information as well as accessing external systems to ensure the inmate being released does not have any holds or is wanted by another jurisdiction. As the inmate is processed out, he or she is run for additional wants and warrants or holds. The inmate's property is returned to the inmate. Most CMSs will allow for the facility to capture a photograph of the inmate at the time he or she is released. These photos will include the property that is being returned to the inmate to neutralize claims by inmates that they did not receive all of their property that they came in with.

The system must capture the date and time of the prisoner's release and who they were released to, if anyone. Often when inmates are released, they are provided with clothing, travel arrangements, e.g., tickets to a specific location, and a limited amount of cash. The system must track this information. The released inmate may also be required to report to a parole facility. The system must capture both the specific parole facility and parole officer and the pertinent information that the inmate will need to contact the parole agency. If the inmate is a sex offender, the police agency in the community in which the sex offender will reside must be notified. The system should be able to forward the required information to the appropriate police department. All of this information needs to be captured by the CMS.

Victim information and victim notification

To be in compliance with federal laws pertaining to victim's rights, victims must be notified whenever a prisoner is up for a parole hearing or whenever the prisoner is going to be released. Modern CMSs must track these hearings and generate the necessary victim notification to the victims. These modules must comply with the federal mandate to track an inmate's victims and notify them of the prisoner's activity such as court appearances, being released, or being executed (Cisco, n.d.).

This module must link each of the inmate's victims to the inmate so that the system can track these victims and provide the appropriate notifications. Inmates often have multiple victims, which may also span multiple crimes. As an example, a rapist might have victims throughout multiple states or multiple cities throughout the United States. The system must be able to track these victims. Figure 9.3 is an example of inmate–victim relationship tracking.

One of the issues that hinders the tracking of the victims is that victims often do not notify officials when they move or change phone numbers or e-mail addresses. To aid corrections officials, the system must track the victim's name, address, telephone, e-mail address, work place name, work place address, and work place phone. In addition to this basic information pertaining to the victim, to track and maintain contact with the victim, the system must be able to also track at least three friends or relatives of the victim. The purpose is to be able to locate the victim in the event the victim fails to notify authorities of their change in address. The system should capture the friend or relative's name, address, telephone number, and e-mail address.

Schedule management

Inmates are scheduled for a variety of things such as parole hearings, court hearings, trials, doctor's appointments, work release, and other activities that require tracking. The CMS must be able to capture this information and provide the necessary information on an individual inmate level.

Court scheduling

Regardless of the type of correctional facility, inmates are often required to make court appearances. These court appearances can be for any variety of reasons—arraignments, pretrial hearings, trials, posttrial sentencing hearings, appeals, and other court requirements. In today's modern jails and prisons, many of these activities occur via video conferencing, and the inmate never has to leave the facility. This does not negate the need for the CMS to be able to schedule these events. The system must be able to capture the inmate ID, date and time of the hearing, type of hearing, location of the hearing, attorney's name(s), attorney's address, attorney's phone number, attorney's e-mail, court and courtroom, case number, court results, and comments. These are the minimum system requirements to manage inmates and the court process. This information needs to be maintained as part of the inmate's file.

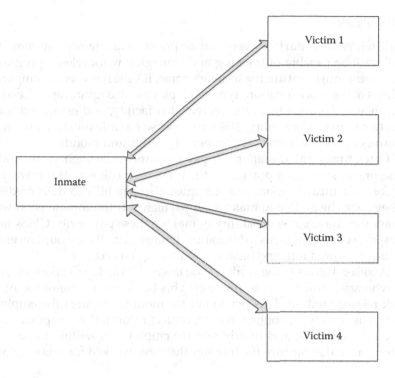

Figure 9.3 Inmate–victim relationship.

Medical and dental scheduling

As discussed previously, medical treatment of inmates occurs in all correctional facilities. This is being complicated today because of the length of prison terms; corrections are experiencing significant increases in geriatric patients as well as all others. Many prisons maintain medical facilities at the correctional institution. Others, particularly county and city jails, outsource medical treatment to local physicians and dentists. As with any patient, follow-up visits are often required. To accommodate this requirement, the CMS must be capable of scheduling for inmates medical and dental appointments. This module should be linked to the medical modules discussed earlier. The module must include the inmate's name and ID number, the physician to be seen, the physician's address, the physician's phone, the physician's e-mail, the date and time of the appointment, the location of the appointment, the security required, the correctional officers assigned, the associated incidents, and the next appointment information (if any). The system must be linked to the medical system for treatment tracking.

Work release

Work release is a part of every jail or prison management system. The CMS must be capable of tracking and managing work release programs. The system must capture the inmate's name, ID, the name of the employer, address of the work location, type of employment, beginning and ending work hours, distance from the correctional facility, and estimated travel time to and from the facility. The work release module must also track the amount of time the inmate works per day, week, and month.

Often times, the inmate must pay reparations for their crime and in some prison systems a portion of the inmate's income goes toward paying for their incarceration. Inmates must also pay bills to their creditors if they have the ability to make such payments. If the inmate is on work release they have some capability of making these payments. CMSs must be capable of tracking this information. It must track the amount received, the amounts paid out, and balances remaining on account.

Another feature of the work release module is tracking various employers who are willing to hire inmates. This becomes a submodule of the work release module. This portion of the module captures the employer name, business type, contact person, contact information, employee type the employer seeks, and hourly rate the employer is willing to pay. The system must also capture the inmates that have worked for this employer.

Community CMS

Few would disagree that our prison system throughout the United States has been under a great deal of stress over the past two to three decades. Our "get tough on crime" approach has resulted in longer crime sentences and mandatory jail sentences that have caused significant prison overcrowding. Overcrowding is ramped and recidivism continues to run high. Many believe that most prisons, county, state, and federal, are nothing more than warehouses of criminals. This has turned our prisons into institutions of punishment as opposed to rehabilitation and reintegration institutions. The reality is that many of these people will be released from prison and will become the responsibility of community corrections.

In today's criminal justice environment, community corrections encompass what was traditionally referred to as probation and parole. Although community corrections is the new term, the roles of probation and parole still exist as they did in the past and not all jurisdictions have adopted the encompassing term of community corrections. As we proceed in defining the information technology requirements of community corrections, we will define the traditional roles as probation or a parole function.

Presentencing investigation

A traditional role of probation is presentencing investigation. Presentencing investigations occur after a person has been found or pled guilty to a crime. Before sentencing, the judge will request a probation report with sentencing recommendations. These investigations encompass several critical elements. They include mental health assessments, criminal history assessments, personal and demographic information, family histories, work history, other cases pending, special needs, etc. (Loryxsystems, n.d.). Risk assessment is a critical issue in determining a person's suitability for a community corrections program. The presentencing module must capture all of this information and allow the data to be analyzed and provide risk assessment information to be used in reporting to the court.

Case management

Case management is the core of community corrections. A CMS must be capable of providing a case management module that will track a person who is on probation or parole. A case management module would include the following submodules:

- Master name index
- Case file

Master name index

The case management module requires an integrated master name index that captures specific information pertaining to the person being supervised. This is similar to the MNI found in the CMS or a law enforcement RMS. It captures the specific information pertaining to the subject as well as that person's involvements in the criminal justice system. This system should allow the user to search on a person's name using Soundex to see all of his or her involvements. From the MNI, the user can move to view a specific individual and all data associated with him/her.

If the community corrections system is linked to another justice system, e.g., corrections system and police RMS, a single master name index should be used. In essence, it should be linked to the enterprise system as opposed to maintaining a duplicate MNI.

Case file

The community corrections system must provide the ability to maintain case files on all parolees or probationers. This is a comprehensive file that captures each case and includes victim information, witnesses, investigation reports, property information, court information, attorneys associated with the case, and information pertaining to the subject. A case file is maintained on each person supervised in community corrections.

Jail and prison management external systems interface requirements

Jail and prison management systems require interfaces to several external systems. Typically, jails and prisons require the ability to access state and national criminal history databases. In addition to state and federal databases, these systems also require access to court systems, probation, and parole systems as well as many other databases outside of the criminal justice system. As an example, many prison management systems require access to medical insurance databases, or access to social welfare systems.

The precise external interfaces will vary significantly from correctional facility to correctional facility. There is no set number or type of interfaces that might be required. The key in a modern CMS is the ability to exchange data. This is why it is critical that CMSs follow NIEM standards for data exchange.

Integration with AFISs and mug shot systems

Typically, jail and prison management systems are integrated with AFISs. AFIS systems are large, complex systems that are costly to implement and maintain and are not as effective when implemented in a single agency. Single agencies or small jurisdictions do not have the benefit of drawing from other agencies in the surrounding areas. AFIS systems are far more effective when implemented on a regional basis. AFIS systems typically are installed in large counties or in multicounty jurisdictions. This provides a much larger database and the cost to implement and maintain a regional database is more equitably shared.

Before the development of AFIS technology, police and sheriff's departments manually captured fingerprints from people arrested for crimes. This information was capture through the use of a special ink that would be rolled onto a glass platform. The booking officer would roll the arrestee's fingers through the ink and then roll them onto a form, provided by the FBI. Typically, they would roll prints onto three fingerprint cards. One card was sent to the FBI, one was often sent to the state, and the third was retained by the agency. Utilizing the Henry fingerprint classification system, fingerprints were classified and stored according to their classification. State agencies also received the fingerprints and stored them in their files as did the agency collecting the initial prints. When a crime occurred where fingerprints were lifted from the crime scene, which are often partial prints, the captured prints would be sent to the FBI to try and obtain a match. State and local agencies that maintained fingerprints might also attempt to match those prints. Because of the number of crimes that occur, it was not feasible to manually search fingerprint cards for every crime; in fact, the FBI would only search their files for a major crime, e.g., homicide, a significant robbery, rapes, etc. In reality, fingerprints did little good to solve the majority of crime, but citizen expectations were often very high about the effectiveness to solving crime through fingerprint identification. Often citizens would become upset with police officers because the officer would not take fingerprints at a typical residential burglary. Officers knew that it would be futile to do so.

The development of AFIS technology enhanced fingerprint technology and its usefulness to criminal justice agencies. Fingerprints could be processed in an automated fashion, which significantly enhanced the ability to rapidly identify the fingerprints and link them to the person to whom they belonged.

References

Cisco (n.d.). Jail Management Software (JAMS) [Computer Software]. Available from http://www.cisco-ps.com/jams/.

Gagne, A. (2015). CrimeStar Inc. (Version 10.6) [Computer Software]. San Jose, CA: CrimeStar Corporation.

InterAct Public Safety (n.d.). Jailtracker Software. Available from http://www.jailtracker.com/software_detail/software_details01.html#Anchor2.

Loryxsystems (n.d.). Presentencing Investigations. Available from http://www.loryxsystems.com/solutions/probation_parole.html.

Maruschak, L.M. (2004). HIV in prisons, 2001. Bureau of Justice Statistics. NCJ-202293. Available from http://www.ojp.usdoj.gov/bjs/.

Miles, C. A., & Cohn, J. P. (2006, January). Tracking prisoners in jail with biometrics: An experiment in a navy brig. *NIJ Journal, 253.*

Office of Justice Programs (2007, June). Largest increase in prison and jail inmate populations since midyear 2000. Available from http://ojp.gov.

Seymour, S., Baker, R., & Besco, M. (2001, July). Inmate tracking with biometric and smart card technology. *Corrections Today, 63,* (4).

chapter ten

Prosecutor information management systems

Like all criminal justice information systems, prosecutorial systems share data with other justice agencies.

List of definitions

LEAA—Law Enforcement Assistance Administration
MNI—master name index
POSSE—Police Operations Support System Elementary
PROMIS—prosecutor management information system

Prosecutorial system

Prosecutor offices, like all components of the criminal justice system, generate an enormous amount of data. For many years, these data existed in paper files, which was extremely cumbersome to handle and difficult to access. The advent of computer technology has allowed prosecutors to store and retrieve this needed information. Like all criminal justice information systems, prosecutorial systems are part of the need to share data across justice agencies. In this chapter, we explore the history of these systems, the evolution of their use today, and what the future holds for prosecutorial information systems.

History of prosecutorial systems

Prosecutorial software came into being in the early 1970s. With the cost of computer technology coming down, it became affordable to implement prosecutorial information management systems for most prosecutorial agencies throughout the United States. The development of the first Prosecutorial System occurred through funding provided by the Law Enforcement Assistance Administration (LEAA), now the Bureau of Justice Assistance (BJA). Inslaw, a nonprofit Washington, DC, firm at that time built this system and named it prosecutor management information system (PROMIS). The federal government funded PROMIS, which

233

consisted of a series of modules intended to track prosecutorial workload and to manage the processes performed in a prosecutor's office. Like the police operations support system elementary (POSSE) and other systems of that time, PROMIS was a pioneering new ground for prosecutor offices. From the original PROMIS system, other prosecutorial management systems have evolved. In this chapter, we discuss the various modules that are typically a part of a prosecutorial information system.

Prosecutor record management information system overview

Most integrated prosecutorial systems perform a combination of functions and tasks required to accommodate the processing and storage of data. Much like their police record management system counterparts discussed previously, prosecutor systems consist of several core modules. Good prosecutorial systems typically consist of the following modules:

- Case manager
- Master name index
- Victim/witness
- Master calendaring
- Attorney assignment
- Property and evidence tracking
- Document management
- Juror tracking
- Discovery
- Worthless checks
- Restitution tracking
- Child support
- Reports
- Integration with other criminal justice agencies (police, courts, corrections, etc.)

In the following subsections, we discuss each of these modules that are typically found in a good prosecutor's management information system.

Case manager

The case manager is the primary module that captures information pertaining to a case. This information comes from the initial crime and arrest report. The police department sends the report over to the prosecutor's office by the police department or other law enforcement agency attempting to file charges on an individual. The information can be entered from the arrest report, or it can be electronically sent to the prosecutor's system from the law enforcement record management system. Figure 10.1 depicts a typical screen that captures data by a prosecutor's case management module.

The case information screen is the heart of the criminal case management options of this program. Adding, updating, and searching new screens occur through this screen. To set up a new case, the end user pushes the "Add Case" button and enters the data as prompted on the screen (Microfirm Software Corporation, 2012). The information captured in the case manager screen contains the information pertaining to the case, the defendant(s) involved, the police department filing the case, the grand jury information, if applicable, and other basic information about the case.

Master name index

Like the master name index (MNI) typically found in a police record management system, a prosecutor's system has a similar MNI. Contained within the MNI are the names of defendants, witnesses, jury members, and anyone else that might be associated with a case. The MNI provides a listing of all of a person's involvements in a case or multiple cases. Searching of last names occurs through Soundex search routines. More sophisticated systems use specialized name search routines that are capable of handling Hispanic surnames, e.g., Jose Hernandez-Gonzales, where the hyphenated names are interchanged. Typically, when entering a last name, the system will provide a list of potential names, as displayed in Figure 10.2.

The user can click on the name, and the system will then open the case displaying all of the information pertaining to that individual and the associated case. The matching list search is a good tool for searching for all past histories of a given defendant. It will retrieve a person's previous involvements and case numbers for review. With a well-written system, the user can call up additional information and screens associated with the case, as shown in Figure 10.3.

Victim and witness tracking

The tracking of victims and witnesses is critical to a prosecutor. The loss of a case occurs because prosecutors were unable to locate the victims or witnesses by the time of trial. All modern-day prosecutor systems must be able to track victims and witnesses through the MNI. The "Victim and Witness Information Screen" keeps track of the victims associated with the case. The MNI screen lists the general information relating to the victim or witness of a case. The victim and witness information manager

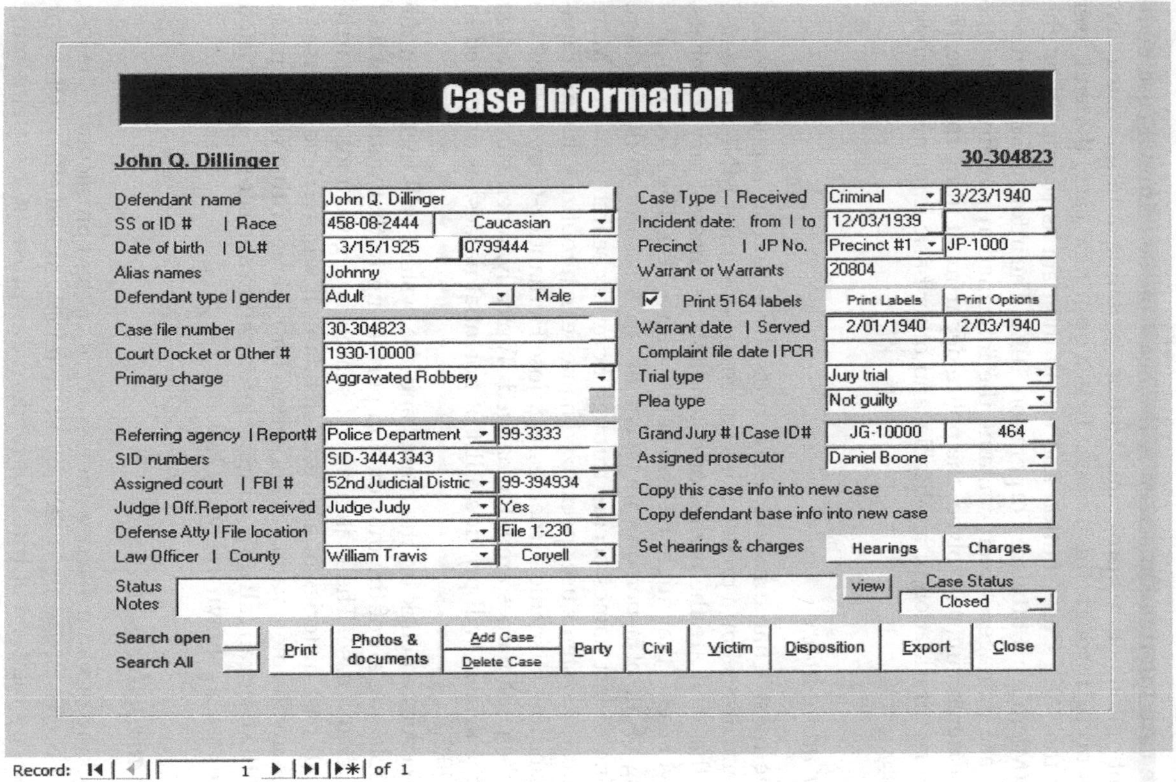

Figure 10.1 Case manager. (From Microfirm Software Corporation, Microfirm, Version 6, Computer software, Carrollton, TX: Microfirm Corporation, 2015.)

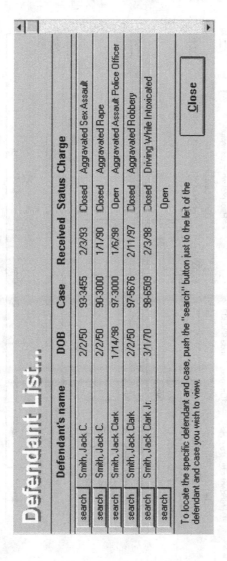

Figure 10.2 Master name search defendant list. (From Microfirm Software Corporation, Microfirm, Version 6, Computer software, Carrollton, TX: Microfirm Corporation, 2015.)

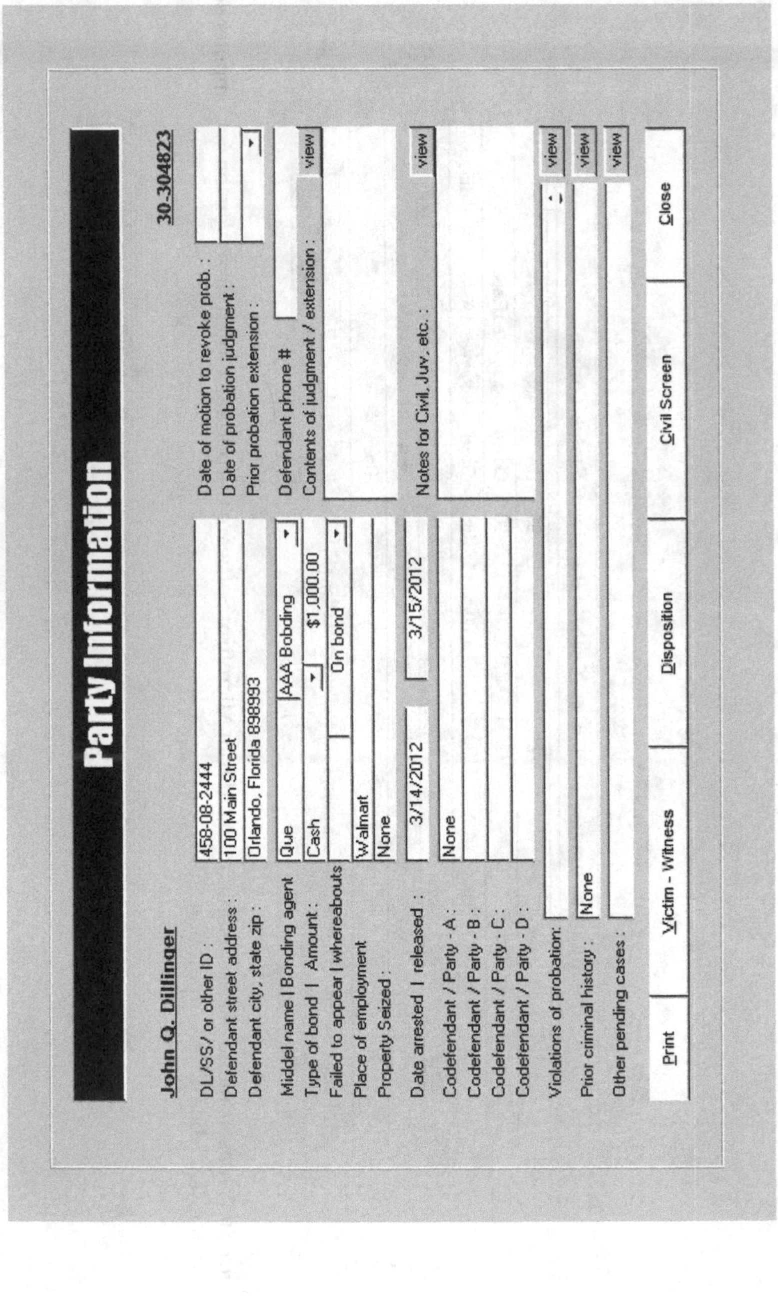

Party Information

John Q. Dillinger   30.304823

DL/SS/ or other ID : 458-08-2444
Defendant street address : 100 Main Street
Defendant city, state zip : Orlando, Florida 898993

Middel name | Bonding agent : Que | AAA Bobding
Type of bond | Amount : Cash | $1,000.00
Failed to appear | whereabouts : On bond
Place of employment : Walmart
Property Seized : None

Date arrested | released : 3/14/2012 | 3/15/2012

Codefendant / Party - A : None
Codefendant / Party - B :
Codefendant / Party - C :
Codefendant / Party - D :

Violations of probation:
Prior criminal history : None
Other pending cases :

Date of motion to revoke prob. :
Date of probation judgment :
Prior probation extension :

Defendant phone # :
Contents of judgment / extension :   view

Notes for Civil. Juv. etc. :   view

view
view
view

Print | Victim - Witness | Disposition | Civil Screen | Close

Figure 10.3 Party information. (From Microfirm Software Corporation, Microfirm, Version 6, Computer software, Carrollton, TX: Microfirm Corporation, 2015.)

contains additional case information such as address, phone numbers, and services provided by the victim. The case ID number links the victim's information on this screen and the victim and witness information manager together. The following is a victim/witness screen that captures critical information pertaining to the victim or witness. As described previously, a master name search will identify victims and witnesses. Figure 10.4 depicts a victim–witness tracking system.

Analysis and disposition

Maintaining the analysis and disposition of cases is critical to most prosecutor offices. Good prosecutor systems will track this information on a case-by-case basis. The system tabulates this information to determine statistics that are vital to analyzing productivity. The information can also prove helpful to the prosecutor should the defendant be involved in other or future cases. In the system represented in this book, the analysis and disposition screen is where the user keeps notes about the disposition and analysis of the case. In most systems, this area is unlimited in the amount of space the user has to write and keep notes on a case. Some systems link this to a word processor for unlimited text entry. In this model system, this screen allows access to the multiple offenses and plea offer screens. Figure 10.5 depicts the analysis and disposition screen.

Master calendaring

Prosecutor offices typically maintain a master calendar that keeps track of all activities. This includes meetings as well as all court hearings, such as arraignments and trials. In most systems, the individual attorney can keep track of his or her personal schedule, which also updates the master calendar. It lists all appointments and hearings in order by date and time. In some systems, the user may view a graphical calendar as a reference to the calendar. Vertical and horizontal bars allow people to increase their viewing ability of the data. When printing the master calendar, it will automatically print a graphical representation of the calendar, which was last viewed on the appointment scheduler.

The master calendar includes all individual appointments and all hearing/trial dates between any two dates. Figure 10.6 depicts a typical master calendar.

Many prosecuting attorney offices maintain their calendars through a third-party package like Microsoft Office. The record management system passes information to programs like Microsoft Outlook to keep calendars for each deputy prosecutor as well as the office as a whole. This is an effective tool for all calendaring needs.

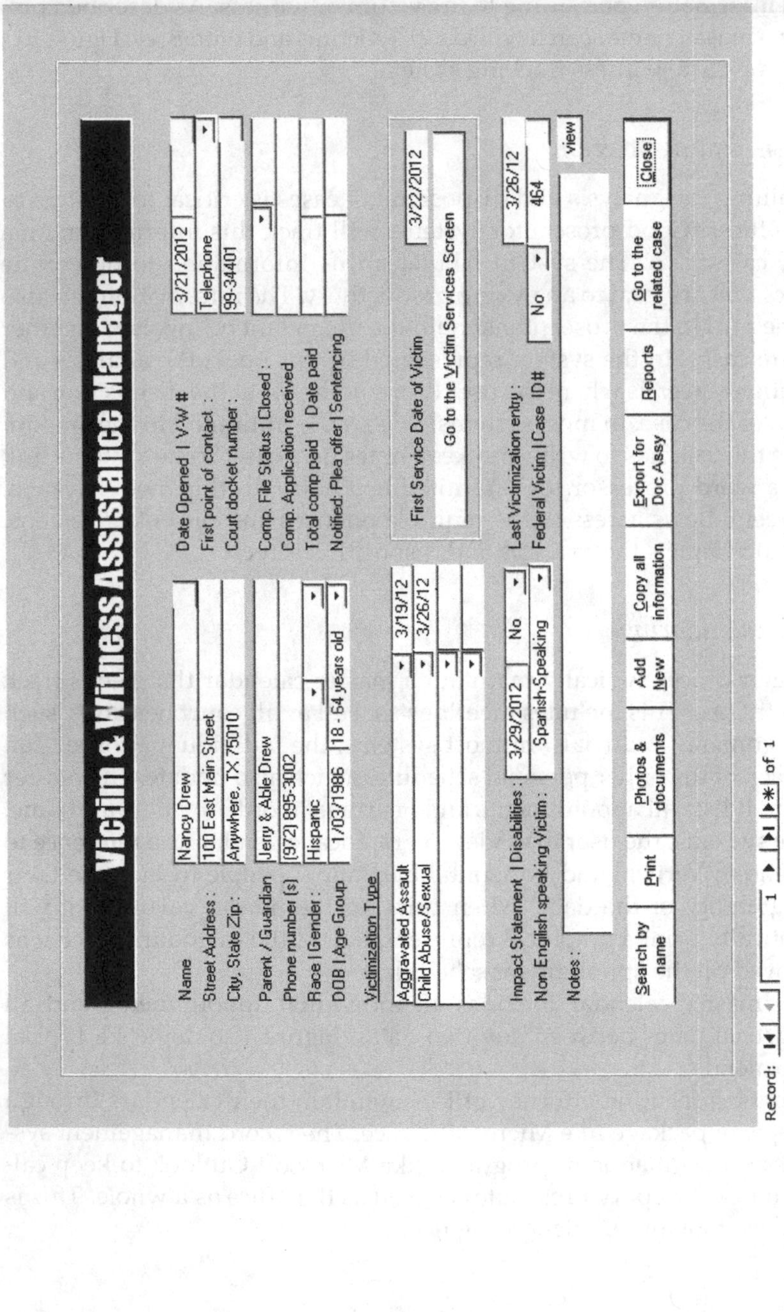

Victim & Witness Assistance Manager

Name	Nancy Drew
Street Address :	100 East Main Street
City, State Zip :	Anywhere, TX 75010
Parent / Guardian	Jerry & Able Drew
Phone number (s)	(972) 895-3002
Race I Gender :	Hispanic
DOB I Age Group	1 /03/1986	18 - 54 years old

Date Opened I V-W # — 3/21/2012
First point of contact : — Telephone
Court docket number : — 99-34401
Comp. File Status I Closed :
Comp. Application received
Total comp paid I Date paid
Notified : Plea offer I Sentencing

First Service Date of Victim — 3/22/2012
Go to the Victim Services Screen

Victimization Type

Aggravated Assault	3/19/12
Child Abuse/Sexual	3/26/12

Impact Statement I Disabilities : 3/29/2012 No
Non English speaking Victim : Spanish-Speaking
Notes :

Last Victimization entry:
Federal Victim I Case ID# — 3/26/12
No — 464 — view

Search by name | Print | Photos & documents | Add New | Copy all information | Export for Doc Assy | Reports | Go to the related case | Close

Record: 1 of 1

Figure 10.4 Victim–witness tracking screen. (From Microfirm Software Corporation, Microfirm, Version 6, Computer software, Carrollton, TX: Microfirm Corporation, 2015.)

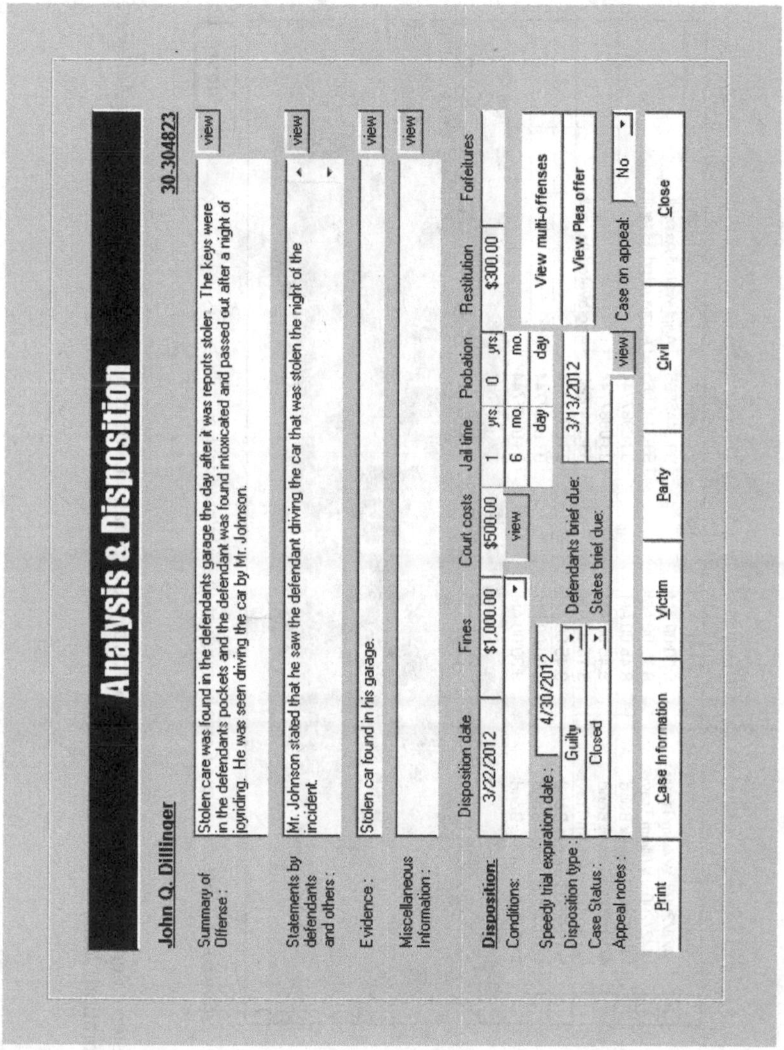

Analysis & Disposition

John Q. Dillinger   30.304823

Summary of Offense :	Stolen care was found in the defendants garage the day after it was reports stolen. The keys were in the defendant's pockets and the defendant was found intoxicated and passed out after a night of joyriding. He was seen driving the car by Mr. Johnson.	view
Statements by defendants and others :	Mr. Johnson stated that he saw the defendant driving the car that was stolen the night of the incident.	view
Evidence :	Stolen car found in his garage.	view
Miscellaneous Information :		view

	Disposition date	Fines	Court costs	Jail time	Probation	Restitution	Forfeitures
Disposition:	3/22/2012	$1,000.00	$500.00	1 yrs.	0 yrs.	$300.00	
Conditions:			view	6 mo.	mo.		
				day	day	View multi-offenses	

Speedy trial expiration date : 4/30/2012   Defendants brief due: 3/13/2012

Disposition type :   Guilty   States brief due: View Plea offer

Case Status :   Closed

Appeal notes :   view   Case on appeal: No

Print   Case Information   Victim   Party   Civil   Close

Figure 10.5 Analysis and disposition screen. (From Microfirm Software Corporation, Microfirm, Version 6, Computer software, Carrollton, TX: Microfirm Corporation, 2015.)

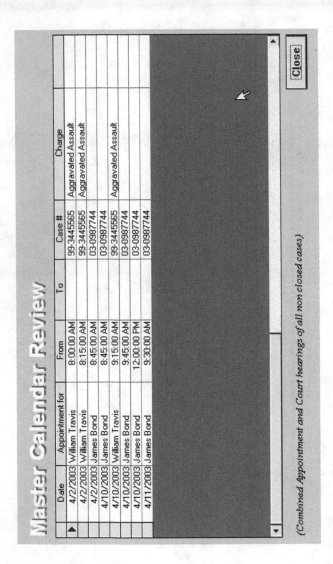

Figure 10.6 Master calendar. (From Microfirm Software Corporation, Microfirm, Version 6, Computer software, Carrollton, TX: Microfirm Corporation, 2015.)

Attorney assignment

In most prosecutor offices, and particularly in large offices, it is necessary to maintain attorney case assignments. In most county prosecutor offices, the distribution of workload occurs based on a function such as case filings, misdemeanor cases, and felony cases. A good prosecutorial system will provide for the assignment of workload based on area of responsibility. It will track the cases assigned to each deputy prosecutor. Supervising attorneys can track the progress of cases assigned to each deputy prosecutor and balance workload among the deputy prosecutors. They can also track the outcome of the cases assigned.

Closely related is the plea or settlement offer. Plea bargaining is a prime function within any prosecutor's office. A good prosecutor system will track all of the associated critical information. The system also tracks the conditions of the plea offer and who made the offer. It also tracks the offer date, offer deadline, fines, court costs, jail time, probation, restitution, and forfeitures. Figure 10.7 depicts a typical offer screen.

Property and evidence tracking

For the most part, the maintenance of property and evidence associated with a case is in the property and evidence room within a police department. Chain of custody is critical to a case. The defendant can claim evidence tampering upon breakage of the chain of custody. This was a critical issue during the famous O. J. Simpson trial for the murder of Nicole Simpson. Evidence needs to be tightly controlled. When the prosecutor obtains evidence to bring to trial, they must be able to show that the evidence has gone from the police department's evidence room to their custody and that it was never out of their control. This includes all evidence that comes into their control, including documents and photographs. If the evidence requires laboratory work, the prosecutor will order the evidence be taken to the lab by the police and not go through the prosecutor's office. On the other hand, police often pass documents and photographs directly to the prosecutor. These are items of evidence just like blood samples, DNA evidence, or any other piece of evidence. A good prosecutor's system will provide a means of tracking evidence. Figure 10.8 depicts a system that captures this tracking.

Document management

Linking documents to a case is crucial because the prosecutor's office does not generate all documents associated with a case office. The initial case report itself typically comes from a law enforcement agency. There are many other documents that the prosecutor's office receives that originated outside the system. As an example, a laboratory report on a piece of

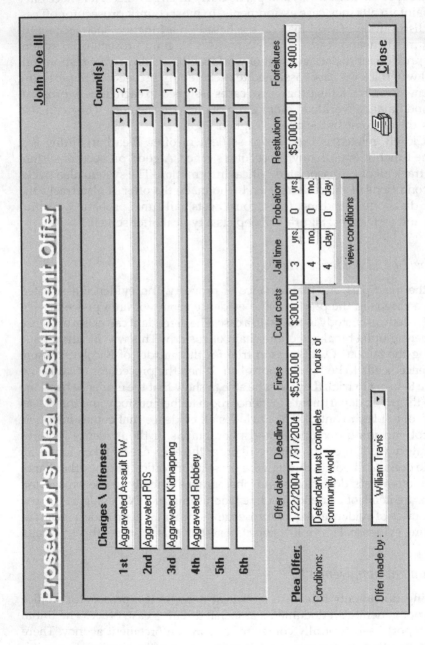

Figure 10.7 Settlement/plea offer screen. (From Microfirm Software Corporation, Microfirm, Version 6, Computer software, Carrollton, TX: Microfirm Corporation, 2015.)

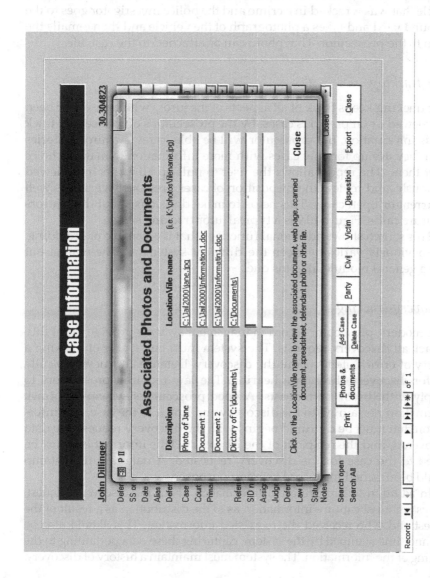

Figure 10.8 Document and photo tracking. (From Microfirm Software Corporation, Microfirm, Version 6, Computer software, Carrollton, TX: Microfirm Corporation, 2015.)

evidence will often come in as a written report. The prosecutor can scan that report and link it to a case so that when someone accesses that case, the laboratory report is a part of the case file. Photos can be obtained in the same fashion. As an example, the prosecutor requests a photo of a vehicle that was wrecked in a crime and the police investigator goes to the impound yard and takes a photograph of the vehicle and then e-mails the photo to the prosecutor. That photo can be attached to the case file.

Juror tracking

Juror tracking keeps track of all aspects of the jurors who have either been interviewed or on previous cases. By the prosecutor's office keeping track of this information, the prosecutor will be able to review juror histories when they are up for new cases with more information to make a choice about them. The report allows the user to pull up all jurors interviewed previously, and review the disposition of cases previously closed as well as current or open cases. This helps to make decisions about these jurors on future cases. Figure 10.9 is a typical juror tracking screen.

This screen shows additional functions that it is capable of providing. This obviously varies between the different systems on the market but have a general module like this one.

Discovery tracking

Most modern prosecutor record management systems provide the ability to track all discovery requests. The system must be capable of tracking a variety of critical items about the discovery. Defense attorneys typically call for discovery through a hearing. The law required prosecutors to comply with discovery requests. A good prosecutor's system will track information pertaining to the discovery and link it to the case. The information that must be captured begins with the discovery request, the data discovered, and the recipient of the discovery. This information must be linked to the case for the discovery requested. A date and time stamp should be attached for record keeping purposes.

In addition to capturing the information about the discovery request, the system must capture information as to the distribution as a result of the request and who received the requested information. This should also be date and time stamped by the system, capturing these data pertaining to the sending of the information. The system must maintain a history of discovery.

Worthless checks

Just about every prosecutor's office throughout the country must deal with worthless checks. Worthless checks include checks written on closed

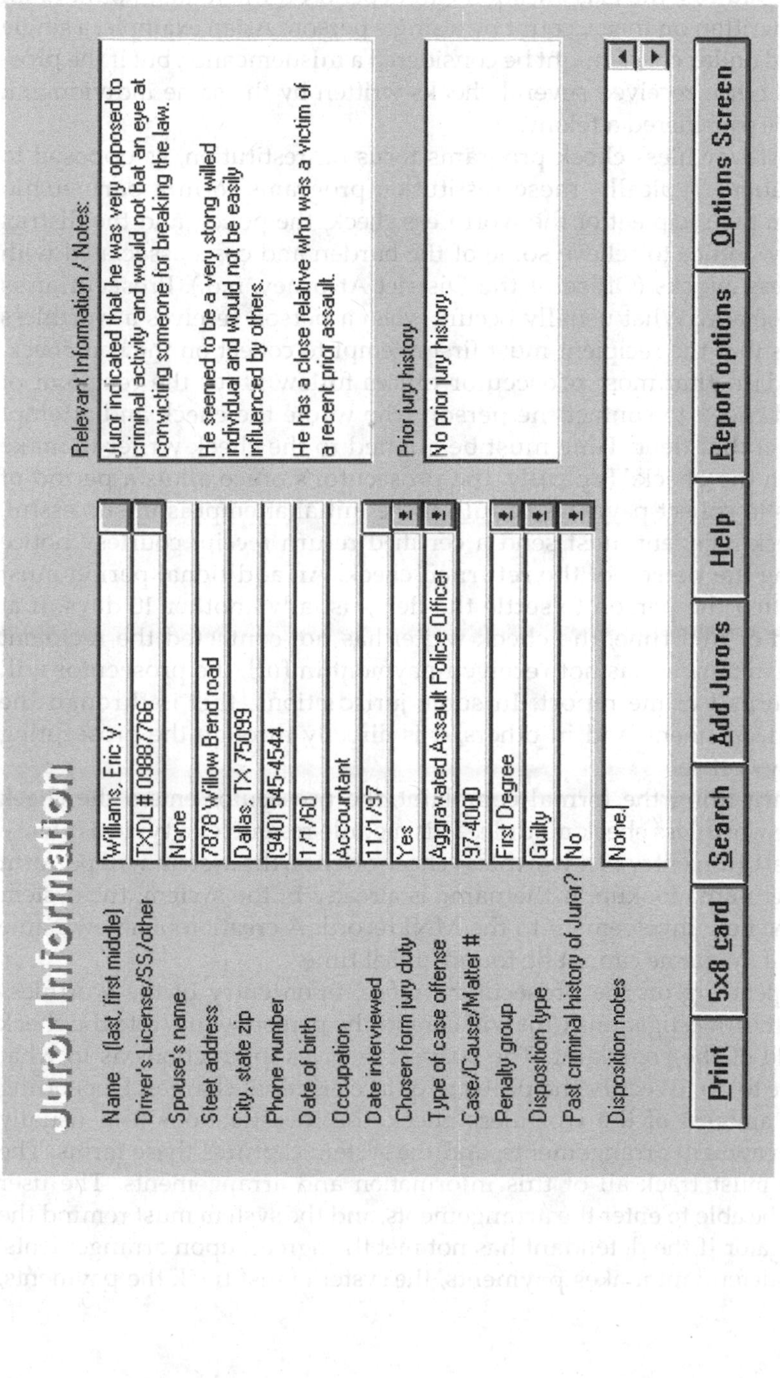

Juror Information

Name (last, first middle)	Williams, Eric V.
Driver's License/SS/other	TXDL# 09887766
Spouse's name	None
Steet address	7878 Willow Bend road
City, state zip	Dallas, TX 75099
Phone number	(940) 545-4544
Date of birth	1/1/60
Occupation	Accountant
Date interviewed	11/1/97
Chosen form jury duty	Yes
Type of case offense	Aggravated Assault Police Officer
Case/Cause/Matter #	97-4000
Penalty group	First Degree
Disposition type	Guilty
Past criminal history of Juror?	No
Disposition notes	None.

Relevant Information / Notes:

Juror indicated that he was very opposed to criminal activity and would not bat an eye at convicting someone for breaking the law.

He seemed to be a very stong willed individual and would not be easily influenced by others.

He has a close relative who was a victim of a recent prior assault.

Prior jury history

No prior jury history.

Print | 5x8 card | Search | Add Jurors | Help | Report options | Options Screen

Figure 10.9 Juror tracking screen. (From Microfirm Software Corporation, Microfirm, Version 6, Computer software, Carrollton, TX: Microfirm Corporation, 2015.)

accounts, overdrawn accounts, forged checks, and worthless checks, with or without the intent to defraud. A worthless check can be considered a misdemeanor or a felony depending on the amount of the check(s). In many instances, the classification can depend on the total amount of all checks written on that account by a single person. As an example, a single hundred dollar check might be considered a misdemeanor, but if the prosecutor's office received several checks written by the same individual, it might be considered a felony.

Most worthless check programs focus on restitution, as opposed to prosecution. Typically, these restitution programs form a partnership between the recipient of the worthless check, the police, and the district attorney's office to relieve some of the burden and costs associated with worthless checks (Office of the District Attorney, n.d.). Prosecution is not automatic. What usually occurs when a person receives a worthless check is that the recipient must first attempt to collect on the bad check. A standard that most prosecutor offices follow is for the recipient of the bad check to contact the person who wrote the check and attempt to collect that debt. Time must be allotted to the check writer to make good on the check. Typically, the prosecutor's office allots a period of 10 days to collect payment in full. If the initial attempt is unsuccessful, the check recipient must send a certified return receipt courtesy notice advising the person of the returned check. An additional period must be allotted the person to settle the debt, usually another 10 days. If at the end of that time, the check writer has not contacted the recipient and the recipient has not received payment in full, the prosecutor will file a formal crime report. In some jurisdictions, this is through the police department, and in others, it is directly through the prosecuting attorney's office.

When filing the formal complaint, the prosecutor enters the check into the worthless check module. This module resembles a typical offense module. Upon entry of a worthless check offense, the system will perform a master name lookup. If the name is already in the system, the system adds the new involvement to the MNI record. A creation of a new name occurs if the name cannot be found at that time.

Depending on the prosecutor's office, upon entry of the worthless check, the investigations unit will contact the person who wrote the check and told of the complaint. The suspect receives instructions as to what they are to do to rectify the problem or face criminal charges. Depending on the amount of the worthless check, the investigations unit usually makes payment arrangements, and the system captures these terms. The system must track all of this information and arrangements. The user should be able to enter the arrangements, and the system must remind the investigator if the defendant has not met the agreed upon arrangements. As the defendant makes payments, the system must track the payments,

and a release must be filed once completed. The system must track all of
the transactions and final disposition.

Restitution tracking

Like the worthless check module, prosecutor offices require the ability to track restitution ordered by the courts for defendants to pay.
Restitution tracking occurs by the worthless check module. This is often
an accounting-like system that tracks payments received and payments
made to the victims and others ordered specified by the courts. The software must be able to track all restitution payments. The court will often
specify the order of payment whenever there are multiple victims. The
restitution tracking module must be able to track these priorities, the
amount, and the order of payment. As with any financial system, the user
must be able to look up an account and immediately obtain its status and
see the amount paid and the amount still due.

Many of the software packages provide accounting reports similar to
those found in an accounting system. This would include reports showing delinquent defendants, closed accounts, outstanding balances by the
defendant, and other similar reports. Accompanying this module would
be a reminder system that generates automatic reminders for late payments, delinquent accounts, and other reminders as needed.

Child support module

Child support is a key function of the prosecutor's office. A prosecutor
information management system must be capable of managing this vital
task. The child support division of the prosecutor's office is responsible
for several tasks. Child support is a parental responsibility that in and of
itself does not fall under the prosecutor's purview. Unfortunately, not all
parents live up to their responsibility and try to avoid paying their child
support. It is often compounded by the fact that one of the parents receives
some form of welfare. A parent under court order to make child support
payments, and fails to do so, commits a crime. This engages the prosecutor's office in rectifying the situation. The term "deadbeat parents" often
refers to parents who fail to make the required child support payments.

Failure to obey a court order is a violation of the law. The prosecuting
attorney's office is responsible for the enforcement of the court order. Most
prosecuting attorney offices support an investigations unit. This unit is
responsible for follow-up investigations required by the prosecutor. They
often work hand in hand with the local law enforcement agencies but
often work exclusively on the deadbeat parents.

There are multiple ways in which the prosecuting attorney can
become involved in the enforcement of child support orders. A parent

could file a complaint with the local prosecutor's office and, in some locations, through the police or sheriff's office. Typically, this entails the parent filing a report and presenting the court order that specifies the terms of the child support order. Too often, the parent with custody of the child or children receives state funding. When this occurs, the funding agency will seek restitution through the child support owed and will require enforcement. The child support module provides the ability to capture this information. Figure 10.10 depicts a typical initial case entry screen.

The system will also capture information pertaining to each parent. Figure 10.11 depicts a typical screen used to collect these data.

The system will also capture information pertaining to the children the couple had together as well as information pertaining to additional children that both had with other people. This captures the basic information used in managing child support collection efforts. Upon receiving the basic information pertaining to delinquent cases, the prosecutor assigns those cases to investigators for follow-up and management.

A key component in the child support module is collection management. Many of the prosecutor management systems use a similar collection management component as that of a business accounting system. The system must be capable of establishing accounts for each child support case. It must track and calculate the owed amount, the received amount,

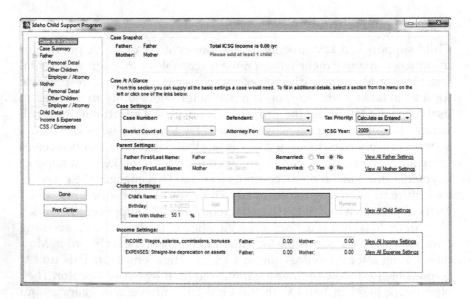

Figure 10.10 Child support case entry screen. (Courtesy of Idaho Child Support, Moonlighting Software, Computer software, Boise, ID: Moonlight Software Corporation, 2015.)

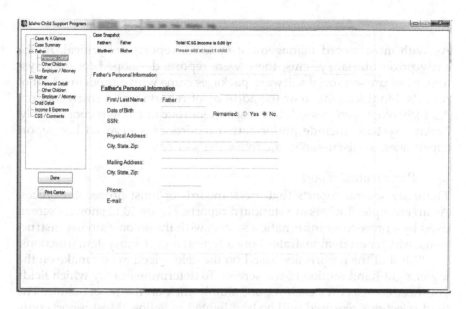

Figure 10.11 Parental information. (Courtesy of Idaho Child Support, Moonlighting Software, Computer software, Boise, ID: Moonlight Software Corporation, 2015.)

and the delinquent payments. Delinquent payments must be managed as they would be in a normal accounting system. The system must report when a payment falls 30, 60, 90 days, or more past due. To manage this process, the system must be capable of producing letters to the delinquent parent, but in addition to the letters, it must be capable of notifying investigators of delinquent accounts for them to take appropriate enforcement action.

Another function that the child support module must be capable of is managing the distribution of the support payments. Many prosecuting attorney offices that have to get involved in enforcing the child support terms charge a fee for this service. Sometimes, that fee may come out of the funds paid, and in some cases, there is an assessment added on to the support payment. This becomes an accounting issue that needs to be handled by the system.

The system must also be able to handle garnishing of wages. To garnish wages, the 'system must be capable of producing the necessary reports and data for the courts to issue the garnishment order. Once approved, the garnishment must be sent to the parent's employer. As the parent changes employers, this must be tracked, and the garnishment transferred accordingly. Lastly, the system must be able to track all of these transactions and the due diligence that has taken place in support of the child support payment compliance.

Reports

As with most record management systems, reports are critical. In the early prosecutorial systems, there were reports developed for each system. Most prosecutorial software packages came with a predefined set of reports. Modifications to or the addition of reports was a costly add-on. As technology progressed, the cost of reports came down considerably. Today's systems include preformatted reports as well as ad hoc report capabilities, as discussed in the following sections.

Preformatted reports

There are several reports that are standard for most prosecutor offices. As an example, dockets are standard reports. Figure 10.12 shows a screen used by a prosecutor information system with the accompanying instructions, which best demonstrates how a typical report subsystem functions.

"Most of the reports are based on the field selection you make on the lower right-hand section of the screen. To determine exactly which fields you need to select for each report, simply click on the report name. The field selections required will be highlighted in yellow. Most reports only require one selection; however, some reports require two selections. On all reports asking for dates, use the following format: mm/dd/yy. January 1st, 2000 will be input at 01/01/2000.

All reports on this screen show you a print preview of the report prior to printing. Once viewed on screen, you may zoom in and out for better viewing, move from one page to the next, escape the preview without printing, and print the report.

Note: The reports with 'P' in the button allow you to search for cases by partial spelling of a charge. This allows you to retrieve a report by specific words within the specific charge. For example, the keyword 'assault', DWI, or aggravated would include all cases where that specific word was included in the charge. This allows you to retrieve categories of crimes by using key words for the report. (Microfirm Software Corporation, 2012)

Ad hoc report generator

Prosecutor information systems require the ability to produce ad hoc reports using any data element and combination of data elements captured by the system. The ad hoc report generator must be simple to use and not require information services personnel to develop and run these reports. The ad hoc report generator must be capable of performing calculations on specified fields. There are several commercially available report writers used by many companies that provide this ad hoc reporting capability. Some firms also provide their own ad hoc report generators. The

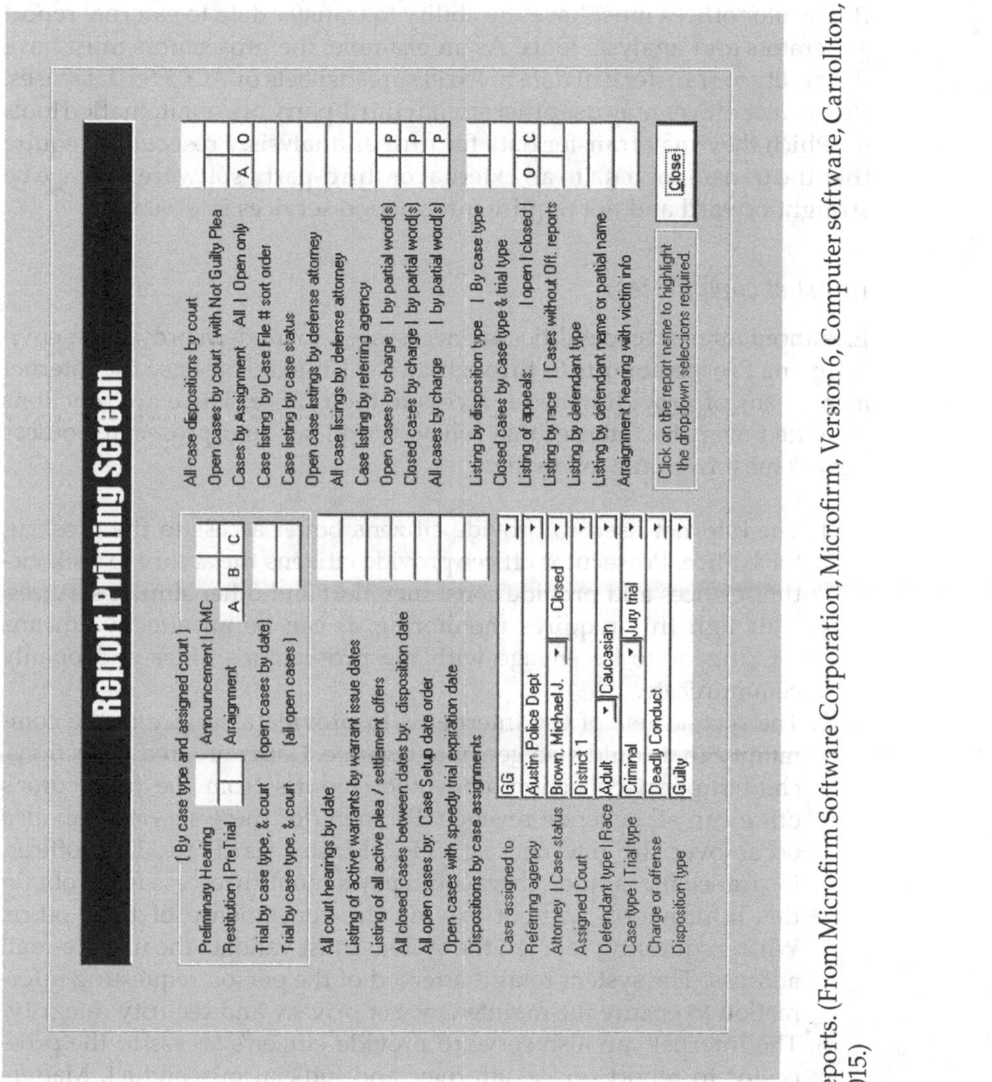

Figure 10.12 Reports. (From Microfirm Software Corporation, Microfirm, Version 6, Computer software, Carrollton, TX: Microfirm Corporation, 2015.)

key is for them to be easy to use and not require a computer programmer to develop.

Transfer data to external report generators

Prosecutor offices must have the ability to transfer data to external report generators and analysis tools. As an example, the prosecutors must have the ability to transfer call data to Excel spreadsheets or ACCESS databases. Prosecutor offices may use other similar third-party office automation tools to which they may transfer data for further analysis. Prosecutors require that the transfer of data to an external or third-party software package be straightforward and not require information services intervention.

Internet capabilities

Enhanced Internet capabilities are necessary in a modern prosecutor environment. Prosecutor offices throughout the United States use the Internet as a means of providing better access to their office. There are functions provided over the Internet that relieve workload, and prosecutor offices benefit most from the following:

1. The Internet used to provide citizens better access to the prosecutor's office. Prosecutor offices provide citizens the ability to seek victim services and provide consumer alert and other similar services. Although this requires monitoring, it can be an effective means for citizens to be engage with the prosecutor's office and openly communicate.
2. The second use of the Internet is to provide a service to the community that could also generate revenue. Court-ordered collections, child support collection, and other reports from the prosecutor's office can all generate revenue. Payment for these services can also occur over the Internet, e.g., Visa, Master Card, etc. Law offices, insurance firms, and others could pay a monthly access fee to obtain this information without leaving the convenience of their office. When requesting reports, the system must validate the user's e-mail address. The system retains a record of the person requesting information to ensure the maintenance of privacy and security integrity.
3. The Internet can also serve to provide citizen's access to the prosecutor to report police, attorney, and judicial misconduct. Matters involving the use of force, especially when death or serious bodily injury occurs, are often the most scrutinized matters involving a peace officer. The community has a right to know whether or not an officer lawfully used deadly force in the application of his or her duties. It is incumbent upon the prosecutor's office to investigate

officer-involved shootings and deaths that occur while a person is in the custody of a peace officer (Los Angeles District Attorney, n.d.).

4. Some prosecuting offices provide online consumer protection forms that allow citizens to download these forms and complete them and submit them either manually or through the Internet.

5. The prosecuting attorney office often provides a host of services to the citizens, which are too many to discuss in detail but pertinent to note that the Internet can and is a vital tool for many prosecuting attorney functions.

Data warehousing and data mining capability

Prosecuting attorney offices house a great deal of data. The ability to access these data by various units within the prosecutor's office is critical. Storing these data also has legal ramifications. The state typically requires the retention of felonies and misdemeanors for a specified period. Certain data have a long useful life, whereas other data have minimal value. A good prosecutor attorney's system can store large amounts of data. It can provide the ability to access that data in a variety of ways.

To be a useful tool, data warehousing and data mining must be easy to use and not geared toward the power user but rather the casual user. The system must have the ability to allow inexperienced users to establish queries that will allow them to access stored data in a variety of ways. Data mining should not require any sophisticated computer skills. Queries should be simple to establish, and end users should be given the choice to view the information at their workstation, to save the data to a local storage device, or to print the data in a report format.

References

Idaho Child Support (2015). Moonlighting Software [Computer Software]. Boise, ID: Moonlight Software Corporation.

Los Angeles District Attorney (n.d.). Justice System Integrity Division. Retrieved from http://da.co.la.ca.us/jsid.htm.

Microfirm Software Corporation (2012). Retrieved from http://da.co.la.ca.us/jsid.htm.

Microfirm Software Corporation (2015). Microfirm (Version 6) [Computer Software]. Carrollton, TX: Microfirm Corporation.

Moonlighting Software (2015). [Computer Software]. Boise, ID: Moonlight Software Corporation.

Office of the District Attorney (n.d.). Bad Check Restitution Program. Retrieved from http://da.Sonoma-County.org/content.aspx?sid=1023&id=1711.

chapter eleven

Court management information systems

Court management systems serve as the enterprise database designed to aid in the management of trials, scheduling of courtrooms, collection of fines, and other judicial tasks.

List of definition

MNI—master name index

Introduction

For many years, like its other criminal justice counterparts, courts functioned in a manual mode. Like other criminal justice counterparts, the courts were extremely paper intensive. Most courts have two divisions, civil and criminal, each with specific and unique requirements. In more recent times, we see highly specialized courts such as family courts and juvenile courts. All state and federal courts have appellate divisions that lead to state and federal supreme court. The concern of all courts, considered core to any court information management system, consists of the following:

- Person information for criminal and domestic-related cases
- Statewide criminal case history for a person
- Domestic violence case and protection order history for a person (Washington State Courts—Judicial Information System, http://www.courts.wa.gov/jis)

There is a further breakdown of these courts. In most jurisdictions, we find courts broken down as follows, with many variations across the country:

- *Courts of limited jurisdiction*—often referred to as municipal courts, minor courts, traffic courts, and justice of the peace. Typically, these courts handle traffic citations, preliminary hearings, misdemeanor crimes, minor civil cases, and other minor adjudications. Typical functions are as follows:
  - Case filing
  - Calendaring
  - Docketing
  - Case maintenance
  - Finding/judgment and sentence recording
  - Accounts receivable and collections
  - Receipting/cashiering
  - Trust accounting
  - Checking and banking
  - FTA and warrant processing
  - Management and statistical reporting (http://www.courts.wa .gov/jis/?fa=jis.display&theFile=caseManagementSystems)
- *Superior courts*—the next level of court in the judicial system. They are not always referred to as superior courts; it depends on the state. They are superior to the lower courts discussed earlier and thus the name superior court. The superior court often hears felony-type cases, appeals from the lower court, civil cases above a certain amount of money; and any case that is not specifically designated to be heard by another court level. At this level court, the information system must address each of the items listed previously plus the following:
  - Manage and report superior court cases, including filing date and dates for court proceedings
  - Record case participants
  - Record charges filed against defendants
  - Provide case status
  - Monitor time-in-process relative to advisory case-processing time standards
  - Document charge and case results, together with judgment amount, sentence, and case completion
  - Record petitions, pleadings, orders, and other documents filed within a case (http://www.courts.wa.gov/jis/?fa=jis.display&the File=caseManagementSystems)
- *Juvenile courts*—can be part of a lower court, superior court, or stand-alone court. The establishment of juvenile courts was to address

issues that are unique to juveniles. Juvenile courts were not always a part of the justice system, and there is still controversy that surrounds these courts and the handling of juveniles in general. Juvenile court information systems are similar to other court software and function the same as lower and superior courts.

- *Appellate courts*—this court is different from the trial courts. They do not typically engage in any collection of funds or other lower court processes. They do have case scheduling requirements and managing of cases that are on appeal. They do not deal with juries or jury selection. The software typically maintains a record of events for cases on appeal and tracks issues in cases (http://www.courts .wa.gov/jis/?fa=jis.display&theFile=caseManagementSystems). Lower division appellate courts, as well as state supreme courts, use this software.

Current court management information systems support all of these levels of court and courtroom processing. In this chapter, we will explore this software and its use within the judicial system.

Court docket module

In order for a case, be it civil or criminal, to come before the court, there must be some form of a case filing. All courts, be it courts of limited jurisdiction or the U.S. Supreme Court, the highest court in the U.S. judicial system, must have a means of filing cases that it needs to address. These cases then become part of a court docket. The court docket is essentially a calendar of cases to be heard by a court. Court dockets schedule both criminal and civil cases.

In the older manual system, the filing of a case occurred through a series of paperwork that an attorney, or other citizen, completed and brought to the court clerk to be filed and scheduled for a hearing. In today's computerized court environments, this occurs through an automated process that has significantly reduced workload on the court clerk's office. Many of the former manual processes associated with case filings, which resulted in the court docket, occur electronically for both criminal and civil cases. As an example, law enforcement can file criminal cases by logging into the court system and entering the required case information. Under the old manual process, most law enforcement agencies had a person, or in larger agencies a number of people, whose sole job was to bring a case to the prosecuting attorney's office for filing. The prosecuting attorney would review the case and either request additional information from the law enforcement agency filing the complaint or file it with the appropriate court. In today's environment, this occurs electronically.

In the case of traffic citations, electronic ticketing (e-ticketing) allows police officers to cite a driver for a vehicle code violation, and upon completion of the citation, the system automatically uploads the citation from the laptop, tablet PC, or other computer device directly into the court docketing system. E-ticketing eliminates the need for a police clerk to file the ticket with the traffic court.

From the civil side of the court, citizens and attorneys can also file cases electronically. In many systems across the United States, the courts charge an access fee to file cases electronically. This benefits an attorney's office because they do not have to have employees or other attorneys go down to a court simply to file a case. Citizens can also file minor cases electronically. Overall, this reduces workload on the court clerk's office.

The following screen depicts a typical case entry screen used to enter case information. This case information formulates the court docket. Throughout the course of the case, the addition of information to other modules as well as the initial record occurs. Figure 11.1 shows a sample court case data screen.

From this screen, the end user can access other critical components associated with this case and also input information pertaining to the case. Information can be entered into the software in several ways. The court can use the stand-alone system, or in support of integrated justice information systems (IJISs), it can be connected to the other software. As an example, the court system may interface with the prosecutor's system or the police software, depending on the jurisdiction and associated legal structure, to document their reports and arrests. Officers enter information into their program that can later be uploaded to the court system, eliminating redundant data entry and the risk of errors. For instance, the officer enters the personal information about each party, the offense committed, when committed, the day the offender must appear in court, and other pertinent information. All of this information is in a standard police report. Tying these two software products together limits or eliminates duplicate data.

Court management software can automatically number every new docket entered into the system. The court defines the numbering scheme entered during the setup process. This enables the court to keep a consistent track of how many cases have passed through their court.

Each court docket acts like a file for each case. The docket contains information about all of the parties, the offenses, the fines/costs, the court minutes, and the correspondence involved in the case. Most of the information can be viewed from one screen (see Figure 11.1). Additional information can be viewed with just one mouse click from the main docket screen.

A single screen displays all court dockets for a court or all courts within a jurisdiction from which they can click on a docket and view all information for that case. Figure 11.2 depicts a docket listing screen.

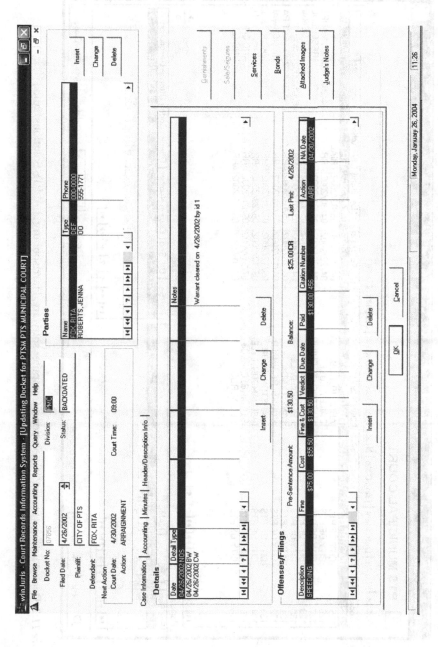

Figure 11.1 Court case data screen. (From PTS Solutions, Computer software, Harrisonburg, LA: PTS Solutions, 2015.)

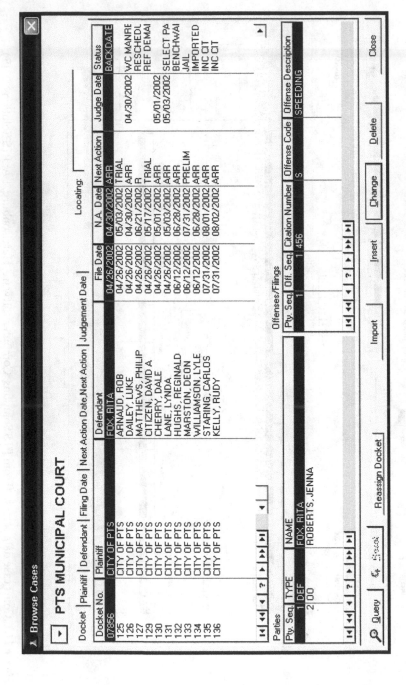

Figure 11.2 Docket listing. (From PTS Solutions, Computer software, Harrisonburg, LA: PTS Solutions, 2015.)

From this screen, the end user can also view basic information about the case as well as the parties involved. The end user can access other information by clicking on an icon. They can look at information pertaining to a plaintiff or a defendant as well as other information. By clicking on the docket, the end user can access the court case data screen. From that point, they move to other critical screens that contain pertinent information about the case.

Court clerks can print daily dockets that display defendants due for court on that day. The list can be printed on a docket sheet. For live court minute entry, clerks highlight a line and click minute entry. This brings up the minute and sentencing screens. If they have multiple defendants who need the same minute parameters, they can tag multiple items and complete the minutes in a batch format. Figure 11.3 depicts a typical daily docket.

The user can view the case by highlighting and clicking on a docket item or print the docket item by highlighting it and clicking on the print key. Figure 11.4 depicts a printed sample of a court docket.

The standard today is for automated dockets. Judges can access these dockets through a terminal or workstation that is on their bench. Printed court dockets are rare to see, but there are those that prefer the printed format. These dockets are also available to citizens through Internet connections to the court system.

Master name index

As with other criminal justice information systems, court management systems also maintain a master name index (MNI). The MNI provides the same functionality in a court management system as found in a police record management system. The court MNI tracks the names of involved parties in a criminal or civil case. This includes the defendant (civil or criminal), plaintiff (civil), witnesses, victims, police officers, and attorneys. In a well-designed system, each party in the case has their name added to the system only once. Once added to the ID file, the person's name appears on a drop-down menu and can be selected into the next case in which the person has involvement. This eliminates duplicate work for the court clerk and also helps maintain an activity history on individuals entered into the system. The ID file documents information such as addresses, date of birth, personal ID number, telephone numbers, employer, height, weight, hair/eye color, gang information, known associates, aliases, etc. Figure 11.5 depicts a typical master name record.

The MNI uses a Soundex routine when searching for a name. Soundex is a programming methodology that allows the end user to enter a name based on how the name sounds as opposed to the precise spelling of the name. Too often there are multiple spellings of a name and the end user may not know the exact spelling. The user does not have to

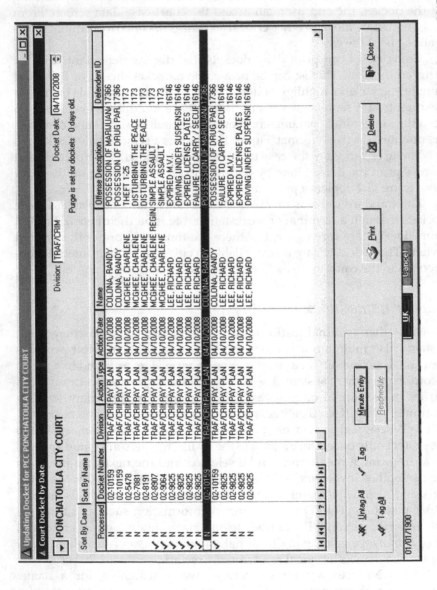

Figure 11.3 Daily court docket listing. (From PTS Solutions, Computer software, Harrisonburg, LA: PTS Solutions, 2015.)

```
PTS MUNICIPAL COURT
DOCKET NUMBER: 07856                                    PROCESSING DATE: 03/11/2004
CITY OF PTS                            VS.FOX, RITA
─────────────────────────────────────────────────────────────────────────────────
Court Date:          Judgement Date:        Offense: SPEEDING
Last Action/Date: ARR    04/26/2002   Next Action/Date/Time:
Case Status:BACKDATED  Defendant Plea:
─────────────────────────────────────────────────────────────────────────────────
Defense Attorney:
─────────────────────────────────────────────────────────────────────────────────
Disposition: ARRAIGNMENT PRESENT IN COURT WITHOUT COUNSEL, RIGHTS ADVISED, SENTENCING: SENTENCE DATE
             4/26/2002. THE FINE WAS DECLARED    $75.00 THE COST WAS DECLARED    $55.50 FOR A TOTAL OF    $130.50



─────────────────────────────────────────────────────────────────────────────────
Warrant Number: 5                    Date Issued: 04/30/2002   Date Served:
─────────────────────────────────────────────────────────────────────────────────
Sentencing Information: Fine:        75.00Costs:       55.50 Extra Costs:        0.00 Restitution:        0.00
                        Restitution To:
─────────────────────────────────────────────────────────────────────────────────
Citation Number:456                  Violation Date/Time:04/26/2002  11:00
Agency: RPD
DL#:               State: MS     SSN: 000-00-0000
Last: FOX                        First:RITA                   Middle:
Employer:
Address: 4116 PICOT
City/State/Zip: MOSS POINT           MS          Phone: (228) 000-0000
Race:B      Sex: F      Height:     Weight:      DOB: 10/25/1974
Officer: JENNA ROBERTS
─────────────────────────────────────────────────────────────────────────────────
Violation:S        SPEEDING
BOND FORFEITURE                    Collected:    0.00    Owed:    0.00
COURT CONST                        Collected:    0.00    Owed:    0.00
```

Figure 11.4 Printed court docket. (From PTS Solutions, Computer software, Harrisonburg, LA: PTS Solutions, 2015.)

spell the name correctly in order for the system to find the possible name. Most systems use the popular Soundex routine known as the New York State Identification and Intelligence System (NYSIIS) to determine if the name already exists in the MNI. NYSIIS became popular because of its ability to search hyphenated names by comparing the two last names, e.g., Hernandez-Gonzales and Gonzales-Hernandez and presenting both names as possible hits.

When completing a name search, the system displays a list of names, as depicted in Figure 11.6, from which the end user can then click on the name that he or she is looking for and display that record.

Sentencing and rulings

Each level of court deals with criminal offenses that range from minor infractions to major felonies. Courts also deal with lawsuits and final decisions in these cases. The results of each must be tracked.

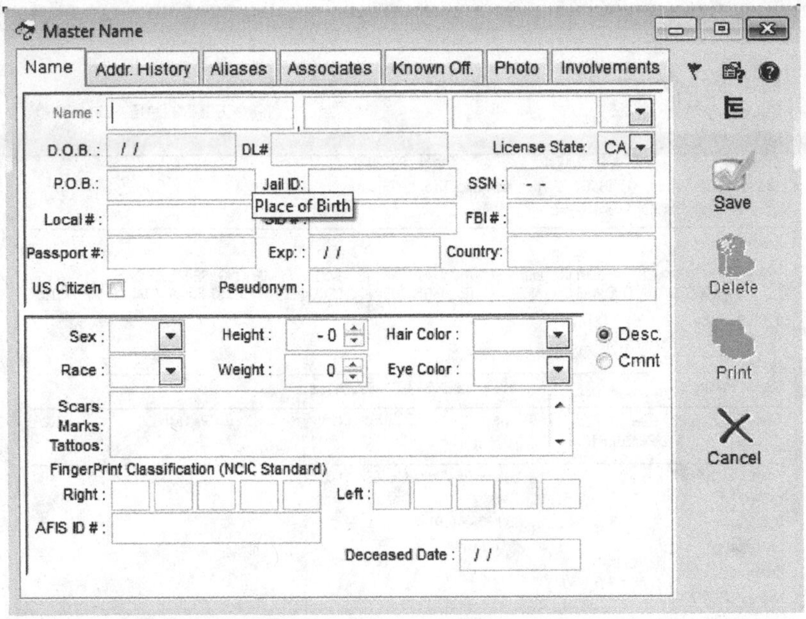

Figure 11.5 Master name index record. (From PTS Solutions, Computer software, Harrisonburg, LA: PTS Solutions, 2015.)

In criminal cases where the defendant is guilty, the judge will sentence the subject based on the discretion provided by law. In some instances, the judge may sentence a subject a number of ways such as a fine, jail time, probation, restitution, or some other assessment or use all of these sentencing options. As an example, it is common for a judge to sentence a convicted subject to serve a year in the state penitentiary, fine him or her $10,000, require the subject to make restitution to the victim, and serve a probationary period after release from prison. The court management system must be capable of tracking all of this information. In the case of restitutions and fines, it is not uncommon for the convicted person to be given a payment plan to make payments on the fines and restitutions. It is also not uncommon for the monies to require payment distribution. The sentencing information needs to be tracked. In those cases where the subject's sentence is a prison term, the sentencing details must be recorded and forwarded to the appropriate jail or prison. If the system meets integrated justice information requirements, the sentencing information is transferable to the appropriate corrections facility. The corrections system updates and manages the sentence from that point forward. Figure 11.7 depicts a typical court management system sentencing screen.

Most court management systems include a full court accounting package to handle the processing and tracking of the financial side of the

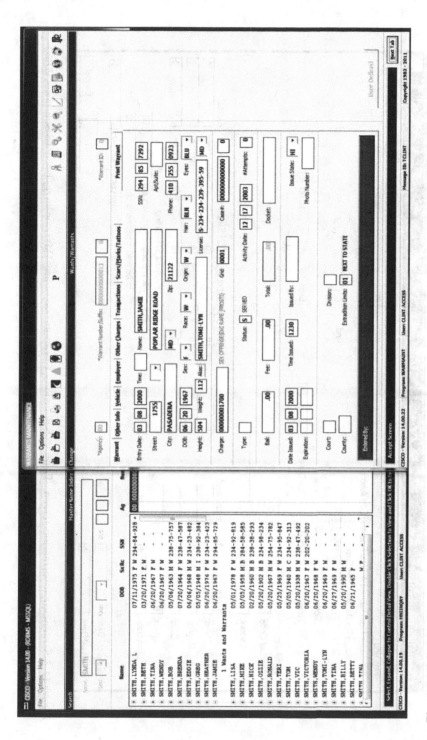

Figure 11.6 Master name index name list. (From Moonlighting Software, Computer software, Boise, ID: Moonlight Software Corporation, 2015.)

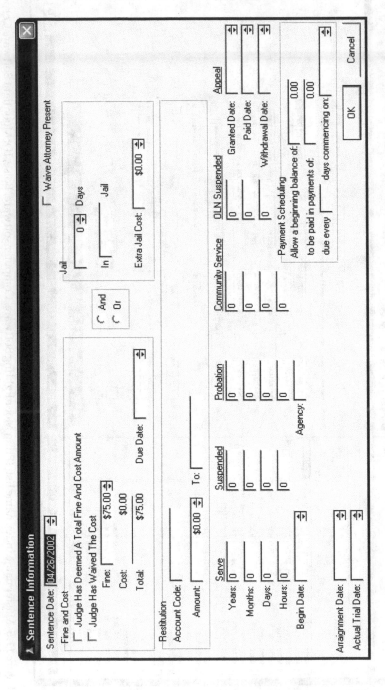

Figure 11.7 Sentencing information screen. (From PTS Solutions, Computer software, Harrisonburg, LA: PTS Solutions, 2015.)

sentencing. The system automatically inserts that based on the offense attached to the docket. The system automatically generates a receipt for payment or cash bond transactions owed. The system stores all receipts in a file that can be displayed at any time. Typically, the system will show the receipt number, date, and time. Other information such as who received the money and applicable notes are available.

At the end of each day, a receipts report can be printed that the clerks can use to balance their cash drawers. The report will show all of the money collected on that day. The court can also print out a daily distribution report that will show the amount of money paid out each day. Each of these reports can also be printed weekly or monthly, depending on the needs of the court. Just like other point of sale systems, these systems can be linked to credit card machines where credit cards can be accepted and interfaced to the appropriate banking system to post the monies from the credit cards.

Courts can write and print checks from the system. With the appropriate system, tracking of these checks occurs using a built-in checking account register. At the end of the month, the court can also reconcile their bank statement using the system. The system includes other various reports and tracking systems such as defendants' balance summary, income/expense report, and aged accounts receivable reports. Figure 11.8 depicts a typical accounting system log of case information and all associated fines.

The accounting system must be capable of capturing the information for a transaction like any other accounting system. Figure 11.9 shows a typical transaction of entry of a cash bond that displays the payment fields. The system displays different fields for fines or costs.

The accounting component must also serve to notify the prosecutor's office whenever a person has failed to meet their court ordered payment requirements. This requires that the system track all contacts with the subject, attempts to collect by date and time, and failed agreements. The system must provide a delinquent listing on a daily basis to follow-up with these delinquent accounts. When it is determined that the subject violated the court ordered terms, all of this information must be sent to the prosecutor. This either occurs manually or electronically depending on the integration of the court and prosecutor systems. In addition, the system must be capable of establishing garnishments, to garnish wages, bank accounts, and other assets of a subject under court order to pay fines and judgments. It must track these garnishments, the accrued amounts, or the generated amounts to date from interest, court costs, attorney percentage, commissions earned, and refunds. The following is a typical screen used to capture this information. Figure 11.10 depicts a sample vendor accrual screen.

Upon collecting the funds, they must be distributed to the appropriate person or group as required. The system must be capable of producing

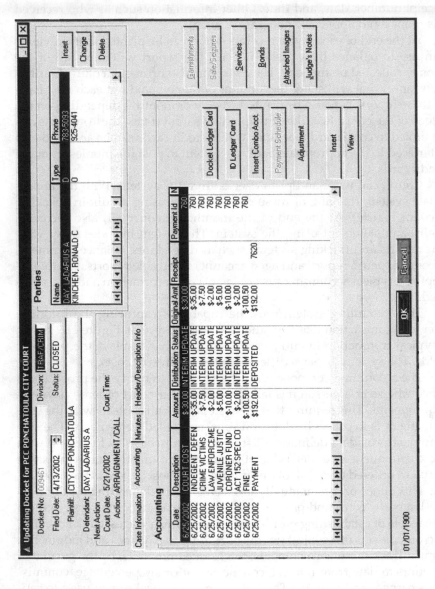

Figure 11.8 Case accounting screen. (From PTS Solutions, Computer software, Harrisonburg, LA: PTS Solutions, 2015.)

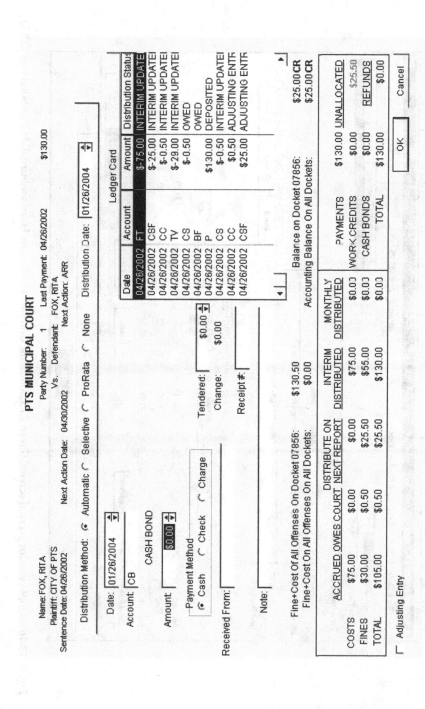

Figure 11.9 Individual financial transaction screen. (From PTS Solutions, Computer software, Harrisonburg, LA: PTS Solutions, 2015.)

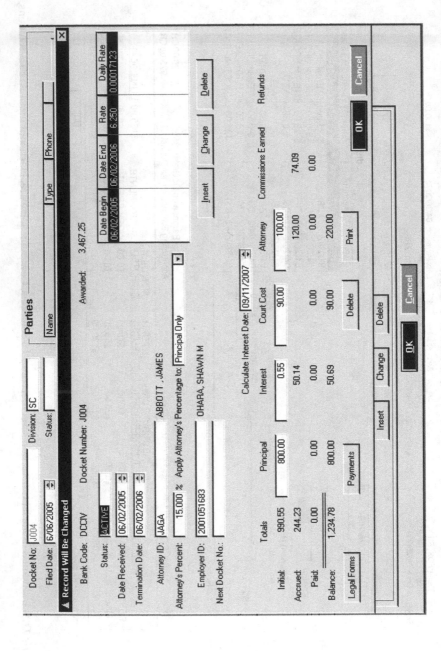

Figure 11.10 Sample vendor accrual screen. (From PTS Solutions, Computer software, Harrisonburg, LA: PTS Solutions, 2015.)

a distribution report on a daily basis as well as at the close of the month. Again, these are normal accounting functions. It should be possible to review this information online as well as producing in a report format that would allow for on screen review with the option of printing a hardcopy. Reports are produced that pertain to a receipt such as drug cases, traffic, and criminal. The system must be capable of examining each receipt. To create these reports, the system must provide the end user with the ability to specify the report they intend to run. Figure 11.11 is a sample report selection screen.

In this system, as in many others, there are two types of accounting reports that are beneficial to courts, interim or daily and monthly. A distribution report is a report showing paid fines and costs and are ready to distribute to the agencies and entities due the fine/cost money. Figure 11.12 is a sample of an interim distribution report.

It is also possible to view the receipts daily, weekly, monthly, or annually. This is usually a report run for a day or in some cases run for multiple days depending on the system. Many court systems have multiple registers where these receipts can be collected.

The court administrator runs this monthly report at the end of each month. The monthly report collects data from each of the interim reports run for the month. Figure 11.13 presents a sample distribution report.

There are multiple forms of payments that courts receive. The following subsections describe the recording of these payment forms required of the system.

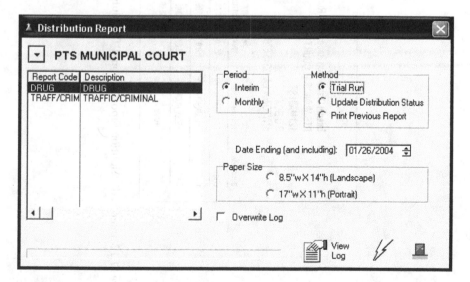

Figure 11.11 Sample report selection screen. (From PTS Solutions, Computer software, Harrisonburg, LA: PTS Solutions, 2015.)

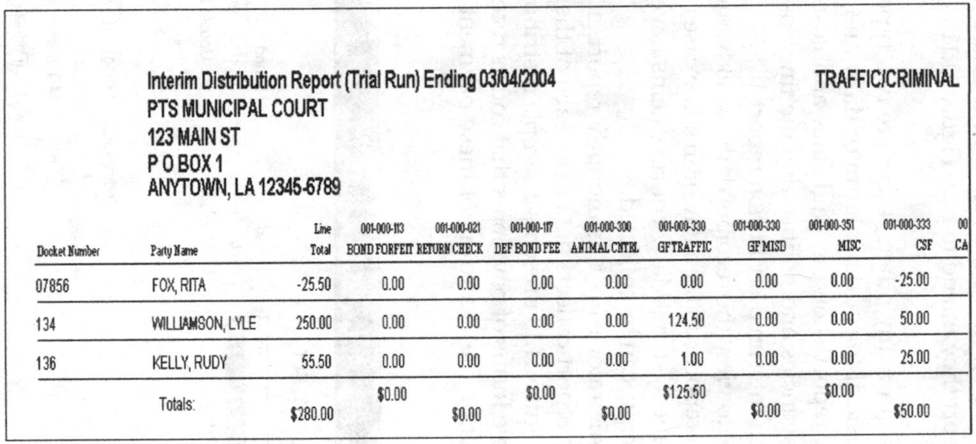

Docket Number	Party Name	Line Total	001-000-183 BOND FORFEIT	001-000-021 RETURN CHECK	001-000-117 DEF BOND FEE	004-000-300 ANIMAL CNTRL	004-000-330 GF TRAFFIC	004-000-330 GF MISD	001-000-351 MISC	001-000-333 CSF	00 CA
07856	FOX, RITA	-25.50	0.00	0.00	0.00	0.00	0.00	0.00	0.00	-25.00	
134	WILLIAMSON, LYLE	250.00	0.00	0.00	0.00	0.00	124.50	0.00	0.00	50.00	
136	KELLY, RUDY	55.50	0.00	0.00	0.00	0.00	1.00	0.00	0.00	25.00	
	Totals:	$280.00	$0.00	$0.00	$0.00	$0.00	$125.50	$0.00	$0.00	$50.00	

Interim Distribution Report (Trial Run) Ending 03/04/2004   TRAFFIC/CRIMINAL

PTS MUNICIPAL COURT
123 MAIN ST
P O BOX 1
ANYTOWN, LA 12345-6789

Figure 11.12 Interim distribution report. (From PTS Solutions, Computer software, Harrisonburg, LA: PTS Solutions, 2015.)

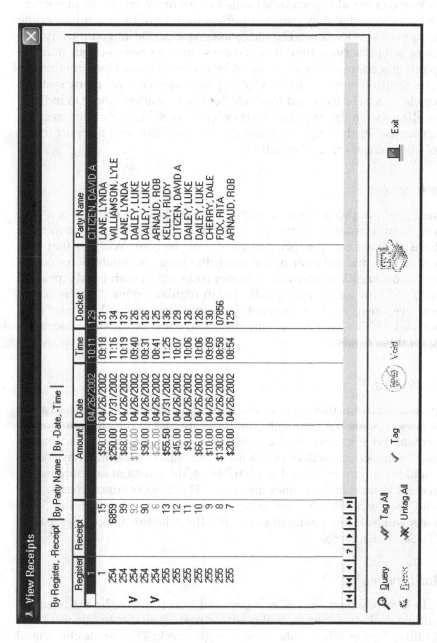

Figure 11.13 Distribution report. (From PTS Solutions, Computer software, Harrisonburg, LA: PTS Solutions, 2015.)

Work credit payments

Work credits are also sometimes called community service or public service work. A judge may assign a person found guilty of a minor crime community service time. The judge assigns a period of community service or public service time that the court management system must be capable of accounting for as payment for his or her fines. Upon completion of the required community service or public service time, many systems provide a report forwarded to a judge or the probation officer to indicate compliance with the required court order. If the subject does not meet the requirement in the required time, the system must send a report to the probation officer for further action.

Cash bond

This is just another term for a payment made prior to court. It is a payment. Courts usually use the term "cash bond" when they use a method where a person can pay prior to court, but the court will put that payment on hold and not distribute it until after their court date. Some courts want to differentiate how much money collected in cash bonds (prior to court) and how much money collected in regular payments (after court). Some even keep the two payment types in a separate bank account (PTS Solutions, 1999). Court management systems must be capable of accounting for these funds.

Unallocated

Unallocated funds usually refer to undistributed funds. With these funds, the subject made the payments, but for some reason the allocation of the payment did not occur to the fines/costs, so the payment was "unallocated." Some courts will place payments on "hold," meaning they choose to hold the payment instead of distributing the payment or applying the payment immediately to fines and costs. The most common reason they "hold" payments is when a defendant pays prior to his court day. Some courts will hold the payment until after the scheduled court day passes (PTS Solutions, 1999).

Multipayment

Multi-item payment describes a payment that needs to be made across multiple dockets. Often in civil courts, a party (usually an attorney) will pay filing fees or other costs using a single check. That single check (and accompanying receipt) pays the fees/costs for multiple clients. What is accomplished with multi-item payment is to be able to assign that same check number to multiple payments across multiple dockets and defendants and issue a single receipt for the check (PTS Solutions, 1999).

Garnishment

Garnishment is a process used in civil courts that describe the process of taking money directly from the wages of the losing party to a case to pay a judgment.

Let's say the judge decides that Mr. Jones owes money to Ms. Smith; this award to Ms. Smith is a judgment. However, Mr. Jones cannot pay the judgment up front because he does not have enough money. The judge may choose to take the money out of Mr. Jones's paycheck that he gets every two weeks from his job at Wal-Mart until Mr. Jones satisfies the judgment to Ms. Smith.

The judge will force Wal-Mart to pay the court a portion of Mr. Jones's salary. The court will then pay this money back to Ms. Smith's attorney so that he can give it to Ms. Smith. This is a garnishment (PTS Solutions, 1999). Garnishments can also occur through criminal sentences in the same manner.

At the end of the day, most courts will print a daily transaction log that shows all of the receipts taken in that day. These are similar accounting reports that a normal accounting package provides. Figure 11.14 shows a sample of this daily cash receipts transaction log.

Warrants

Courts must have the ability to create warrants. Judges often issue bench warrants for a variety of reasons. As an example, the judge will likely issue a bench warrant for that person's arrest if that person failed to appear in court after receiving a subpoena to appear on a certain date and time and did not show up. If a subject is out on bail and does not appear in court on the date and time assigned, the court revokes that person's bail, and the judge will issue a bench warrant for that person's arrest.

Upon the issuance of a warrant, the clerk enters the information into the system through the warrant module. The warrant module must also be connected, through an interface, to upload the data to the state and NCIC warrant system. Access to the state and NCIC warrant systems occurs through a system interface. Figure 11.15 depicts a typical warrant data entry screen found in a court management system.

From the information entered in this module, a hard copy of the warrant that includes the mug shot of the subject can be printed for distribution. Figure 11.16 depicts a sample of a hard copy of a warrant.

Court management systems also provide the ability to search the warrant file. This can occur directly through the warrant module or an MNI

Cash Register Receipts Report

PTS MUNICIPAL COURT
123 MAIN ST
P O BOX 1
ANYTOWN, LA 012345-6789

Register Number	Receipt Number	Docket Number	Party Name	Cash/Check#/Charge	Amount
04/24/2002					
255	7	125	ARNAUD, ROB	CASH	$20.00
				Register Total	**$20.00**
				04/24/2002 Total	**$20.00**
04/26/2002					
1	15	131	LANE, LYNDA	CASH	$50.00
1	16	129	CITIZEN, DAVID	CASH	$66.00
				Register Total	**$116.00**
254	v 6	125	ARNAUD, ROB	CASH	$0.00
254	90	126	DAILEY, LUKE	CASH	$90.00
				Register Total	**$90.00**
255	8	07856	FOX, RITA	CASH	$130.00
255	10	126	DAILEY, LUKE	CASH	$66.00
255	11	126	DAILEY, LUKE	CASH	$9.00
255	12	129	CITIZEN, DAVID	CASH	$45.00
				Register Total	**$250.00**
				04/26/2002 Total	**$456.00**

Figure 11.14 Daily receipt transaction log. (From PTS Solutions, Computer software, Harrisonburg, LA: PTS Solutions, 2015.)

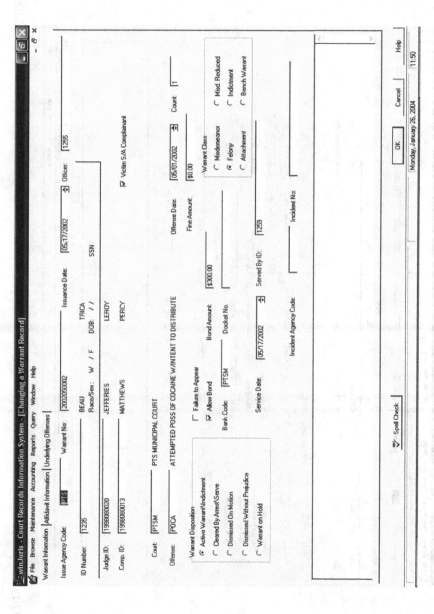

Figure 11.15 Sample warrant entry screen. (From PTS Solutions, Computer software, Harrisonburg, LA: PTS Solutions, 2015.)

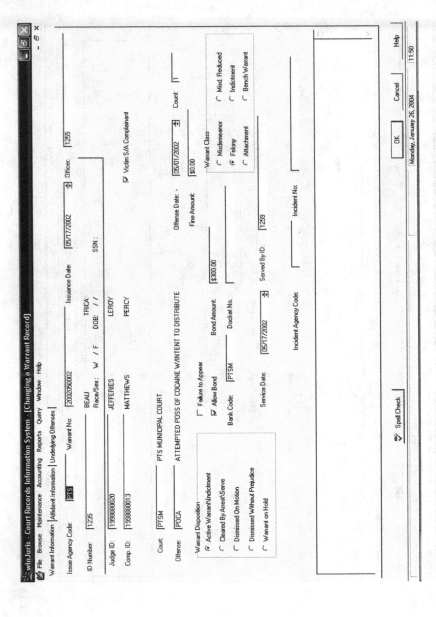

Figure 11.16 Sample hard copy warrant. (From PTS Solutions, Computer software, Harrisonburg, LA: PTS Solutions, 2015.)

search. This search capability uses the same features and functions found in the MNI, including the Soundex search capability. The master warrants file can display active warrants or all warrants (including served, on hold, etc.). When a name search occurs directly through the warrant module, the following selection screen appears. Selecting one of the records listed would display the warrant record. Figure 11.17 depicts a sample warrant file listing.

Electronic ticketing

Not all court levels deal with traffic citations; this is usually a function of a lower court. In earlier court management systems, traffic citations would be forwarded to the court. The court usually had a staff of data entry clerks that would manually enter each and every citation. Electronic ticketing significantly enhanced this process. There are a number of electronic ticketing systems developed that provide the ability for police officers to enter traffic citations electronically at the time they issue the citation. There are a number of different devises used to issue these citations, including handheld devises as well as laptop computers. Police officers issue the citation and print a copy of the citation through an in-car printer. The system uploads the citation directly to the court of jurisdiction. Figure 11.18 depicts a typical electronic tick screen.

The system uploads the information captured from this citation into the court management system docketing module for traffic court processing. The citation file can keep track of all tickets given to the court by law enforcement. The screen documents offenses, vehicle information, blood alcohol content, etc.

Court minutes

Throughout court cases during trials, court reporters take minutes that document everything that occurs in the courtroom. After court, the clerk can document the activities of the proceeding using the minute section of a court management system. From here, the clerk can insert the plea, the verdict, the next court date, and the sentencing information; reduce/waive the fine or cost amount(s); and issue a warrant or set up a partial payment schedule. Most of the minutes can be entered using drop-down menus. The information in these drop-down menus is fully customizable by the court.

Court scheduling

The court scheduling module in most court management systems allows for court assignments and appearances to be created easily with seamless

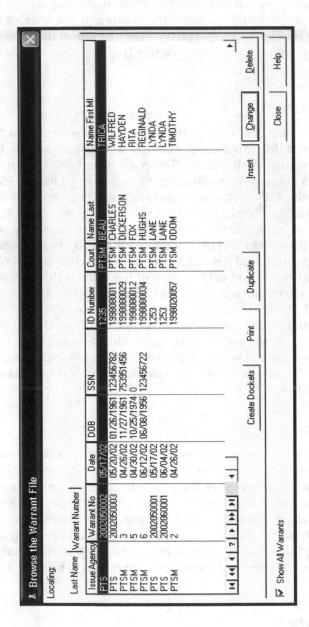

Figure 11.17 Sample warrant file listing. (From PTS Solutions, Computer software, Harrisonburg, LA: PTS Solutions, 2015.)

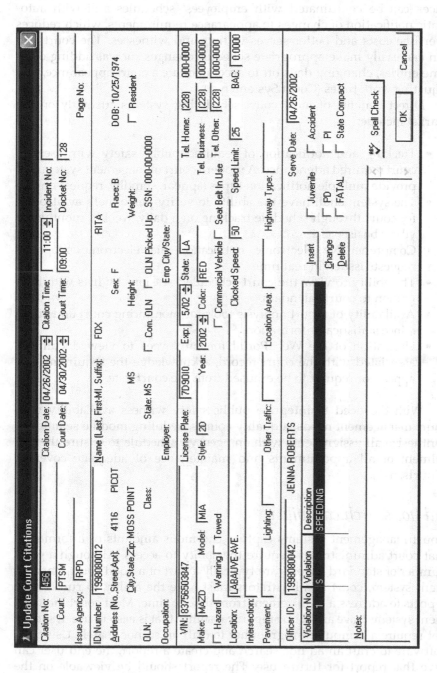

Figure 11.18 Sample electronic citation system. (From PTS Solutions, Computer software, Harrisonburg, LA: PTS Solutions, 2015.)

integration and consideration of scheduling information. Court appearances can be coordinated with employees' schedules and with automatic notification of changes to appearance requirements, which reduces overtime costs and better serves victims and witnesses. The court liaison can easily make appropriate schedule changes such as adding overtime entries, changing days off to accommodate a court appearance, and adjusting work times (Court System, n.d.).

Direct benefits of most court scheduling systems currently on the market include:

- Tracking and notification of required public safety witnesses for court required attendance. A modern court management system will provide multiple notification types (appear, standby, request-only).
- The system shall have the ability to verify personnel's availability for court through schedule tracking on a daily, weekly, monthly, or yearly basis.
- Comprehensive electronic notification via electronic subpoena requests issued in real time.
- The ability to view the court scheduled sessions by lists with integration to court calendars.
- Availability of report analysis tools for monitoring court and attendance statistical information.
- Utilization of the Web Portal for employees to view documents associated with the court record, acknowledge the requirement to appear, or request to be excused from the court date.

With the need to integrate public safety witness availability with court management needs, a quality court scheduling module seamlessly synthesize all assignments with an agency's schedule to ensure the fulfillment of all appointments and maintenance of adequate coverage (Courts, n.d.).

Ad hoc search capability

Court management systems capture enormous amounts of information that court administrators require the ability to access. Although a great number of standard reports are typically a part of a good court management system, court administrators must have the ability to run ad hoc reports to address a requirement from time to time. Most court management systems have an ad hoc report capability that is easy to use. It should not require a computer programmer to craft an ad hoc search. Using the software to craft an ad hoc search and create a report, the end user can save that report for future use. The report should be viewable on the screen or formatted for hard copy printout.

Standardized reports

In today's information technology environment, standardized reports are not as critical as they once were. Many third-party report-generation software packages provide the ability to generate reports without computer programming knowledge. That being said, most court management systems have a series of standardized reports. It is not uncommon for court management systems software vendors to have a large number of standardized reports, many of which they built for other courts and then put them into their list of reports.

Integrated justice information systems and court management software

Court management software is a part of IJISs. This software must be National Information Exchange Model (NIEM) compliant so that data can be easily shared between court management systems as well as police, prosecutor, and corrections systems. The ability to share information across the justice systems is critical. In the past, information has always gone up the justice system. Police would make the initial arrest, and the prosecutor would either file or not. If the prosecutor filed, the information would be passed to the courts, but the final disposition was never known by the police.

Unfortunately, it has always been a difficult task to pass information back down the chain. As an example, it is not uncommon for police not to know the final adjudication of a case. The police arrest a subject for a felony, but the prosecutor files the case as a high-grade misdemeanor. When it gets to court, it is plea bargained to a low-grade misdemeanor. In the meantime, the police still hold a felony arrest on this person.

The court's role in the IJIS system is to provide information for the police, prosecutors, and corrections and include this information in the case record. Name search can occur, which will provide access to court cases. These are critical to sharing information within the criminal justice system.

References

Court System. (n.d.). Retrieved from http://www.ptssolution.com/court-records -software.html.

Courts. (n.d.). Retrieved from http://www.vcssoftware.com/content/solutions /court-scheduling.php.

Moonlighting Software. (2015). [Computer Software]. Boise, ID: Moonlight Software Corporation.

PTS Solutions. (1999). Court Management Systems [Computer Software]. Harrisonburg, LA.

PTS Solutions. (2015). [Computer Software]. Harrisonburg, LA: PTS Solutions.

chapter twelve

The challenges of implementing a criminal justice information system

The implementation of criminal justice information systems is an arduous process that requires significant planning and oversight if it is to be successful.

List of definitions

Central processing unit
FRS—functional requirement specification
Input/output
IT—information technology
PMI—Project Management Institute
RFP—request for proposal

Critical success factors in implementing criminal justice information systems

The implementation of any criminal justice information system requires a tremendous amount of effort and considerable expertise, not just on the part of the vendor selected to provide the system but also on the agency for the implementation. To this point, we have discussed the main systems used in the criminal justice environment. In the following subsections, we will discuss the implementation of these systems and the challenges faced by agencies when implementing these critical systems.

Many criminal justice agencies have learned that it requires a level of expertise to identify their information technology (IT) needs. Most criminal justice agencies do not have that expertise on staff and will often hire a consulting firm to help them through the procurement process. In some instances, they will hire a professional project manager to oversee the implementation of the system. In large agencies, they may have a trained project manager in their IT department who is capable of providing the necessary project management.

Functional requirement specification

Most criminal justice agencies will begin the process through the development of a functional requirement specification (FRS). The basis of the FRS is a comprehensive needs assessment. The process begins by reviewing all documentation prepared by the agency in support of the project. As part of this initial review, the consultant typically reviews previous reports prepared by outside entities, inside entities, or consultants. This occurs prior to their coming on site, so they have an idea of the challenges with developing and implementing a criminal justice system.

Once on site, the consultant reviews and assesses all of the processes performed by the justice agency they are working with to implement a new IT system. The consultant assesses both current and future needs of the agency. They will conduct a comprehensive needs assessment/needs analysis of the agency or each of the participating agencies if it is an integrated system. This occurs through detailed assessments of each operating unit within the justice agency such as police, prosecutor, or courts. This usually entails meeting with key individuals and the working staff to ensure the technology meets the needs of the people it serves.

The on-site needs assessment must address business issues, functional issues, and technical issues. Figure 12.1 depicts the components of a sample of a computer-aided dispatch (CAD), a record management system (RMS), and a mobile computing system.

The functional requirement specification captures these needs, as defined in the next section.

Development of an FRS

The development of a specification document requires that the agency's needs be appropriately identified and categorized as well as documented. This is a critically essential component in this process and consists of the three critical assessments: business, functional, and technical requirements.

Business issues

Business issues cover a significant portion of any project. The author defines business issues as those project components that must be satisfied to function within the culture of each of the departments. Business requirements transfer into functional needs, and they encompass the following:

Technical issues
– Hardware issues
– Software issues
– Networking issues
– CDMA, radio, Wi-Fi, etc.
– Interoperability

Functional issues
– CAD, RMS, mobile
– Required interfaces
– Communications
– Future needs
– Data throughput

Business issues
– Goals, objectives
– Required tasks
– Cost benefit
– On going support
– Special programs

Figure 12.1 Project components.

- The current business practices used to conduct day-to-day functions in the organization and how IT can enhance the efficiency in performing these required tasks.
- What are the department's goals and objectives and how can IT assist the department in achieving and implementing those goals and objectives?
- Required training both at the time of implementation and after implementation. The issues addressed are how difficult is the system(s) to train? Does it require follow-up training by the vendor?
- What level of system support is required post implementation? The installation of a new system with enhanced capabilities will likely require additional or different support demands than are currently being experienced. It is important to assess the impact on the agencies information systems support staff.
- What are the financial costs of implementing the new system, and what are the ongoing support costs for such a system? Too often, agencies fail to recognize the true support costs. As an example, most vendors provide upgrades to their software, providing the entity is paying an annual support fee. What is rarely recognized is that there can be significant additional cost associated with an upgrade if the agency must rely on the vendor to actually upgrade their system.
- Upgrades and enhancement are critical toward the integration of current and future systems. The system to be implemented must be capable of accommodating this growth. Just as importantly, the vendor selected must be capable of keeping pace with critical changing business practices so often experienced in the criminal justice environment.
- The business issues include the development of a comprehensive implementation plan that correlates with budgetary cycles.
- The development of a realistic implementation plan must be part of the business issues.

These are only a few of the many business issues that require consideration when developing an FRS and implementing a new enterprise system.

Functional issues

The functional issues pertain specifically to the processes performed through the course of normal business. These processes include the required interactions with other emergency service and justice agencies within the city and or county such as courts and emergency management agency. The approach to obtaining functional requirements entails careful examination of the work tasks required. Consultants will conduct an on-site analysis to verify these needs. In the development of the comprehensive functional design specification, they will carefully construct information-flow diagrams to ensure that the flow of data is consistent with how the agency performs their required tasks. The consultant will identify those requirements where IT can improve departmental operations. The result of the functional requirement analysis is an FRS that specifies the required functionality of an integrated system.

Technical issues

Critical to the needs assessment and consequently the FRS is the technology issues to meet the functional and business needs. The technical component requires a solid architecture capable of supporting the data flow volumes associated with the criminal justice agency's needs. The technical components include the following:

- Hardware (file servers, workstations, printers, laptops, PDAs, etc.)
- Software (CAD, records, and mobile computing)
- Internal and external interface requirements
- Integration requirements with other internal and external systems

Figure 12.2 helps to visualize how the business and functional issues come together. It highlights that the basis of technology surrounds the needs of business and functional requirements, and not the reverse. It depicts the requirement process.

After the completion of the functional requirement specification, the agency can then move on to the acquisition phase, using the FRS as the blueprint for the system to be acquired and installed.

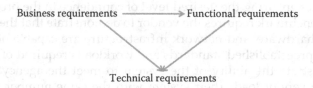

Figure 12.2 Requirement process.

Development of the request for proposal

Criminal justice agencies typically acquire the system that is going to meet their needs identified in the FRS by developing a comprehensive request for proposal (RFP) that they distribute to the vendor community that provides these types of systems.

The consultant develops the necessary RFP/statement of work as specified in this requirement. The basis for this procurement document is the FRS as describe in the previous section.

Upon the development of the RFP, the consultant typically provides the client with a draft RFP for their review. The consultant meets with the client to review the draft and document any requested change, to review last minute issues, and to establish a final calendar of events for the proposal. The consultant will then make the necessary changes and finalize the RFP released to the vendor community for their response.

After the final closing date and the receipt of the proposals, the consultant will typically assist the justice agency in evaluating the proposals to determine the best proposals. The agency, with the consultant, usually narrows down the vendors to what they often refer to as the "short list." Usually, this is three to five vendors that are invited to go through a more detailed selection process. This next phase of the process typically entails an oral presentation, where the agency asks the vendor to present their company and the proposed products. In the earlier days of criminal justice information system procurement, this was typically an opportunity to ask the vendor questions and for the vendor to demonstrate their product(s). Today, this part of the procurement process has become far more sophisticated.

Consulting firms now conduct what some refer to as a benchmark test. Benchmark testing requires vendors to demonstrate their systems ability to meet the criteria specified in the RFP. The benchmark tests their proposal under similar workload the agency can expect when they go operational. Benchmark testing provides the ability to observe the system under nearly realistic conditions. Traditional approaches used in the past consist of a review of the vendor's proposal, an oral interview, a software demonstration, and reference checks on the vendor's existing client base. Normally, this process consumed a half to a full day to complete but fell well short of ensuring the desired level of confidence in the product.

The benchmark requires the vendor to demonstrate that the proposed software, hardware, and network infrastructure are capable of performing to the preestablished standards and workloads required of the client. To demonstrate the ability of the system to meet the agency's requirements, the vendor loads their system with the same number of records that the agency is likely to load before going operational. The consultant then conducts performance tests over a network where they adjust the network load. The consultant also requires that the vendor provide test software that can vary the central processing unit and disk input/output. The purpose is to simulate the number of users and activity on a normal working system. The consultant then has them enter data and inquire the system just like it would occur in the real world. They then include the recorded results as part of the contract. The system that best meets the performance criteria is the one selected for the agency.

The development of the final contract encompasses all of these findings and helps to establish the system acceptance test. Developing the contract must be specific. The vendor provides many promises during the procurement phase. The agency also specifies several requirements; it is critical that the contract reflect these requirements. In addition, the contract must also include a payment plan based on useable deliverables. These contracts should include a timeline that includes penalties for not meeting the scheduled dates. These are all part of the contract phase.

Implementing the system

Implementing the selected system requires an organized and well-managed process. The reality is that most criminal justice agencies lack experience at the implementation of complex, integrated systems. Some agencies are wise enough to understand this issue, and they usually have successful implementations. Others think that they can handle this on their own, or they put all of their trust and faith in the company they hired to implement the information system.

Project management is a critical factor in the implementation of a new system. Project implementation consists of two key components if the IT system is going to be successful. The management of the project is critical to successful implementation. Equally important is to manage the change that is going to occur with the implementation of a new system. The author's involvement in the implementation of hundreds of IT systems across the country provided him with experience with many successful implementations. Unfortunately, he has also seen poorly implemented systems that did not follow these two key elements, which in turn failed or created significant difficulties. To ensure successful projects, the author supports the philosophies and principles developed and put forth by the Project Management Institute (PMI). The PMI's principles and practices address these issues.

In the following subsections, we address project management and change management associated with the implementation of new systems.

The role of the "executive" champion

The implementation of a substantial criminal justice system such as an RMS requires significant support from the leader of the organization, such as the chief of police. The head of the organization must support the implementation of the new system at all levels. It is crucial for others in the organization that report to the executive, either directly or indirectly, to understand that the implementation of the new system is critical to the organization and vital to the key executive. This executive championing is crucial to a successful implementation.

As a leader, simply stating support for the project is not enough. The executive manager must also play a significant role. The author by no means believes the executive has to take a day-to-day role in the project but must provide guidance. According to Dr. Ireland (2006),

> Executive management sets strategic goals for the organization and uses projects to meet those goals. The requirements of the strategic goals must flow down to projects, and the Executive Managers must ensure the projects have a direct alignment with the goals. Any change to the strategic goals might be cause for a change to projects such as to terminate, modify, or continue under different project goals.

In criminal justice environments, it is not likely that the chief executive is going to have a day-to-day hand in the implementation of a system, although that might occur in smaller organizations. Typically, the chief executive in a justice organization will appoint or hire a qualified project manager to handle the details of the implementation of a project. A good chief executive will require biweekly or monthly reports where he or she can be briefed on the status of the project. In these meetings, the project manager can raise the risk factors to the attention of the chief executive and obtain direction where and when necessary. Keeping an open line of communications is critical in the implementation of an IT project.

Critical to the project is the assurance that the chief executive is behind the project, as demonstrated through the processes discussed previously.

The role of the project manager

Obviously, the role of the project manager is significant and critical to the successful implementation of a criminal justice information system. Often we see justice agencies appoint someone from within their organization to serve as the project manager. Although this is usually appropriate with large agencies that often have significant IT professionals, most medium and small agencies do not have qualified personnel to serve as project managers. It is not uncommon for the medium and smaller agencies to contract with IT professionals that are capable of providing quality project managers.

The project manager is responsible for the day-to-day management of the project. He or she must be skilled in a variety of areas. The project manager must be able to communicate both verbally and in the written word. He or she must be able to schedule resources both within the organization and with external resources. He or she must have a thorough understanding of the system(s) to be installed and must work with the selected vendor to ensure the systems are implemented as anticipated. He or she must be able to control scope creep and control costs. The project manager must also be able to time manage the project to ensure enough time allotted by not just the vendor but equally important the agency. These are only a few of the skills required of a project manager. The success of the project typically depends on the project manager.

The project manager must be able to manage every aspect of the project. He or she must know when the project is in difficulty and be able to identify the source of those difficulties. Equally important, the project manager must know how and when to engage the resources that are available to him or her. There are many tools to help the project manager with these issues.

The end user and managing their expectations

The end user is the reason for a new system, to provide greater efficiencies and to improve the end user's productivity. Obviously, the implementation of a new system does not always achieve these goals. Not meeting the end user's needs occurs for many reasons. The problem can stem from the requirement-gathering phase and throughout the project. Other than system failure, the most prevalent reason is improperly managing their expectations.

The acquisition process in government is a long one. As an example, the implementation of a police RMS usually is 2 years in the making. During this time, there is a great deal of talk that occurs about the new system and what it will do for the organization. The end users begin to develop expectations as to how the new system is going to improve their work environment. Often, many of these expectations are exaggerated. If the project executive and the project manager do not manage these expectations appropriately, the agency runs the risk of end user disillusionment, which can lead to the rejection of the new system.

Establishing appropriate end user expectations is critical. A good project manager will engage the end users throughout the project process to make them feel that they have had input into the new system's design and implementation. There are also many other issues that must be addressed by the project manager to ensure the appropriate assimilation of the end user with the new system. As an example, if the agency is replacing an older system that has been working in the agency for a long time, the end user is accustomed to that system when doing their primary job.

Training is one of the best ways to ensure that the end user will know how the new system accomplishes what they need to do. The author has seen good systems fail because of poor training, and mediocre systems succeed because of good training. There are currently two forms of training used in the implementation of justice systems in today's technology environment: (1) the traditional means of classroom training, where the vendor comes on site with a training team and the vendor's team provides all personnel training, and (2) "train the trainer," which is preferred by the vendor and many agencies because of costs. With this option, the agency will select from within their own staff those who will provide training to the other employees. These selected few receive full training on the system by the vendor; they in turn go out into the organization and train all the others.

Both of these training methodologies can be effective in the right environment. The problem with the train-the-trainer, however, is that often a loss of information occurs between the time that the trainer receives training and the time that they begin training the end user. It has also been recognized that the level of software sophistication must also be taken into account. Highly complex systems are not good candidates for train-the-trainer programs and should not be left to train the trainer. The train-the-trainer method with less complex systems is possible and works successfully. The key is knowing the environment as well as the capability of the end user. As an example, if the agency is replacing an older system but the end user is computer oriented, the train-the-trainer method may be a more viable solution than an agency where the end user is going from paper to automation. However, agencies moving from old IT to modern-day technology may have the same difficulties with the train-the-trainer method as an agency being computerized for the first time, perhaps more.

The following is an actual case study that demonstrates this problem (Ioimo, 2009):

In 2005, the San Jose, California, Police Department moved to replace their existing CAD system in their combined communication center that they used since 1989. San Jose is a major U.S. city. It is the ninth largest city in the United States. This is an extremely busy communication center.

The call takers and dispatchers were used to their old character-based CAD system, which was replaced with a new system with a graphical user interface front end.

The decision was made that to implement the new CAD system and to save money training the end users, the train-the-trainer approach would be used. There were a number of issues that were not adequately addressed at the time of this decision. As an example, with one hundred employees to train, the length of time to train everyone was not adequately considered. This meant there were many call takers and dispatchers that were trained early but waited over a month before the system went operational. This proved problematic in that once they did go live, much of what they had learned had been forgotten.

When San Jose went live, havoc occurred in the communication center. Call takers and dispatchers could not remember how to perform critical tasks. The volume of calls created a very busy environment. As the evening progressed, it got busier, and the dispatchers could not keep pace. The people that were the trainers were at the dispatch center, but because there were so many people having difficulties, they could not keep up with the requests for assistance. Oftentimes, the trainers themselves had forgotten how to do certain tasks.

The officers in the field had new mobile computer software to match the new CAD system. Their system was working well as the officers were comfortable using the new mobile software. The officers became concerned about the new CAD system and believed it was becoming a safety issue. The Police Officer's Association brought a lawsuit against the city.

In the end, it was determined that training was the issue; although there were some software issues, the software was not the problem, but the training caused a safety issue. The vendor was made to retrain the call takers and dispatchers. Once they went operational after the training, there was no problem, and the system has been working fine ever since.

This case study demonstrates the need for the appropriate training and managing expectations of the end user. Both the executive manager and the project manager have responsibilities in this area. Both should work to keep the expectations as to the new system's capabilities realistic and not over build its capabilities.

Project planning

Project planning is a core element of project management. Whenever a system is being implemented, a detailed plan needs to be put into place. The plan must be comprehensive and include the specific tasks required to ensure the successful implementation of the system. Too often, cities and counties will accept the project plan provided by the vendor. This plan typically addresses the company's requirements but often fails to include the tasks the justice agency is required to complete to ensure the project's success. Likewise, agencies want to hold the vendor responsible for time delays by providing financial penalties when the vendor goes a certain period of time past the deliverable due date, e.g., if the code tables are 45 days past due, the vendor is charged a fee. Although they want to hold the contractor financially liable, they do not accept penalties when they are late with a needed piece that impacts the project schedule. This is an issue that is slowly being addressed in this environment.

There are several software packages that assist in project planning. These software packages provide the ability to track each task and record information pertaining to that task. Project planning software also tracks costs; thus, the project manager can determine if the project is under or over budget. Figure 12.3 depicts a sample project plan and Gantt chart for an actual consulting project.

Although this is a high-level plan, there are many other critical elements to the plan that the software is capable of producing that assists the project manager in planning and managing the project.

Scope creep and how to manage it

A significant problem that many criminal justice agencies face when implementing an information system is scope creep. The continuous addition of requirements after the completion of the initial design phase and the software development and implementation of the system has begun causes scope creep (Scope Creep Definition, n.d.). In the early days of criminal justice information systems, this was a serious problem, primarily because agencies were not sure of what they needed, and as the project progressed, it saw the addition of new items. The problem with scope creep is that it adds risk to the project, and it can cause substantial budget overages to occur.

Scope creep occurs for a variety of reasons, some legitimate and some not. The important thing is for the project manager to manage scope creep. Ideally, once the project is underway and a contract is executed between the agency and the contractor, the deliverables should not change. Obviously, we live in a real world, and that is not always possible. Changes are going to occur. The larger the project and the longer it takes to implement the system, the likelihood of scope changes occurring increases, sometimes substantially.

Legitimate changes in scope typically occur because of a change in the law that requires database or process changes. As an example, the author was in the process of helping a major city implement a new police RMS. When the project began, the agency was reporting crime to the FBI using the traditional uniform crime reporting format. Just before the scheduled "go live" date, the state required that all agencies report using the state's version of the National Incident-Based Reporting System.

ID	WBS	Task Name	Duration	Work	Start	Finish	Timeline
1	1	EMERGENCY COMMUNICATION CAD/AFR CONSULTING PROJECT	220 days	1,499.73 hrs	Mon 11/3/14	Fri 9/4/15	
2	1.1	Project Management	220 days	0 hrs	Mon 11/3/14	Fri 9/4/15	
3	1.2	Pre Onsite Review	10 days	0 hrs	Mon 11/3/14	Fri 11/14/14	
4	1.3	RWCC collect requested documents and forward to PSCI	2 days	0 hrs	Mon 11/3/14	Tue 11/4/14	
5	1.4	RWCC Site Pre and Meeting Support	2 days	0 hrs	Mon 11/17/14	Tue 11/18/14	
6	1.5	TASK 1: Review Operational Requirements	13 days	144 hrs	Wed 11/19/14	Fri 12/5/14	
7	1.5.1	Business Issues	2.5 days	40 hrs	Wed 11/19/14	Fri 11/21/14	Ralph Ioimo,William Bridenburg
8	1.5.2	Functional Issues	2.5 days	40 hrs	Fri 11/21/14	Tue 11/25/14	Linda Hill,Ralph Ioimo
9	1.5.3	Technical Issues	5 days	40 hrs	Wed 11/26/14	Tue 12/2/14	Tom Davey
10	1.5.4	Budgetary Analysis	3 days	24 hrs	Wed 12/3/14	Fri 12/5/14	Ralph Ioimo
11	1.5.5	RWCC Onsite Support	13 days	0 hrs	Wed 11/19/14	Fri 12/5/14	
12	1.6	Needs Assessment/Functional Requirement Specification Development	32 days	852 hrs	Mon 12/8/14	Tue 1/20/15	
13	1.6.1	Introduction section	2 days	16 hrs	Mon 12/8/14	Tue 12/9/14	Ralph Ioimo
14	1.6.2	Global Requirements	3 days	24 hrs	Wed 12/10/14	Fri 12/12/14	Linda Hill
15	1.6.3	CAD/Mobile and Field Automated Reporting Requirements	20 days	640 hrs	Mon 12/15/14	Fri 1/9/15	Ralph Ioimo,William Bride
16	1.6.4	Develop Functional Requirement Specification	15 days	120 hrs	Mon 12/8/14	Fri 12/26/14	Ralph Ioimo
17	1.6.5	Raleigh County Review of Functional Requirements	10 days	0 hrs	Mon 12/29/14	Fri 1/9/15	
18	1.6.6	Joint PSCI-RWCC Needs Assessment/Functional Requirements Review	2 days	32 hrs	Mon 1/12/15	Tue 1/13/15	Ralph Ioimo,Tom Davey
19	1.6.7	Finalize Needs Assessment/Functional Requirements Specification	5 days	20 hrs	Wed 1/14/15	Tue 1/20/15	Ralph Ioimo[25%],Lindi
20	1.7	TASK II: Request for Proposal Development	28 days	112 hrs	Wed 1/21/15	Fri 2/27/15	
21	1.7.1	Introduction to RFP	2 days	8 hrs	Wed 1/21/15	Thu 1/22/15	Ralph Ioimo[50%]
22	1.7.2	Description of required services	3 days	12 hrs	Fri 1/23/15	Tue 1/27/15	Ralph Ioimo[50%]
23	1.7.3	Minimum Qualifications	1 day	4 hrs	Wed 1/28/15	Wed 1/28/15	Ralph Ioimo[50%]
24	1.7.4	Proposal Process	1 day	8 hrs	Thu 1/29/15	Thu 1/29/15	Linda Hill
25	1.7.5	Evaluation Section	3 days	12 hrs	Fri 1/30/15	Tue 2/3/15	Tom Davey[50%]
26	1.7.6	Functional Requirements Section	5 days	20 hrs	Wed 2/4/15	Tue 2/10/15	Ralph Ioimo[50%]
27	1.7.7	Pricing	1 day	4 hrs	Wed 2/11/15	Wed 2/11/15	Ralph Ioimo[50%]
28	1.7.8	Develop Evaluation Criteria	3 days	12 hrs	Thu 2/12/15	Mon 2/16/15	Tom Davey[50%]
29	1.7.9	Review Proposal with RWCC	4 days	12 hrs	Tue 2/17/15	Fri 2/20/15	Ralph Ioimo[25%
30	1.7.10	Final Modification of Proposal	5 days	20 hrs	Mon 2/23/15	Fri 2/27/15	Ralph Ioimo[50%
31	1.8	TASK III: Selection Process	84 days	391.73 hrs	Mon 3/2/15	Thu 6/25/15	
32	1.8.1	Release RFP to Vendors	1 day	0 hrs	Mon 3/2/15	Mon 3/2/15	
33	1.8.2	Vendor Response	45 days	0 hrs	Tue 3/3/15	Mon 5/4/15	
34	1.8.3	Vendor Conference RWCC and PSCI	2 days	16 hrs	Wed 3/18/15	Thu 3/19/15	Tom Davey
35	1.8.4	Evaluation of Proposals RWCC and PSCI	3 days	14.4 hrs	Mon 5/4/15	Wed 5/6/15	Ral
36	1.8.5	Conduct Benchmark Test RWCC and PSCI	10 days	160 hrs	Thu 5/7/15	Wed 5/20/15	
37	1.8.6	Conduct Reference Checks	3 days	24 hrs	Thu 5/21/15	Mon 5/25/15	
38	1.8.7	Vendor Recommendation and Support Services	5 days	40 hrs	Tue 5/26/15	Mon 6/1/15	
39	1.8.8	Vendor Contract negotiations RWCC and PSCI	15 days	113.33 hrs	Tue 6/2/15	Mon 6/22/15	
40	1.8.9	Finalize Contract Negotiations RWCC and PSCI	3 days	24 hrs	Tue 6/23/15	Thu 6/25/15	
41	2	TASK IV: Project Management	62 days	456 hrs	Mon 6/29/15	Tue 9/22/15	
42	2.1	Onsite meetings required throughout the project PSCI and RWCC	20 days	120 hrs	Mon 6/29/15	Fri 7/24/15	
43	2.2	Review of Vendor Documentation as required PSCI and RWCC	10 days	80 hrs	Mon 7/27/15	Fri 8/7/15	
44	2.3	Monthly Status Reports RWCC Review	12 days	96 hrs	Mon 8/10/15	Tue 8/25/15	
45	2.4	Vendor Contact and Management	20 days	160 hrs	Wed 8/26/15	Tue 9/22/15	
46	3	TASK V: System Acceptance	38 days	186.67 hrs	Wed 9/23/15	Mon 11/16/15	
47	3.1	Oversite of system testing PSCI and RWCC	20 days	106.67 hrs	Wed 9/23/15	Tue 10/20/15	
48	3.2	Oversite of "go live"	10 days	80 hrs	Wed 10/21/15	Tue 11/3/15	
49	3.3	Project Complete	0 days	0 hrs	Mon 11/16/15	Mon 11/16/15	

Figure 12.3 Sample project plan.

This was a substantial change to the purchased software. Because it was a law change, it had to be made in order for the new system to be compliant with state law. This type of scope creep can occur during the implementation phase of a computer project.

On the other hand, desired changes or desired additions that are not specifically required for the success of the project are the types of scope

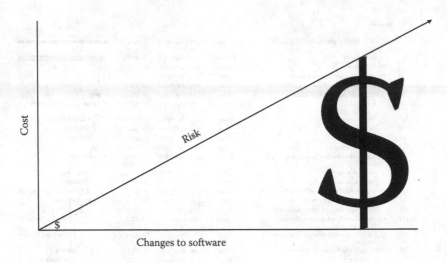

Figure 12.4 Scope creep risk.

changes that need to be avoided. This typically occurs when a project is in progress and someone in the agency argues the need to include a new workgroup application that was not previously planned. As an example, the author worked with an agency that specifically stated in their initial functional requirement specification that they would not need a property and evidence workgroup because they had just purchased one that was meeting their needs. The property room manager went to a conference where he saw a new property and evidence system that he believed would be perfect for his property and evidence room. He argued that it should be installed with the new RMS. The project manager argued against implementing the new workgroup application because it was going to set the project back by 3 months and would add $120,000.00 to the project. They would have to obtain that money because the project was already at its financial limit. This is a typical problem that increases risk, costs, and time to a project. Figure 12.4 graphically depicts this problem.

A critical project manager responsibility is the ability to control scope creep. If allowed to run unchecked or checked very little, the cost will go up exponentially, as will the project risk. Criminal justice information system implementations should avoid intentional scope creep at all costs. Unavoidable scope creep should be managed by the project manager and kept to as minimal as possible.

Test plans and procedures

Critical to the implementation of criminal justice information systems is making sure the system is capable of meeting the agency's needs and the agency is receiving what it contracted for from the contractor. To ensure this occurs, the system should be thoroughly tested before it goes operational. Testing should occur at three levels: component level, integration level, and system level. Component level testing consists of testing the subcomponents of the total system. As an example, a component to a police RMS might be the property and evidence module. This module would be tested on its own, which helps to identify where problems exist.

Integration testing is the next phase in the testing process. Each module and interface that comprise the entire system were independently tested. Then as other modules and components become available and installed, they were tested again to insure that the integration is successful and that the new component, when added to the system, does not cause problems. Many times, we find integration testing disregarded. Typically, it is time consuming and requires performing significant testing. Many contractors choose to disregard integration testing until the final system test. Conducting the integration testing with the addition of new components allows the end user and the contractor to identify a faulty component at the time it is implemented.

Upon the completion of the system implementation, a comprehensive system-level test should be conducted. The system test tests all components of the system. The secondary phase of system-level testing is the "go live" test. With this component, the system must continuously run for a contracted amount of time, usually 30 days. If the system continuously runs without errors, the testing ends.

Prior to any software or interface testing, a set of test plans and test procedures must be developed at two levels, the component level and the system level. The test plans must address how testing will occur at each level. They should identify each system component that requires testing. The test procedures specify exactly how to test each component of the system; they should specify the approach for the integrated system. As an example, in a criminal justice RMS, a component could be a single module, such as an arrest module. Upon completion of that component, it would be tested to insure it meets all of the requirements and works as specified in the design document. Upon completion of all modules and the completion of the system integration, a systemwide test will take place to insure that all components work together and that the system as a whole meets the specified requirements.

During each of the testing phases, the errors must be recorded. The best process used is to divide the errors into three levels of severity. Level 1 errors are catastrophic errors. They are errors that cause the entire system to crash; hence, end users are unable to process until the completion of error repairs. When a level 1 occurs, all processing stops; this also stops the testing period. Upon fixing the error that caused the catastrophic failure, the system level testing restarts as does the time clock for the amount of time the system must stay operational before accepted.

Level 2 errors are serious errors, but they do not bring down the entire system and/or there are ways around the problem. They are serious enough that the system cannot be accepted with these errors. The system can still function in other areas; therefore, the system test can continue, but system acceptance cannot occur until all fixes take place and the system runs without further level 1 or level 2 errors.

Level 3 errors are not serious enough to prohibit the system from going live, nor do they stop the 30-day continuous operational process. These are minor software errors, such as a misspelled word on a screen or some other minor issue that does not detract from processing. These are errors that must be fixed but do not stop the system from going live, nor do they detract from the 30-day operational requirement. The contractor must fix these minor errors within the first year of the system's operation.

System acceptance occurs once the new system is free of level 1 and level 2 errors for a straight 30 days of operation.

Bringing a new system operational

There are other issues, however, that need to be considered when bringing a new system operational. It is not uncommon for an agency to implement a core or enterprise system as well as several workgroup applications. Critical to the success of the new system is to implement the system in phases. Typically, the core or enterprise system is the first to be implemented, followed by other workgroup applications. As an example, in a police department, the RMS is the core or enterprise system first installed and brought operational. Once the RMS is operational, the next most prominent workgroup application is implemented, followed by the next until all workgroups are operational. Figure 12.5 depicts sample multi-workgroup implementation.

The previously mentioned diagram is a typical law enforcement agency implementation. The order of implementation is dependent on the agency's needs. In a typical law enforcement agency, they would likely implement the RMS first, followed by the field mobile computing system, and then one of the other workgroups.

Bringing a new system operational in a phased approach as described earlier is the most manageable. Although the "big bang" approach may have worked for the development of the universe, it is not viable for the implementation of new IT systems. The phased approach provides the ability to manage the implementation to ensure assimilation occurs in an orderly manner.

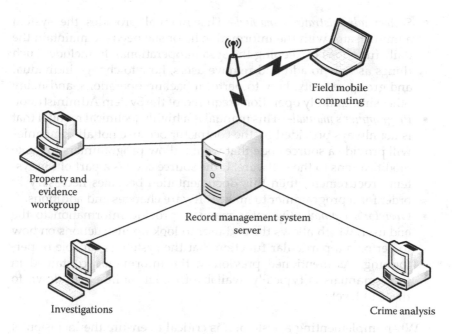

Field mobile
computing

Property and
evidence
workgroup

Record management system
server

Investigations

Crime analysis

Figure 12.5 Sample multi-workgroup implementation.

System documentation

System documentation is critical for the successful implementation and continued daily operations of criminal justice information systems. With early software development, documentation consisted of manual documents. If the system administrator or the end user required information or needed to know how to perform a specific function, they would open the manual and look up the specific task and follow the instructions provided to complete the task. In today's environment, the automation of this process occurs at several levels. Although it is often possible to print the required manuals, most systems use automated manuals linked to the software in ways that allow the end user to access information down to the field level usually by placing the cursor in the field they are seeking information about and by pressing the F-1 Help Key or right clicking on the mouse and select help.

The implementation of criminal justice information systems typically includes the following documentation, which are typically online but may also be printed for those who need hard copies:

- *System specifications*—These specifications serve as a blueprint for the installed systems. The agency can use these documents for the implementation of additional systems and to modify existing ones as may be necessary in the future.

- *System administrator's manual*—This manual provides the system administrator with the information he or she needs to maintain the daily functions of keeping the system operational. In includes such things as how to add and remove users, how to change individual and group security, how to perform backup operations, and many other similar daily operations required of the System Administrator.
- *Programmer's manual*—This manual is a highly technical manual that is not always provided by the contractor because not all companies will provide a source code that would allow programmers to make modifications to the software. If the source code is a part of the system procurement, then this documentation becomes necessary in order for a programmer to make software changes and additions.
- *Operator's manual*—Operator manuals provide information to the end user, which allows the end user to look up instructions on how to perform a particular function that the system is capable of performing. As mentioned previously, the information contained in these manuals is typically available through online help down to the field level.

When implementing a system, it is critical to ensure the inclusion of this information. It is also critical to test the manuals during the component- and system-level testing to ensure that the information is accurate and instructions have kept up with the changes and modifications that have occurred over time.

Daily support for installed systems

Managing the systems on a daily basis requires appropriate support staff. Most support for installed criminal justice systems comes from either city or county IT departments. Larger agencies employ their own IT staff. As an example, one of the author's clients has its own IT department, which consists of a staff of 108 IT professionals that consists of systems administrators, systems analysts, network analysts, and computer programmers. The department's IT staff supports an in-house developed RMS. They are currently in the process of implementing a commercial off-the-shelf RMS, which will change the staffing level considerably.

Smaller agencies do not have nearly the staffing of a large agency as the one described, but all agencies require system administrator support. It is not uncommon for a systems analyst to be assigned to handle the day-to-day computer system issues. In small agencies, one person is usually responsible for network, hardware, and software support. In large agencies, there can be staff assigned to support each of these areas.

Change management ensuring systems are used to their fullest potential

The implementation of criminal justice systems typically creates significant change. In most instances, that change is positive. However, realizing the benefits of a new system and adopting the required changes and assimilating those changes into the daily routines of the end users can be challenging. Regardless if an agency is implementing an information system for the first time or if they are replacing an existing system, change is going to occur, which will directly impact the agency and the end user. This change must be managed at all levels, or significant problems can arise that can cause another good system to fail.

In implementing a new system, there are two elements to a successful implementation, the technological element and the human element. The author has already discussed the approach to the technology implementation, testing, and system acceptance. The human element requires a change management plan that addresses how change is going to be brought about with the people who need to use the system. The implementing agency often neglects this area. They assume training will adequately address the end-user issues. The changes that occur as a result of the implementation of the new technology are disregarded.

New technology invariably forces users and agencies to do things differently. With the implementation of more technology, processes once done separately collapse into a single process. As an example, the officer turned in the handwritten crime reports at the end his or her shift. A supervisor reviewed the report, and once approved, the report went to the record's bureau where a records clerk would enter the data into the RMS. With the implementation of field mobile computing, the officer enters the information into his or her laptop and forwards it to the shift supervisor for approval. Once approved, the system uploads the report to the RMS and automatically populates the RMS database. What is no longer necessary is for the records clerk to have to enter that data. Given this new workflow, decisions must be made as to what is the new role of the records clerk. Obviously, this creates a great deal of uncertainty among employees.

A change management plan would assess this system before implementation, and decisions can be made in advance of when it goes live. Clearly, job functions are going to change at the least. If there is a need to reduce staff, which also needs to be planned, are the personnel going to be laid off or is the staff reduction going to be handled through attrition? It might be necessary to add technical staff. A change management plan addresses all of these issues.

In today's criminal justice information system environment, most systems have a significant amount of capability rarely used to its fullest by the agency. Often, we find that agencies request information through the RFP process and often pay for the additional capabilities but then never implement those components of the system that they bought. There are several reasons for this, but typically it surrounds the implementation process where these items are not properly addressed. In some instances, the end users do not realize that a specific capability exists because training did cover that capability. Change management planning would ensure that this does not occur and that all aspects of the system are addressed during training and that there is an implementation plan in place that addresses these new capabilities.

Change management is critical to the successful implementation of criminal justice information systems. Although this can add to the cost of a project, which is why many agencies do not contract with change management experts, it can also ensure the success of the new system(s).

User groups and criminal justice information systems

One of the major differences between criminal justice information systems and information systems in other environments is that most of the criminal justice software suppliers support user groups. User groups serve multiple purposes for companies that provide these systems. Membership in the user group provides the agency with technical support. Typically, technical support can be provided from 8:00 a.m. to 5:00 p.m., 5 days a week or 24 hours per day, 7 days per week. Obviously, the 24-hour, 7-day support will cost more money, but as agencies become more and more computerized, it is the preferred support level.

The user group also meets on an annual basis to discuss issues with the vendor that pertains to the software. These issues range from faults with the software to future requirements. There are usually many requirements for changes that the users bring forth at these meetings. The vendor typically captures each suggested software change. Usually, it is not feasible for the vendor to address each change requested by the end users. To address this, the vendor will have the user group members prioritize the changes. The vendor will usually commit to a specific number of changes that they will make before the next release of the software. All user group members receive the enhanced software as part of their membership fees.

Most vendors provide one software upgrade release per year included as part of the user group fee they charge the agency. The user receives the upgrade to install on their system without assistance from the vendor, other than perhaps telephone support. They do usually provide written instructions. There are instances, however, where the installation of the upgrade requires a substantial effort, and most agencies must contract with the vendor to implement the upgrade. Smaller agencies are likely to require the vendor to implement the complicated upgrades. The vendor does not charge for these enhancements; they are part of the user group fees. What they are charging for is the services to implement the enhancements.

There are other times when the vendor will charge the end user for a version release. A version release is typically a significant change in the existing software. As an example, a recent vendor in the marketplace provided a complete software rewrite, making their software fully XML compliant. This required that the end user totally upgrade their system, eliminating their old software to implement this new version. This upgrade also required data conversion. The vendor did charge the agency for the new software, the data conversion, and the training. The charge was considerably less than what an agency would pay were they not part of the user group.

Many end users elect to hold off on implementing version upgrades. A version upgrade would be like going from version 5.7 to 6.0. This typically occurs because the agency wants other agencies to test the software first before they implement the upgrade. In other words, they want to make sure the software does not have serious "bugs." This is a standard practice, particularly with large agencies that have high volumes of data and significant system usage. Most vendors understand this conservative approach to implementing a new version of the software. This becomes problematic when an agency falls several versions behind the most current. Vendors establish a maximum number of previous versions that they will support. If an agency falls too far behind, it no longer can obtain support for the software. The vendor does not want to support many different versions of the software, so they establish a specific number of back versions that they will support.

Managing system growth and budgeting for change

As agencies become more computerized, system growth occurs naturally. System growth also becomes an issue in several ways over time. Upon implementing a new system, and as long as it is implemented correctly, it should meet all of the agency's current requirements. Over time, new features and functional requirements begin to emerge. These can occur as a result of changes in the laws, new processes or procedures, or other changes that the existing system is unable to meet or address. When this occurs, agencies adapt in different ways, but often they will implement a stand-alone system to address the new requirement. The computer industry refers to these as "stovepipes."

These stand-alone systems do not integrate with the core system or the enterprise database. They usually require specialized software, and they are not supported by the IT staff of agencies. Before long, there are multiple "stovepipes" throughout the organization. This becomes costly and operationally hazardous. As an example, the author worked with one large agency in the development of an FRS for the procurement of a new system. During that process, we discovered that various units throughout the department had either developed systems of their own to address specific problems or purchased third-party applications. Redundant data entry was occurring throughout the department. Agencies hired multiple people to do the necessary data entry. The installation of the existing core system occurred 10 years prior. Many things had changed in that time, and the old system could not keep up with the requirements. In the end, the new system was able to eliminate all of these redundant systems, saving the agency approximately ten million dollars.

Another agency that the author worked with had a similar problem. The core system was so outdated that the detectives no longer relied on it, and a detective with some computing skills built a system that the unit began to use. They would enter their own crime reports, arrest reports, and wants and warrants. The records division was also entering this information, but not in a coordinated manner. A problem occurred when a detective arrested and booked a man on a warrant that was in the detective's system but patrol previously cleared this warrant and removed it from the main system.

These types of problems occur because the criminal justice agencies tend to cling to old, outdated systems. These systems need to be updated on a regular basis. They also need to be maintained and kept current with the upgrades the vendors provide. The hardware and the software should be depreciated at industry standard rates and replaced when fully depreciated with the last technology. This avoids the stovepipes discussed previously.

References

Ioimo, R.E. (2009). San Jose Computer Aided Dispatch Study. Public Safety Consultants, Inc., 2009.

Ireland, L. (2006). *Executive management's role in project management*. Retrieved from http://www.asapm.org/asapmag/articles/ExecRoles.pdf.

Scope Creep Definition (n.d.). Retrieved from http://www.pcmag.com/encyclopedia/term/50891/scope-creep.

chapter thirteen

The future of technology in law enforcement

Technology is moving faster and faster as is its influence on police operations.

List of definitions

ALPR—Automated License Plate Reader
ESRI—Environmental Science Research Institute
FBI–CJIS—Federal Bureau of Investigations–Criminal Justice Information Systems
FirstNet—First Responder Network Authority
GIS—Geographic Information Systems
IACP—International Association of Chiefs of Police
LTE—Long Term Evolution
NLETS—National Law Enforcement Telecommunications System
PERF—Police Executive Research Forum

Introduction

Predicting the future of technology in law enforcement is a challenge because of the rapid rate of change in technology (some would call it a tsunami of change) and the simultaneous invention of new operating modes for policing. Making any useful predictions for more than 3 years into the future becomes more speculative than scientific, and anything much further out than 3 years becomes a guess. Despite this reality, futurists, including the Society of Police Futurists International writing in 2015, are optimistically attempting to predict the state of the art in 2020, which has some attraction as a measuring point if, for no other reason, it ends the current decade (Society of Police Futurists International, 2015).

This chapter will operate on this same general time frame, as any attempt to predict the nature of technology let alone its application in law enforcement beyond 2020 is not likely to envision the nature of technology or law enforcement much beyond this milestone. Even within this time frame, the accuracy of any predictions given herein decays rapidly beyond approximately 12 months.

There exists a very distinct linkage between innovations in technology and innovations in police operations. The introduction of two-way radios in policing resulted in the widespread introduction of mobile police patrol. Although some critics have decried the isolation that such technology may have created between the police and the public, there is no doubt that this technology innovation shaped the future of police patrol practices. During the past several decades, there are many other examples of how technological innovations such as the mobile computer have shaped the nature of police operations and practices. The opposite is also true—as new modes of policing have been explored; such innovations have provided opportunities for technological innovations. As only one example, the emphasis on data-driven policing in the 1990s stimulated the market for geographic information systems (GISs) in policing (see Federal Communications Commission, 2015).

Given the recognition of the linkage between technology innovation and operations innovation, the changing models of police operations provide a basis for suggesting how technology will evolve to support policing objectives and strategies. These forces, when combined with the emerging environmental changes, give us some guidance in estimating the development of new technology that may be invented even if it does not exist today. These factors become the drivers for changes in the application of technology in law enforcement.

This chapter will begin with a discussion of the drivers and then will attempt to predict the basis for technological innovation suggested by these drivers and current and near-term technological innovations that may be relevant to law enforcement.

Driving forces influencing technology adoption

As discussed previously, the two categories of drivers leading to the adoption of new technology are the changes in policing models and the environmental factors that police must deal with as the nature of crime and society changes.

Changes in policing models

A more common practice for early cloud computing adaptors seems to be a fixed monthly cost per user, which is paid out of operating budgets rather than with large capital expenditures. An example of a current cloud-based offering following this model is the product offered by Datamaxx, which provides full NCIC and NLETS access over a cloud-based network that fully complies with FBI CJIS security requirements with 24/7 technical support at a cost of $10 per user per month.

The practice of policing has undergone a steady evolution through early post World War II models toward a much more sophisticated response that has seen the introduction of community-based policing, data-driven policing, intelligence-led policing, and most recently what has been called predictive policing. From the discussions at meetings of national policing organizations such as the International Association of Chiefs of Police (IACP), the Police Executive Research Forum (PERF), and others, it is clear that there is an emerging reemphasis on the police function of prevention as opposed to what has been called the 911 model or a model responsive to calls about crimes or incidents. Police agencies are therefore seeking technologies, such as those provided by business intelligence software products or their more modern incorporation of predictive analytics, to assist in determining where the next criminal incidents will occur. Today, a number of police agencies are using predictive analytics software to estimate the location of potential crimes and thereby assign resources to prevent them. This form of policing will significantly change policing in the future.

There has also been an emerging trend connected to the prevention model that has been built on the notion of "hot spot" policing, where resources are assigned to patrol or monitor the locations where the highest number of serious crimes occur. These strategies rely on the use of spatial analysis capabilities of the GIS software that has been applied to this market, and further enhancement of GIS capabilities, including predictive capabilities, is likely to find a way into law enforcement. The evolving interest in "hot spot" policing has been reinforced by the research conducted by Braga and Weisburd (2010) on location-based policing. The changes in police operations and the corresponding reliance on technology in the form of spatial analysis software will continue to grow as police make even more radical changes in operations in support of the location-based policing model. At a recent conference, several police chiefs reported on the fact that they had abolished the beat concept in favor of allocating resources to probable locations as a function of the time of day. This kind of radical innovation in operations will lead to the need for more sophisticated resource allocation software.

Environmental factors driving innovation

No summary of the environmental factors influencing the adoption of new technology would be complete without reference to the financial crisis that the nation experienced beginning in 2007 to 2015, which has resulted in the reduction of approximately 10% of the police personnel in the country, according to the PERF.

Cloud computing and administrative functions

Another important part of the approach to cloud computing that concerns law enforcement executives is the nature of the applications that are selected as being appropriately provided by cloud computing. The initial applications that have been implemented or proposed for government purposes have mostly been associated with what are sometimes called administrative functions. It is fairly common for government agencies to explore and, in some cases, to implement the use of cloud computing for such applications as e-mail and document storage and retrieval. Companies have continued to expand offerings for cloud-based e-mail, word processing, and other office automation functions. These functions are web-based applications requiring only a browser to operate.

Law enforcement has been slow to adopt the use of cloud computing. As part of city or county operations, law enforcement agencies have seen their e-mail and document creation and storage migrate to the web and to a cloud computing model only because the whole of a city or county is making such a change.

Some agencies, sometimes driven by central government approaches, will turn to cloud computing for administrative functions such as personnel management, training, customer relations, and vehicle maintenance, just to name a few. In cases where very high application availability in support of a direct mission is not a requirement, using cloud computing—even public cloud computing—makes economic and policy sense.

There are a host of cloud computing-based applications that are useful to law enforcement that either supplement or enhance on-premise information technology applications. A good example is the robust offering from ESRI of a cloud computing–based GIS (Environmental Research Systems Institute, n.d.). Bair Analytics has implemented a regional crime analysis system that provides a cloud-based analytical tool for data visualization that agencies can use at no cost to share incident data across geographical boundaries and share such data with the public (Bair Analytics, n.d.). Taser has added a cloud-based service of creating and maintaining a digital evidence locker originally designed as a place to store and manage (with full chain of evidence management) the video files taken from officers wearing miniature video cameras (Taser International, Digital Evidence Management, n.d.). SST offers its ShotSpotter Flex offering as a cloud-based service, in this case using the Intrado NG 911 conformant cloud service to provide a subscription-based service of the ShotSpotter capabilities (Urgent Communications, n.d.).

Cloud computing and mission critical functions

The use of cloud computing for mission critical IT functions in law enforcement is not well developed. There are only a few agencies at the time of this writing that claim to be using cloud computing for such critical functions as access to state and federal crime data bases, computer-aided dispatch (CAD), records management systems (RMSs), or intelligence systems. Some of the subsystems that support these mission critical purposes do operate in a web mode, and some of the actual applications have been built to use Internet technology, including browser-based operations, but these applications tend to be run on servers controlled by and on the premises of the police department or communications center. In some cases, the servers running these critical systems are part of the city or county data center, but even this remote placement has caused problems over the years.

Supporting systems, such as GISs, are available today in the public cloud and can be used in support of mission critical functions such as CAD and RMS. One of the possible models for the deployment of cloud computing is often called the hybrid mode, where some of the core functionality remains on local servers but uses the cloud for supporting functions and as a backup for data storage and disaster recovery.

There is also a growing acceptance of the concept of using multiple clouds to ensure the recoverability of data in the event of a problem with any given cloud services provider. There are now cloud provisioning software packages that can handle the use of multiple clouds for these purposes, and this approach reduces the concern about there being a single point of failure in the cloud.

From the perspective of law enforcement, there are very significant differences and perceived risks between the public, private, community, and hybrid models of cloud computing. Fundamental concerns about the lack of control of applications running under the public cloud are lessened by the adoption of the private cloud restrictions and are even further mitigated by a hybrid model.

If the commercial model holds true in the law enforcement world, then it is reasonable to expect that the largest agencies might be attracted to the construction of their own private cloud. By contrast, smaller agencies are more likely to eventually embrace the public cloud model unless coalitions of agencies combine to create their own private or community clouds.

It is important to note that there is often an assumption that cloud computing is something for large agencies to pursue. Actually, the greatest benefits may come to smaller agencies: The smaller the agency, the greater the percentage of benefit. Given the reality that smaller agencies cannot often afford to acquire and maintain their own computer system for law enforcement purposes, the concept of cloud computing—predominantly the community model—tends to be quite attractive.

In a study by the IJIS Institute in 2012, 80% of the police executives responding express concerns about the risks of cloud computing and articulated the specifics that made them apprehensive. They mostly were concerned about ensuring that the data were secure and could not be modified inappropriately and that they could retrieve the data if they wanted to move it elsewhere (Wormeli, 2012). However, the perceptions of police executives are changing. In a follow-up survey sponsored by the IACP and SaveGov, conducted by the Ponemon Institute, 54% of the respondents said they were considering cloud computing at least for functions such as e-mail and disaster recovery (IACP, 2013).

The pervasive use of video

As of November 2015, law enforcement agencies have already begun to take advantage of higher definition, lower cost, and smaller video cameras for a variety of purposes. This trend will continue and will result in even smaller, cheaper, and more powerful devices and transmission capabilities.

What has held back the proliferation of video in law enforcement work at least for those applications that might be termed mobile is the lack of available bandwidth. A live video feed requires many times more bandwidth than the exchange of data, and the kinds of gigabyte availability just have not been available to law enforcement for widespread deployment. However, the advent of the FirstNet program approved by congress to spend more than $7 billion to implement a nationwide broadband data capability will remove the fundamental impediments to the use of video, inasmuch as the LTE standard on which FirstNet is built will accommodate the larger bandwidths needed for transmitting video through the Internet between vehicles and base stations. The Federal Communications Commission is also pushing forward with other initiatives designed to make broadband capabilities accessible throughout the nation, particularly in rural areas (see FFC, 2015).

Setting aside the limitations on deployment resulting from a lack of available bandwidth, the future holds a promise of much greater use of video and the potential for new applications not currently available. The potential uses of video in law enforcement will include, but not be limited to, the following service areas.

Video surveillance and monitoring

Video is already being expanded as a means of surveillance across urban areas throughout the world. In the PERF study of technology in policing conducted in 2012, 23% of police agencies claimed that they were already streaming video from fixed surveillance cameras to police vehicles, and 81% of the responding agencies planned to do so by 2017 (PERF, 2012). As bandwidth and additional cameras become available, most major cities and suburban departments will explore the wider use of video as an alternative to patrol. What is only just beginning is the development of sophisticated video analytics such that the fixed cameras and associated processing systems have sufficient intelligence to identify suspicious circumstances with the view of the camera so that alerts can be generated without requiring human monitoring of hundreds or thousands of cameras.

Police in some cities have already begun to negotiate the online real-time access in an integrated fashion to commercial surveillance cameras operated by businesses, particularly in high-risk areas. Making the private deployment of surveillance video an integrated part of the police capability offers benefits both for the detection of suspicious behavior and for the postincident investigation. Atlanta, Georgia police are hoping to monitor 762 cameras integrating police and private security camera locations there (AJC.com, 2012).

Automated license plate readers

Fixed and mobile automated license plate readers (ALPRs) have emerged from the prototype status into production systems, and police agencies are rapidly implementing these systems to spot stolen or wanted vehicles and report their location. The technology has become affordable, and according to the 2012 PERF study, 85% of agencies plan to acquire or increase their use of ALPR in the next 5 years. There have been privacy issues raised by critics of these devices, but there is widespread support among police agencies for this technology. Initially, ALPR systems were deployed mostly as stand-alone systems and had no thorough integration with external systems, but in the coming years, this is likely to change.

A developing trend is to ensure that the ALPR systems whether fixed or mobile are well integrated with CAD, message switching, and RMS. The need to check the stolen or wanted status of vehicles, determine owner information, extend the database checks to owners of the vehicle, and other purposes means that when a license plate is scanned, it should be submitted to a variety of databases. Typically, this means integration with a CAD system or, if separate from CAD, the message switch that connects to state and NCIC systems. Agencies are already seeing the need to have ALPR outputs as part of the agency's RMSs and to ensure that the ALPR results are integrated with queries from the RMS to local, state, and federal systems if the results are to be credible and useful.

Mobile video systems

Video cameras were first placed in police vehicles to document activities during a traffic stop so as to protect the officer from allegations of misconduct by dissatisfied citizens. The early adopters wanted to ensure that there was a way to produce documentation that showed that the officer did not use excessive force or otherwise mistreat the person stopped. Many of the early mobile cameras were installed with large hard drives in the vehicle because of the lack of bandwidth to forward streaming video from the vehicle to a communications center. Many such installations still exist, but this mode of operation introduces logistical challenges of transferring the video recordings to a repository and then also providing a way to search and retrieve a particular set of footage.

Advancements in camera technology, including miniaturization and reduced costs, have led many police agencies to replace in-vehicle systems with cameras worn by the officer, if for no other reason than to record better images while the officer is outside the vehicle. Many midsize agencies have been implementing this capability, and more are seeking funding to do so. In addition, as the bandwidth becomes available, the use of cameras on the officer will be connected to the network so that the real-time image can be viewed by the watch commander or communications manager in the police department and the communications center. This reverse streaming capability is important for officer safety as well as documenting the activities of an officer to protect against unfounded accusations of inappropriate police behavior. In the future, on-scene video images created by these mobile cameras will inform the tactical commanders that may be in remote facilities.

Further development of social media

After having been formally introduced in 2004, Facebook has acquired nearly 1.49 billion monthly active users through November 2015. Other social media have had similar if not as spectacular growth paths in this age of connectivity. Spurred by the high usage rates of the millennial generation, social media traversing has become a habit for many youth and a significant number of adults throughout the world.

Police agencies have responded with enthusiasm, as social media such as Facebook, Twitter, and other sites became a logical place to communicate with young people and increasingly with the population as a whole. According to the IACP Center for Social Media, its survey in 2012 found that more than 82% of police departments used social media (Federal Communications Commission, 2015). The uses for these tools start with the need to communicate policy, strategy, how to get services, pay fines, and know about crime trends and then move to using the tools to support the investigative process. One midwestern city has a task force of 30 investigators scouring a variety of social media sites to discover leads about crimes. This unit has been highly productive in the evidence found on the Internet.

Police departments have evolved their understanding of social media and their practices to take advantage of the advancements in social media.

As an example, police departments in Seattle, Washington and Cambridge, Massachusetts have started a Twitter feed of reported crimes (Annear, 2003). As agencies discover ways to enlist the aid of the community in fighting crime, they begin to use the two-way capabilities of Twitter to collect feedback. Police executives are continually refining their use of blogs, Facebook, and other software to enhance community awareness and participation.

The IACP Center for Social Media contains a robust set of links to resources available to help establish and improve the police use of social media. The resources and illustrative case studies can be found at http://www.iacpsocialmedia.org/Resources.aspx.

There are still unresolved legal issues regarding the right of police to use information gleaned from a person's Facebook or other personal postings, and the IACP has recognized the need for guidelines to address these issues. For example, most police agencies that use social media for investigative support do not submit their findings as evidence but rather use the information to generate leads that may result in more targeted investigations.

The opposition has also become practiced in the use of social media. Drug cartels in Mexico use Twitter to warn their members about the location of police roadblocks. Flash mobs in Michigan use Facebook and Twitter to gather the mob quickly to attack and devastate a fast food establishment. Terrorists in Mumbai made heavy use of social media in coordinating the attacks there.

Despite all the many applications that inventive police staff have created to use social media, it is likely that we will see substantially more innovative and creative solutions in the future. New tools are being created to expedite the search of social media in large memory resident databases so that investigators can identify in real time where flash mobs may be gathering or other crimes are being organized and coordinated. Police agencies are developing real-time crime centers where analysts will have instant access to predictive analytics and other tools for handling "big data" that can quickly handle the kinds of analytics needed to recognize patterns in real time.

Smartphone and tablet technology

The consumer-driven revolution in personal computing that has happened is having a direct impact on police operations, and this will only intensify in the near future. Today's smart phone has become much more than a phone, integrating many functions that have utility in police operations—camera, video capture and display, Internet browser, photo library (mug shots), GPS receiver, document storage, etc. As the competitive races continue, police will benefit from the advancements driven by consumers in large numbers. There will be an enormous amount of new features for this device, to the point where it no longer makes sense to call it a phone. For example, the smartphone is a viable platform for augmented reality where computer-generated graphics augments our visual presentation. Think of pointing the smartphone camera at a building and having the floor plans appear and eventually the display will appear in 3-D without any need for glasses. The room you are looking into will just stick out of the device and give you the 3-D perspective.

The Siri and Google Voice personal assistants will get much more sophisticated, allowing users to customize the tasks that they perform. Biometric security will improve, so that there will be the potential for single sign-on across multiple systems, as swiping your finger across the phone triggers facial recognition in the front camera to confirm your identity.

Then there will be many new apps developed for policing. There are only a few dozen apps in iTunes that have direct application in police or public safety work. They tend to be rather simplistic, as is typical of early generation software applications in any domain. Because of the tools available to lower the barriers to entry in this field, individual police officers and firefighters have written their own applications for the iPhone and Android-based phones (Neugebauer, 2012). Cities and counties are increasingly turning to the production of tailored applications for their own purposes of serving the public, allowing for inquiries about services or crimes to be easily displayed (City of Santa Clara, 2012).

Police agencies are already beginning to use tablets, thanks mainly to the rapid success of the iPad. The enhancements for smartphones will also apply to tablets, and in addition, the tablet will become a much more useful device for entering crime and accident reports than the smartphone. Tablets will also benefit from the voice-enabled research to develop much more capability to control tablet operations by voice, which may lead to further deployment in vehicles as a replacement for laptops.

One of the impediments to progress that will be addressed in the future is the need to integrate smartphone apps with the enterprise information system to provide that seamless interface everyone seeks. Cities and counties have recently been focused on the integration of the mobile apps with the databases in the backroom so that this ideal can become reality. The necessity of this integration when the app deals with data stored in a repository has certain impacts on privacy and security, including determining the applicability of FBI CJIS rules for controlling access to criminal information. Where the mobile app falls under these provisions, specific control measures must be implemented.

The mobility dilemma is complicated by the need to deal with the drive known as BYOD—bring your own device. Law enforcement IT managers, just like corporate IT managers, have to figure out how to allow individuals to bring their smartphones and tablets to work and give them access to the applications and databases they need to do their work. Some CIOs in larger commercial and government organizations shudder at the thought of employees bringing unsecured devices to work and figuring out how to access their work resources, particularly when the employees are computer smart and have the ability to write their own apps using the readily available app development kits that make it extremely easy to create a new app. The army of app developers at large is closing in on 1 billion apps just for the iPhone and iPad user community, and apps built by cities, digitally sophisticated government employees, and freelance programmers continue to flood the iTunes library.

The move toward BYOD is inevitable.

1. State and local agencies cannot afford to equip everyone with this technology.
2. The entry of the digital native population age-group into law enforcement means that they will all bring their own devices whether we ask them to or not.
3. They will use these devices for texting each other, taking pictures, and making videos of their work scenes, and otherwise using the tool that they have already adopted as a key part of their life. Some will even write apps for these devices.

Collaboration technologies

In most of both government and industry circles, a new wind of collaboration is setting the stage for a future less concerned about competition and more concerned about performance and efficiency of using resources. In their new book, Bratton and Tumin (2012) make the case that there is really no choice in the wake of the financial crisis that America has had to weather, combined with the broad necessity not to waste resources. They argue that "In collaboration folks come together, give something up, and get something back that's even better. They achieve something together that none can alone, and are better off for it."

In the wake of disappearing police departments and staff reductions, police agencies throughout the country are much more receptive to sharing resources, finding ways to economize, and collaborating in a way that everyone is "better off for it." Where there is a movement toward a new paradigm such as this one, technology will surely follow and collaboration is no exception. Early attempts at fostering collaboration relied on the conventional social media such as Facebook, blogs, and other means to exchange ideas and resources. Many of these tools will mature and be used solely for this purpose.

There is one particular genre of software that has emerged and will also advance to support major collaborations. Sometimes called "crowd sourcing," this new class of software is designed to encourage collaboration across employees and customers (the public) to engage in the consideration of problem solving and policy setting that has to happen in collaborative projects. Crowd sourcing got its start as companies, government agencies, and philanthropy groups sent out a call for help to attack intractable problems. As this practice became more widespread, software companies emerged that were focused precisely on filling this need. The underlying purpose of crowd sourcing software is at least focused on the objective of creating what has long been called collective intelligence, wherein the wisdom of the crowd outdoes the wisdom of a single person or small group. The idea of organizing the minds of 1,000 smart people to focus on a single problem in a relatively short period of time has resulted in some amazing results. "Companies, nonprofits, and governmental agencies that embrace disciplined collaboration perform better than those with an exclusively decentralized approach, because disciplined collaboration combines the results of all the independent units and results based on collaboration. That kind of performance is hard to beat" (Hansen, 2009).

Crowd sourcing software offers features not found in other social media such as a built-in capability to score input so that the best ideas are ranked by the opinions of the contributors. Also, in these applications, the user interface is designed to foster a simple participation without obfuscating the issue. The software can be used internally for creating the collective intelligence of the force in dealing with difficult problems or externally to gain a collaborative mind-set with the community.

Continuing innovation

Going beyond the further deployment and enhancement of known technologies driven by the forces of change and challenge, there are evocative concepts being considered that will undoubtedly have an impact on policing as practical innovations emerge from what is now a thoughtful discourse. Ray Kurzweil (2012), one of the most prolific inventors and authors about our future, has suggested that the capacity of computers to exceed that of the processing power of the human brain will be a reality yet in this decade, within the range of the time period selected for this chapter. In his latest book, he suggests that we may see driverless cars in public use before the end of this decade and we will be able to augment the capacity of our human brains by artificial digital capabilities in the cloud that will far exceed our individual mental capacities to discern patterns and apply knowledge to decision making.

When driverless cars and intelligent machines that supplement our capacity for analysis are put into practice, they will be adopted in law enforcement. It is easy to see the value in high capacity intelligence analysis capabilities that can, for example, detect the growing possibility of a flash mob gathering to lay waste to a 7-11 store in time to allow the police to be at the scene before the mob arrives.

Innovative technology will become pervasive in law enforcement when the value premise for its acquisition becomes obvious. Executives in law enforcement pay close attention to technologies that improve officer safety and provide clear and present evidence of supporting the law enforcement mission. When the technology becomes an almost invisible part of the police response, serving in a supporting role as opposed to becoming an end in itself, its future is assured. The technologies described previously are on their way to satisfying these criteria for adoption.

References

AJC.com. (2012, October 15). *Atlanta council votes to spend $2 million for video cameras.* Retrieved from http://www.ajc.com/news/news/atlanta-council-votes-to-spend/nSdbc/.

Annear, S. (2003, February 19). *Cambridge Police Embrace Social Media with New Real-Time Tweets about Area Real Crime.* Retrieved from http://bostinno.com/2013/02/19/cambridge-police-embrace-social-media-with-new-real-time-tweets-about-area-crimes.

Bair Analytics (n.d.). RAIDS Online. Retrieved from http://www.bairanalytics.com/software/raidsonline/.

Braga, A., & Weisburd, D. (2010). *Policing problem places: Crime hot spots and effective prevention.* Oxford: Oxford University Press.

Bratton, W., & Tumin, Z. (2012). *Collaborate or perish!* New York: Crown Business.

City of Santa Clara. (2012, August 15). *Police department crime report iPhone app.* Retrieved from http://santaclaraca.gov/index.aspx?page=1839.

Digital Evidence Management (n.d.) Retrieved from https://www.taser.com/products/digital-evidence-management.

Environmental Research Systems Institute (n.d.) ESRI's offering of GIS Services in the Cloud. Retrieved from http://www.esri.com/products/arcgis-capabilities/cloud-gis.

Federal Communications Commission. (2015). *Telecommunication service in rural America.* Retrieved from http://www.fcc.gov/encyclopedia/telecommunications-service-rural-america.

Hansen, M. T. (2009). *Collaboration: How leaders avoid the traps, create unity, and reap big results.* Boston, MA: Harvard Business Review Press.

IACP. (2013). *Guiding principles on cloud computing in law enforcement.* Retrieved from http://www.theiacp.org/About/PressCenter/CloudComputing/tabid/1113/Default.aspx.

Kurzweil, R. (2012). *How to create a mind: The secret of human thought revealed.* New York: Viking.

Neugebauer, C. (2012, August 27). Salt Lake City FBI agent changes how child sex crimes are investigated. *The Salt Lake Tribune*. Retrieved from http://www .sltrib.com/sltrib/news/54721915-78/zimmerman-fbi-tools-child.html .csp?goback =%2Egde_4104229_member_159732653.

Police Executive Research Forum. (2012). *How are innovations in technology transforming policing?* Washington, DC: Author.

Society of Police Futurists International. (2015). *Futures research*. Retrieved from http://www.policefuturists.org/futures-research-2.

Taser International, Digital Evidence Management. Retrieved from http://www.taser .com/products/digital-evidence-management/evidence.

Urgent Communications (n.d.) *ShotSpotter, Intrado enhance partnership to include cloud service*. Retrieved from http://urgentcomm.com/psap/briefs/shotspotter -intrado-cloud-service-20111004.

Wormeli, P. (2012). *Mitigating risks in cloud computing in law enforcement*. IBM Center for the Business of Government. Retrieved from http://www .businessofgovernment.org/report/mitigating-risks-application-cloud -computing-law-enforcement.

Index

Page numbers followed by f and t indicate figures and tables, respectively.

A

Abuses, 167
Accounting system, 269
Activity logging, 79–80
Ad hoc report(s), 146
Ad hoc report generator, 252, 254
Ad hoc search capability, 284; *see also* Court management information system
Administrative crime analysis, 185, 200–202; *see also* Information technology and crime analysis
Analysis/disposition of cases, 239, 241f
Analysis of data, 194–195; *see also* Crime analysis/crime mapping
Appellate courts, 259
Arrest, 121–122, 124
Asset seizures, 143
Association of Public Safety Communications Officials (APCO), 57, 64
Attorney assignment, 243, 244f; *see also* Prosecutor information management systems
Audiences for administrative crime analysis information, 200
Audit trail, 80
Automated fingerprint identification systems (AFIS)
    features of, 136–139
    integration with, 209, 230–231
Automated Information System (AIS) database, 151
Automated license plate readers (ALPR), 315; *see also* Law enforcement, future of technology in

Automated license plate recognition systems, 171
Automated location index (ALI), 54, 56, 86
Automated name index (ANI), 54, 56, 86
Automated vehicle location (AVL) system, 75, 97, 102

B

Bair Analytics, 312
Bar coding, 144
Benchmark, 292
"Be on the lookout" (BOLO), 134
Biometrics, 215, 216
Biometric tools, 170; *see also* Mobile office
Bluetooth technology, use of, 176
Briefing (information), 172–173; *see also* Mobile office
Bring your own device (BYOD), 319
Broadcast messages, 178
Bureau of Justice Assistance (BJA), 233
Business issues, 288, 290; *see also* Functional requirement specification (FRS)

C

CAD, *see* Computer-aided dispatch (CAD)
Call entry, 84
Call pending queue, 93
Call priority, 87–88
Call receipt, 85–87
Call scheduling, 91
Call table, 76–77
Call takers and dispatchers, 74
Card file, 81
Car-to-car text messaging, 166
Case accounting screen, 270f

Case aging, 146
Case management, 229–230; *see also*
    Schedule management
Case manager, 234–235, 236f; *see also*
    Prosecutor information
    management systems
Cash bond, 276; *see also* Court management
    information system
CASS, *see* Crime analysis support system
    (CASS)
Cell tracking, 215; *see also* Inmate tracking
Cellular digitized packet data (CDPD), 11,
    164
Cellular technology, 163
Cellular telephones, 173; *see also* Mobile office
Centralized automated message
    accounting (CAMA) signal
    protocol, 59–60
Change management, 305–306; *see also*
    Criminal justice information
    systems (CJIS), implementation of
Child support case entry screen, 250f
Child support module, 249–251, 250f, 251f;
    see also Prosecutor information
    management systems
Choropleth and thematic mapping,
    combination, 190, 192f
Choropleth map, 190
Classroom training, 296
Cloud computing; *see also* Law
    enforcement, future of
    technology in
  and administrative functions, 312
  and mission critical functions, 312–314
CMS, *see* Corrections management system
    (CMS)
COBOL systems, 8–9
Code division multiple access (CDMA), 164
Code table management, 99
CODIS ("Combined DNA Index System"), 5
Collaboration technologies, 319–320
Collection of data, 193–194; *see also* Crime
    analysis/crime mapping
Command area dispatch (CAD) systems,
    92–93
Command line, 83
Commercial burglary/thefts, 197f
Commissary; *see also* Corrections
    information technology
  commissary inventory tracking
    subsystem, 222
  commissary privileges, 222
  commissary transactions, 222–223

Commissary and food service
    management, *see* Commissary
Communication, 295
Community CMS, 228; *see also* Schedule
    management
Community corrections, 207
Community Oriented Policing Services
    Making Officer Redeployment
    (COPS/MORE) program, 5, 160,
    163
Component level testing, 301
Computer-aided dispatch (CAD) system
  administrative functions, 75, 99–100
  baseline functions, 78–84
  call entry, 84–91
  calls for service data transfer, 78
  case study, 296–297
  code table management, 76–77
  development of, 74
  dispatch process, 91–98
  and E9-1-1 systems, 54
  evolution of, 6–7
  false alarms and, 153
  first, 7
  functional requirement, 48–49
  geofile processing, 89–90
  integration with information systems,
    166
  introduction, 73–74
  mapping, 63f, 100–103
  operations analysis and, 199
  project components, 288–289f
  squad or shift activation, 76
  supervisory functions, 98–99
  system performance requirements,
    74–75
  training support, 78
  unit recommendation and validation
    tables, 77
  voice communications and, 164
  window configurations, 75–76
Computer-generated photo lineups, 17
Computerized criminal history (CCH)
    file, 5
Computer–telephony integration, 87
Consultants, 291
Convertible laptops, 174; *see also* Mobile
    computing
CopLink, 187, 188f
COPS-MORE program, *see* Community
    Oriented Policing Services
    Making Officer Redeployment
    program

Correction management systems, 13–14
Corrections information technology
  commissary
    commissary inventory tracking
      subsystem, 222
    commissary privileges, 222
    commissary transactions, 222–223
  community corrections, 207
  corrections management systems (CMS)
    about, 214–215
    inmate tracking, 215–220
  doctors/dentists/nurses, 220
  history of, 208
  inmate accounting, 221
  inmate medical billing, 220–221
  institutional incarceration, 207
  integration with AFIS/mug shot
    systems, 230–231
  jail and prison management external sys-
    tems interface requirements, 230
  jail booking/intake systems
    about, 208
    components, 209, 210f
    inmate classification, 211–213
    medical history, 213
    personal information, 211
    personal property, 213–214
    subject name, 209, 211
    subject's aliases, 211
  schedule management
    case files, 229–230
    case management, 229–230
    community CMS, 228
    court scheduling, 226
    master name index (MNI), 229
    medical and dental scheduling, 227
    presentencing investigation, 229
    work release, 228
  sentence management
    about, 223
    inmate rehabilitation training,
      224–225
    inmate release and reintegration,
      225
    sentence compliance, 223–224
    victim information and victim
      notification, 225–226
Corrections management system (CMS)
  about, 214–215
  community, 228
  inmate tracking
    cell tracking, 215
    disciplinary tracking, 217

    inmate identification, 216
    medical tracking, 218–220, 219f
    movement tracking, 215–216
    prisoner phone logs, 218
    visitor tracking, 217–218
Cost of convertible laptop, 174
Costs of prisoner medical care, 221
Court administrator, 273
Court case data screen, 261f
Court clerks, 263
Court docket module, 258–263; *see also*
        Court management information
        system
Court management information system
  ad hoc search capability, 284
  cash bond, 276
  court docket module, 259–263
  court minutes, 281
  court scheduling, 281, 284
  electronic ticketing, 281, 283f
  garnishment, 277
  integrated justice information systems/
    court management software, 285
  master name index (MNI), 263–265,
    266f, 267f
  multipayment, 276–277
  overview, 257–259
  sentencing and rulings, 265, 266,
    269–275
  standardized reports, 285
  unallocated funds, 276
  warrants, 277–281, 282f
  work credit payments, 276
Court management software, 260, 285;
     see also Court management
     information system
Court management systems (CMS), 11–13
Court minutes, 281; *see also* Court
     management information system
Court-ordered collections, 254
Court scheduling, 227–228; *see also* Court
     management information
     system; Schedule management
  about, 281
  direct benefits, 284
Courts of limited jurisdiction, 258
Crime analysis/crime mapping
  forms of, requiring information
    technology
    administrative crime analysis,
      200–202
    intelligence analysis, 204–205
    operations analysis, 198–200

predictive policing, 202–203
strategic crime analysis, 197–198
tactical crime analysis, 196–197
GIS and crime mapping, 187–189
history of crime analysis, 182–185
and information technology
analysis of data, 194–195
collection of data, 193–194
dissemination, 195
intelligence analysis, 185–186
intelligence-led policing, 186–187
overview, 181
types of crime mapping, 189–193, 194
Crime analysis/geographic information
systems, 132–136
Crime analysis information, 170; *see also*
Mobile office
Crime analysis support system (CASS)
about, 132
crime pattern detection, 184
crime potentials forecast, 184
crime suspect correlation, 184
crime trend forecast, 184
exception reports, 184
freeware to police, 184
resource allocation, 184
target profiles, 184
Crime mapping, *see* Crime analysis/crime
mapping
Crime pattern detection, 184
Crime potentials forecast, 184
Crime prediction software, 195
Crime suspect correlation, 184
CrimeViewTM application, 132–133
Criminal history systems, development
of, 4–6
Criminal investigative analysis, 185
Criminal justice agencies, workgroup
applications in, 15
Criminal justice enterprise computing,
exploring, 11
Criminal justice information systems (CJIS)
about, 2
correction management systems, 13–14
court management systems (CMS), 11–13
critical success factors in implementing,
287–288
data mining, 14–15
data warehousing, 14–15
development of criminal history
systems, 4–6
evolution, 2–4
evolution of CAD systems, 6–7

exploring criminal justice enterprise
computing, 11
mobile computing, 9–11
record management systems (RMSs), 7–9
workgroup applications in criminal
justice agencies, 15
Criminal justice information systems
(CJIS), implementation of
change management, 305–306
critical success factors in
implementation, 287
daily support for installed systems, 304
end user and expectation management,
295–297
executive champion, role of, 293–294
functional requirement specification (FRS)
about, 288, 289f
business issues, 288, 290
functional issues, 290–291
technical issues, 290, 291f
implementing selected system, 293
new system operational, bringing, 302, 303f
project manager, role of, 294–295
project planning, 296–298, 299f
request for proposal (RFP),
development of, 292–293
scope creep, 298–300, 300f
system documentation
operator manuals, 304
programmer's manual, 304
system administrator's manual, 304
system specifications, 303–304
system growth management/budgeting
for change, 307–308
test plans and procedures, 300–302
user groups/criminal justice
information systems, 306–307
Criminal profiling, 185
Crosstab of data of robberies, 199f
Crowd sourcing software, 320

D

Daily court docket listing, 264f
Daily receipt transaction log, 278f
Daily support for installed criminal justice
systems, 304; *see also* Criminal
justice information systems,
implementation of
Data
collection of, 193–194
mining, 14–15, 255
warehousing, 14–15

Databases, access to, 102–103
Data radio as transport mediums, 162; *see also* Mobile computing
Data transfer to external report generators, 254; *see also* Prosecutor information management systems
Data warehousing/data mining capability, 255; *see also* Prosecutor information management systems
Decentralization of information systems, 178
Defense attorneys, 246
Delinquent payments, 251
Dental scheduling, 228; *see also* Schedule management
Dentists, 220
Department of Motor Vehicles (DMV), 4
Digital photography, 140, 144, 170–171; *see also* Mobile office
Disciplinary tracking, 217; *see also* Inmate tracking
Discovery tracking, 246; *see also* Prosecutor information management systems
Dispatcher, 177
Dispatch operations, and mobile computing, 165–167
Disposing of property, 143
Disposition of cases, 239, 241f; *see also* Prosecutor information management systems
Dissemination, 134, 195; *see also* Crime analysis/crime mapping
Distance learning, 46
Distribution report, 275
Docket listing, 262f
Doctors, 220
Document and photo tracking, 245f
Document management, 243, 246; *see also* Prosecutor information management systems
Driver's licenses, 171
Driving forces influencing technology adoption, *see* Law enforcement, future of technology in
Duplicate call detection, 88–89

E

Electronic citation system (sample), 283f
Electronic ticketing, 281, 283f; *see also* Court management information system

E-mail, 134
E-mail services, 46
Emergency alert, 98–99
Emergency service number (ESN), 56–57
End user and expectation management, 295–297; *see also* Criminal justice information systems (CJIS), implementation of
Enterprise information system, *see* police record management system
Environmental factors driving innovation about, 311; *see also* Law enforcement, future of technology in
cloud computing and administrative functions, 312
cloud computing and mission critical functions, 312–314
Errors, 301–302
Event history, 95
Evolution data optimized (EVDO), 164
Extensible markup language (XML), 27–28

F

Face print, 18
Facial recognition system, 140, 216
False alarms, 153–154
Federal Communications Commission (FCC), 11, 162, 314
Field interview reports (FIR), 126
Field mobile reporting, 168
Field report writing, 167–168, 169f; *see also* Mobile computing
Final contract, 293
Fingerprint(s), 230
Fingerprint card, 137–138
Fingerprint cradle, 172
FirstNet program, 314
Fixed automated license plate readers, 315
Food service management, commissary and, *see* Commissary
Frequency spectrum, 162
Functional issues, 290–291; *see also* Functional requirement specification (FRS)
Functional requirement specification (FRS); *see also* Criminal justice information systems (CJIS), implementation of
about, 288, 289f
business issues, 288, 290

functional issues, 290–291
technical issues, 291, 291f
Funds, unallocated, 276
Fusion center intelligence analysts, 186

G

Gang affiliation, 212–213; *see also* Jail
     booking/intake systems
Gang members, 212
Garbage in, garbage out, 194
Garnishment, 277; *see also* Court
     management information system
General education degree (GED), 224–225
Geographic information system (GIS); *see
     also* Information technology and
     crime analysis
     in crime analysis functions, 132
     and crime mapping, 187–189
     in mobile computing, 161–162
     in policing, 310
Ghost call, 64
GIS, *see* Geographic information system
     (GIS)
Global justice extensible markup language
     data model (GJXDM), 21–22, 27,
     28–30
Global Justice Extensible Structure Task
     Force (GXSTF), 21
Global Justice XML Data Dictionary
     (GJXDD), 29
Global positioning system (GPS)/
     automated vehicle location (AVL)
     requirements, 102
Global positioning system (GPS)
     technology, 62–63, 215
Google Voice personal assistants, 318

H

Hard copy warrant (sample), 280f
Hazard information file, 90
Hearing carry over, 61
Henry fingerprint classification system,
     230–231
High-grade misdemeanor, 285
HIV patients, in state and federal prisons, 220
Homicide
     density map, 191f
     plot map, 189, 190f
     and population density in Washington,
        192f

Hot spot, 164, 191
Hot spot vehicle theft map model, 193f
Houston Police Department, 159
Hypertext markup language, 26–27

I

IACP Center for Social Media, 317
ILD, software package, 187
Incident-based reporting system (IBRS)
     reports, 201
Individual financial transaction screen,
     271f
Information exchange package documents
     (IEPD), 49
Information systems, overview, 1–2
Information technology and crime
     analysis; *see also* Crime analysis/
     crime mapping
     about, 195
     administrative crime analysis,
        200–202
     intelligence analysis, 204–205
     operations analysis, 198–200
     predictive policing, 202–203
     strategic crime analysis, 197–198
     tactical crime analysis, 196–197
Inmate accounting, 221
Inmate classification; *see also* Jail booking/
     intake systems
     gang affiliation, 212–213
     suicide attempts, 212
Inmate identification, 216; *see also* Inmate
     tracking
Inmate medical billing, 220–221
Inmate rehabilitation training, 224–225; *see
     also* Sentence management
Inmate release and reintegration, 225; *see
     also* Sentence management
Inmate tracking; *see also* Corrections
     management system (CMS)
     cell tracking, 215
     disciplinary tracking, 217
     inmate identification, 216
     medical tracking, 218–220, 219f
     movement tracking, 215, 216
     prisoner phone logs, 218
     visitor tracking, 217–218
Inmate–victim relationship, 227f
Innovation, 320–321; *see also* Law
     enforcement, future of
     technology in

Institutional incarceration, 207
Integrated Criminal Apprehension
    Program (ICAP), 182
Integrated justice information system (IJIS),
    285; *see also* Court management
    information system
  about, 260, 285
  initiative, 21
Integrated Justice Information Systems
    (IJIS) Institute, 48
Integration testing, 301
Intelligence analysis, 185–186, 204–205;
    see also Crime analysis/
    crime mapping; Information
    technology and crime analysis
Intelligence-led policing (ILP), 181, 186–187;
    see also Crime analysis/crime
    mapping
Interfaces, 136, 151
Interface testing, 301
Interim distribution report, 274f
International Association of Chiefs of
    Police (IACP), 48, 311
International Association of Crime
    Analysts (IACA), 198
Internet capabilities, 254–255; *see also*
    Prosecutor information
    management systems
Internet for wanted suspects
  advantages, 201
  disadvantages of, 201–202
Intranets, 27
Investigative software, 195
Iris recognition, 216

J

Jail booking/intake systems; *see also*
    Corrections information
    technology
  about, 208
  components, 209
  inmate classification
    gang affiliation, 212–213
    suicide attempts, 212
  medical history, 213
  personal information, 211
  personal property, 213–214
  subject name, 209, 211
  subject's aliases, 211
Jail intake/booking screen (sample), 210f
Jail management systems (JMS), 208, 211

Jail/prison management external systems
    interface requirements, 230
JavaScript, 26–27
Juror tracking, 246, 247f; *see also* Prosecutor
    information management systems
Juvenile contact, 124–125
Juvenile courts, 258

K

Known offenders, 125–126, 195

L

Laptops, significance, 10
Laptop technology, success of, 160–161
Law enforcement, future of technology in
  collaboration technologies, 319–320
  driving forces influencing technology
    adoption
    automated license plate readers
        (ALPR), 315
    environmental factors driving
        innovation, 311–314
    mobile video systems, 315–316
    pervasive use of video, 314–316
    policing models, changes in, 310–311
    video surveillance and monitoring,
        314–315
  innovation, continuing, 320–321
  overview, 309–310
  smartphone and tablet technology,
      317–319
  social media, development of, 316–317
Law enforcement and crime analysis data,
    202
Law Enforcement Assistance
    Administration (LEAA), 8, 132,
    182, 208, 233
Law Enforcement Information Sharing
    Program (LEISP), 36–37, 48
Law Enforcement Information Technology
    Standards Council (LEITSC),
    47–49
Law Enforcement Online (LEO), 46–47
Legitimate changes in scope, 298
Library function, 80–81
License plate checks, 171
Link analysis
  definition, 134
  sample chart, 135
  software, 195, 205

Live scan, 138
Live scan devices, 16
Low-grade misdemeanor, 285

M

Magnetic strips, 171
Managing criminal investigation (MCI),
        19–20
Map(s), 189
Mapping, 189, 193
Master calendaring, 239, 242f; *see also*
        Prosecutor information
        management systems
Master location index (MLI), 116, 119
Master name index (MNI); *see also* Prosecutor
        information management systems;
        Schedule management
    about, 230, 235, 237f
    for court management information
        system, 261–263, 266f, 267f
    in police record management systems,
        108–114
Master name search defendant list, 237f
Master Street Address Guide (MSAG), 56
Master vehicle index (MVI), 114, 116
Medical/dental scheduling, 228; *see also*
        Schedule management
Medical history, 213; *see also* Jail booking/
        intake systems
Medical management in prison, 219
Medical tracking, 218–220, 219f; *see also*
        Inmate tracking
Mental conditions, 213
Message status terminal (MST), 9–10,
        157–158, 158f
Method of operation (MO) data, 182
Mobile automated license plate readers, 315
Mobile computing
    benefit of, 178
    data radio/wireless technology as
        transport mediums, 162–165
    and dispatch operations, 165–167
    features of, 9–11
    field report writing, 167–168
    future of
        convertible laptops, 174
        personal digital assistants (PDA), 176
        tablet personal computers, 174–175
        technology integration, 178
        voice-to-text/text-to-voice systems,
            176–178
    history of, 157–162

mobile office
    about, 168–170
    biometric tools, 172
    briefing information, 172–173
    cellular telephones, 173
    crime analysis information, 170
    digital photography, 170–171
    reference information, 172
    wireless mobile video, 171
    objectives, 157
    security in, 165
Mobile data terminal (MDT), 10, 158, 159f
Mobile office; *see also* Mobile computing
    about, 168–170
    biometric tools, 172
    briefing information, 172–173
    cellular telephones, 173
    crime analysis information, 170
    digital photography, 170–171
    reference information, 172
    wireless mobile video, 171
Mobile video systems, 315–316; *see also*
        Law enforcement, future of
        technology in
Motorola MW 800, 160f
Motorola 4.9 system, 165
Movement tracking, 215–216; *see also*
        Inmate tracking
Mug shot systems, 137–138, 230–231; *see also*
        Police workgroup applications
Multi-item payment, 276–277; *see also* Court
        management information system
Multimedia library, 46
Multiple crimes, 189
Multi-workgroup implementation (sample),
        303f

N

NameSearch®, 110, 111f, 112
National Advisory Commission on Criminal
        Justice Standards and Goals, 8
National alert system, 46
National Center for Missing and Exploited
        Children, 46
National Crime Information Center (NCIC)
    about, 4–6, 37–41, 74, 114
    warrant systems, 277
National Criminal Intelligence Sharing
        Plan (NCISP), 187
9-1-1 national emergency number
    basic, working, 55–56
    cellular phone technology, 61–63

challenges faced by, 58
enhanced, 56–58
introduction, 53–55
next-generation, 66–71
TTY/TDD communications, 60–61
voice over Internet protocol, 64–66
National Emergency Number Association
(NENA), 55, 60, 62
National Incident-Based Reporting System
(NIBRS), 41–46, 298
National Information Exchange Model
(NIEM), 22, 27, 31–36, 49, 285
National Institute of Justice, 202
National Law Enforcement
Telecommunication System
(Nlets), 47
National Organization of Black Law
Enforcement Executives
(NOBLE), 48
National policing organizations, 311
National Sheriff's Association (NSA), 48
N-DEx (Law Enforcement National
Database Exchange), 6
N-DEx (National Data Exchange), 31
NDIS (National DNA Index System), 5
New York State Division of Criminal
Justice, 110
New York State Identification and
Intelligence System (NYSIIS),
110, 265
Next generation 9-1-1 (NG9-1-1), 86
Nonpatrol units, 96
Nurses, 220–221

O

Officer history, 96–97
Online forums, 46
Online messaging/conferencing, 84
Open System Architectures, 9
Operations analysis, 198–200; *see also*
Information technology and
crime analysis
Operator manuals, 304; *see also* System
documentation
Optical character recognition, 171
Overcrowding in prisons, 228

P

Panasonic Toughbook convertible
computer, 174, 175f
Panasonic tough book laptop, 161f

Parental information, 251f
Party information, 238f
Patrol briefing, 172
Pattern maps, 190
Pawnshop, 151–152
Personal digital assistant (PDA), 10, 176, 177f,
217; *see also* Mobile computing
Personal information, 211; *see also* Jail
booking/intake systems
Personal property, 213–214; *see also* Jail
booking/intake systems
Pervasive use of video, 314–316; *see also*
Law enforcement, future of
technology in
Photographs of known offenders, 195
Photo lineups, 17
Pictographs, 137
Pin map, 189, 195
Planning Research Corporation (PRC), 7
Plea bargaining, 243
Plot maps of crimes, 162, 170, 189
Police briefings, 172–173; *see also* Mobile
office
Police computer-aided dispatch (CAD)
systems, *see* Computer-aided
dispatch (CAD) systems
Police cruisers, 168
Police culture, 183
Police enterprise computing system, 11,
12f; *see also* Criminal justice
enterprise computing
Police Executive Research Forum (PERF),
48, 311
Police operations support system
elementary (POSSE), 8, 234
Police record management systems, *see*
Record management systems
(RMS)
enterprise information system, 106–107,
106–129
arrest, 121–122, 124
calls for service, 107–108
citations, 126–127
field interview reports (FIR), 126
incidents, 119, 121
juvenile contact, 124–125
known offender, 124–125
master location index (MLI), 116,
119
master name index (MNI), 108–114
master vehicle index (MVI), 114, 116
wants, warrants, and protective
orders, 127–128, 129f

Police workgroup applications
  automated fingerprint identification
    systems (AFIS), 136–139
  case management, 145–146, 149
  crime analysis and geographic
    information systems, 132–136
  false alarms, 153–154
  investigation, vice, intelligence, and
    narcotic systems, 149–151
  mug shot systems, 139–140
  pawnshop, 151–152
  property and evidence, 140–141,
    143–145
  subpoena tracking module, 154–155
  workgroup applications, 131–132
Policing, community-based, 311
Policing models, changes in, 310–311; *see
    also* Law enforcement, future of
    technology in
POSSE, *see* Police operations support
    system elementary (POSSE)
Predictive policing, 202–203; *see also*
    Information technology and
    crime analysis
Preformatted reports, 252
Premise history file, 91
Premise information file, 90–91
Prerecorded messages, 177
Presentencing investigation, 229; *see also*
    Schedule management
Primary rate interface integrated services
    digital network (PRI-ISDN)
    trunks, 60
Printed court docket, 263, 265f
Printers in patrol cars, 170
Prisoner phone logs, 218; *see also* Inmate
    tracking
Private branch exchange (PBX) systems,
    59–60
Privileges, commissary, 222
The Problem with XML Technology, 28
Programmer's manual, 304; *see also* System
    documentation
Project components, 289f
Project manager, role of, 294–295;
    see also Criminal justice
    information systems (CJIS),
    implementation of
Project plan (sample), 299
Project planning, 296–298, 299f;
    see also Criminal justice
    information systems (CJIS),
    implementation of

PROMIS, *see* Prosecution management
    information systems (PROMIS)
Property and evidence tracking, 243, 245f;
    see also Prosecutor information
    management systems
Prosecuting attorney, 259
Prosecuting attorney offices, 255
Prosecution, 248
Prosecution management information
    systems, 8
Prosecutorial software, 233
Prosecutor information management
    systems
  prosecutorial system
    about, 233
    history of, 233–234
  prosecutor record management
    information system overview
    analysis/disposition of cases, 239,
      241f
    attorney assignment, 243, 244f
    case manager, 234–235, 236f
    child support module, 249–251, 250f,
      251f
    data transfer to external report
      generators, 254
    data warehousing/data mining
      capability, 255
    discovery tracking, 246
    document management, 243, 246
    internet capabilities, 254–255
    juror tracking, 246, 247f
    master calendaring, 239, 242f
    master name index (MNI), 235, 237f
    property and evidence tracking,
      243, 245f
    reports, 252–254, 253f
    restitution tracking, 249
    victim and witness tracking, 235,
      238, 239f
    worthless checks, 246, 248–249
Prosecutor management information
    system (PROMIS), 233
Prosecutor offices, 233, 239, 254
Prosecutor record management
    information system overview,
    see Prosecutor information
    management systems
Public safety answering point (PSAP),
    54–56, 60, 61, 86
Public safety witness, 284
Public Switched Telephone Network
    (PSTN), 64

Q

Quality corrections management software, 224
Quality prison management systems, 223

R

Radio frequency ranges, 162
Radio log, 6–7, 73
Rand Corporation, 19
Rand study, 202–203
Recidivism, 228
Record management system (RMS)
    and CMS, 11
    commercial off-the-shelf, 304
    in crime analysis, 185, 193, 196
    features of, 7–9
    printed reports, 42
    project components, 288
Redundant data entry, 308
Redundantly arrayed independent disk
        drives (RAID) technology, 80
Reference information, 172; *see also* Mobile
        office
Regional Data Exchange (R-DEx), 36
Rehabilitation training, 225
Reports; *see also* Prosecutor information
        management systems
    ad hoc report generator, 252, 254
    preformatted, 252
Report selection screen (sample), 273f
Request for proposal (RFP), development
        of, 292–293; *see also* Criminal
        justice information systems
        (CJIS), implementation of
Requirement process, 291
Resource allocation, CASS and, 184
Restitution tracking, 249; *see also* Prosecutor
        information management
        systems
Risk assessment, 229
Robbery, crosstab of data of, 199f
"Rolodex" system, 79
Rugged tablet PC, 175, 175f

S

San Diego Jail, medical exam room, 219f
Schedule management; *see also* Corrections
        information technology
    case files, 229–230
    case management, 229–230
    community CMS, 228
    court scheduling, 226
    master name index (MNI), 229
    medical and dental scheduling, 227
    presentencing investigation, 229
    work release, 228
Scope creep, 298–300, 300f; *see also*
        Criminal justice information
        systems (CJIS), implementation
        of
Seasonal robbery trends, 198, 198f
Secondary public safety answering points
        (SSAP), 58
Security in mobile computing, 165
Selective router, 57–58
Sentence compliance, 223–224
Sentence management; *see also* Corrections
        information technology
    about, 223
    inmate rehabilitation training, 224–225
    inmate release and reintegration, 225
    sentence compliance, 223–224
    victim information and victim
        notification, 225–226
Sentencing and rulings, 265, 266, 269–275;
        see also Court management
        information system
Sentencing information screen, 268f
Settlement/plea offer screen, 244f
ShotSpotter Flex, 312
Sidekick, 61
Silent dispatching, 166
Single fingerprint identification
        technology, 162
Six-pack, 139–140
Smart card technology, 215
Smartphone, 61
Smartphone and tablet technology, 317–319;
        see also Law enforcement, future
        of technology in
Social media, development of, 316–317; *see
        also* Law enforcement, future of
        technology in
Soundex, programming methodology, 110,
        209, 235, 263, 265
Special Interest Groups (SIG), 46
Spreadsheets, 195, 196
Standardized reports, 285; *see also* Court
        management information
        system
Status timers, 94–95
Stolen vehicle recovery locations, 194f
Stovepipes, 307, 308

Strategic crime analysis, 185, 197–198; *see also* Information technology and crime analysis
Subgeographic reporting districts, 200
Subject name, 209, 211; *see also* Jail booking/intake systems
Subject's aliases, 211; *see also* Jail booking/intake systems
Subpoena tracking module, 154–155
Suicide attempts, 212; *see also* Jail booking/intake systems
Superior courts, 258
Supervisory function
    emergency alert, 98–98
    supervisor monitoring capability, 98
    supervisory workstation, 98
Supporting systems, 313
System acceptance, 302
System administrator, 304
System administrator's manual, 304; *see also* System documentation
System documentation; *see also* Criminal justice information systems (CJIS), implementation of
    operator manuals, 304
    programmer's manual, 304
    system administrator's manual, 304
    system specifications, 303–304
System growth management/budgeting for change, 307–308; *see also* Criminal justice information systems (CJIS), implementation of
System-level testing, 301, 304
System specifications, 303–304
System status management (SSM), 97–98

T

Tablet personal computers, 10, 174–175; *see also* Mobile computing
Tablet technology, smartphone and, 317–319; *see also* Law enforcement, future of technology in
Tactical crime analysis, 185, 196–197; *see also* Information technology and crime analysis
Target profiles, CASS, 184
Technical issues, 291, 291f; *see also* Functional requirement specification (FRS)
Technology integration, 178; *see also* Mobile computing

Test plans/procedures for criminal justice information systems, 300–302
Text messaging, 166
Text-to-voice systems, 176–178; *see also* Mobile computing
Thematic map, 189
Time slice, defined, 3
Traffic court processing, 281
"Train-the-trainer" method, 296
Transmission controlled protocol/Internet protocol (TCP/IP), 164
Trend mapping, 192f

U

Ultra high-frequency (UHF), 162, 163
Unallocated funds, 276; *see also* Court management information system
Undistributed funds, 276
Uniform crime report (UCR), 41–46, 201
Unit history, 96
Unit recommendation, 96
Unit status monitoring, 93–94
Unit validation and recommendation tables, 100
User-definable expert advisor, 80
User-definable medical questions, 213
User flexible systems, 223
User groups/criminal justice information systems, 306–307

V

Vendor(s), 306–307
Vendor accrual screen (sample), 272f
Version upgrade, 307
Very high-frequency (VHF), 162
Victim and witness tracking, 235, 237f, 238, 240f; *see also* Prosecutor information management systems
Victim information/notification, 225–226; *see also* Sentence management
Video, pervasive use of, 314–316
Video surveillance and monitoring, 314–315; *see also* Law enforcement, future of technology in
Virtual Command Center (VCC), 46
Virtual Private Network (VPN), 46–47
Visionics, 18
Visitors in prisons, 217
Visitor tracking, 217–218; *see also* Inmate tracking

Voice over Internet protocol (VoIP), 61
Voice recognition, 216
Voice-to-text systems, 176–178; *see also*
    Mobile computing

W

Wants, warrants, and protective orders,
    127–128, 129f
Warning in transaction log, 223
Warrant(s), 277–281, 282f; *see also* Court
    management information system
Warrant entry screen (sample), 279f
Warrant file listing (sample), 282f
Web Portal for employees, 284
Wi-Fi technology, 164

Wireless mobile video, 171; *see also* Mobile
    office
802.11a-g wireless networking, 11
Wireless technology as transport
    mediums, 162–165; *see also* Mobile
    computing
Work credit payments, 276; *see also* Court
    management information system
Workgroup applications in criminal justice
    agencies, 15
Work release, 228–229; *see also* Schedule
    management
World Wide Web (WWW), 49–50
Worthless checks, 246, 248–249; *see
    also* Prosecutor information
    management systems

Printed in the United States
by Baker & Taylor Publisher Services